LOGIC AND PHILOSOPHY

10/30/74
114 - 15
167 - 177
182 - 90

THE CENTURY PHILOSOPHY SERIES

Justus Buchler and Sterling P. Lamprecht, *Editors*

Logic and Philosophy
SELECTED READINGS

Edited by
GARY ISEMINGER
Carleton College

New York
Appleton-Century-Crofts
Division of Meredith Corporation

for my parents

PREFACE

This anthology has grown out of the conviction that introductory logic can and should be a course of philosophical interest, not merely a mathematics course, on the one hand, nor a kind of "remedial think-ing" course, on the other.

In choosing selections, then, I have sought expressions of opposing views on issues of philosophical interest which, it seems to me, can be made to arise naturally for the reflective student who is introduced to the subject in the currently customary manner, beginning with propositional logic, and who is to be brought at least to the point where he has got some idea of the nature and function of formal sys-tems. I have used material of this kind in an introductory logic course and also in a separate course, presupposing an acquaintance with the fundamentals of modern and traditional logic, which emphasized the philosophy of logic. If the anthology is to be used in the former way, Selections 1–9 make a natural progression, running parallel to the way in which the fundamental ideas of logic are introduced in such textbooks as my *An Introduction to Deductive Logic* (Appleton-Century-Crofts, 1968), and they, together with Selections 16, 17, 20, and 21 can, in general, be understood without reference to quantification theory. Selections 10–15 presuppose a knowledge of quantification theory, while Selections 18 and 19 presuppose this and a knowledge of the traditional logic of categorical propositions as well.

Because of the nature of the selections, grouped around common themes, there are often direct references from some selections to others in the same group. Because of the nature of philosophical problems, connected with one another in intricate and subtle ways, there are often direct references from one group of selections to another, connec-tions between one group of selections and another, and connections between issues raised in the selections and issues not dealt with directly in them. I have tried, in my introductory comments to the three large groups into which the selections fall, to suggest some of the intercon-nections among the issues which are discussed. I have tried, by append-ing annotated Suggestions for Further Reading, to suggest ways the interested reader may delve more deeply into these issues and pursue issues not directly discussed here as well.

v

    I am grateful to Mrs. Deanna Dammer, Miss Sally Steusloff, Miss Gwendolyn Thomas, and, especially, my wife Andrea for help in preparing the manuscript. Carleton College helped to defray the costs of preparation through a grant from the Faculty Improvement Fund.

G.I.

CONTENTS

Preface   v

PHILOSOPHICAL PROBLEMS OF LOGIC   3

Propositions
   1. GOTTLOB FREGE: The Thought   7
   2. A. D. WOOZLEY: Judgement   19
   3. GEORGE PITCHER: Propositions and Meanings   29

Logical Truth
   4. BERTRAND RUSSELL: A Priori Knowledge and Universals   35
   5. HANS HAHN: Conventionalism   45
   6. ARTHUR PAP: Laws of Logic   52

Entailment
   7. WILLARD VAN ORMAN QUINE: Implication and the
      Conditional   60
   8. CLARENCE IRVING LEWIS: Strict Implication   67
   9. ALAN ROSS ANDERSON and NUEL D. BELNAP: Entailment   76

LOGIC AND EXISTENCE   113

Existence and Being
   10. ALEXIUS MEINONG: Kinds of Being   116
   11. MORTON WHITE: The Use of 'Exists'   127

Ontological Commitment
   12. WILLARD VAN ORMAN QUINE: On What There Is   146
   13. WILLIAM P. ALSTON: Ontological Commitments   157

Quantification and Existence
   14. CZESLAW LEJEWSKI: Logic and Existence   167
   15. L. JONATHAN COHEN: Logic and the Empty Universe   182

LOGIC AND LANGUAGE   193

Truth-Functions and Ordinary Language
   16. P. F. STRAWSON: Truth-Functional Constants and Ordi-
      nary Words   195

17. J. A. FARIS: Interderivability of '⊃' and 'If'   203

The Logic of Categorical Propositions
18. FRANZ BRENTANO: Criticisms of Traditional Logic   211
19. P. F. STRAWSON: Orthodox Criticisms of the System   217

Regimentation
20. P. F. STRAWSON: Two Kinds of Logic   227
21. WILLARD VAN ORMAN QUINE: Aims and Claims of
        Regimentation   240

Suggestions for Further Reading   245

PHILOSOPHICAL
PROBLEMS OF LOGIC

Fairly early in many presentations of deductive logic we are told that we can identify valid deductive arguments with logically true "if . . . then" propositions, or at least that there corresponds to every valid deductive argument such a proposition and that every argument to which such a proposition corresponds is valid. The clarification of the concepts employed in this account of validity, in particular the concepts of a proposition, of logical truth, and of "if . . . then," is one of the first tasks for the philosopher of logic.

The issues about propositions are typical of many questions in the philosophy of logic and in philosophy generally. On the one hand, there are those who feel compelled by the force of various arguments to assert the existence of some kind of entities, in this case propositions, which cannot reasonably be identified with any of the perhaps more obvious and unproblematic entities to which these entities are related in various ways, in this case sentences or (perhaps) facts. Frege presents a classical statement of the case for this view, calling the entities he discerns "thoughts," although he is careful to point out that they are not, as we might suppose from the name, identifiable with mental occurrences of any kind. Just the puzzling thing about them, in fact, is where in heaven or earth they might be found, and Frege dwells on, one might even say luxuriates in, their rather mysterious combination of characteristics.

On the other hand, there are those who are repelled by such entities, most often referred to as "propositions," and their odd properties. Woozley's argument is an attempt to accept the main premises of arguments like Frege's and avoid the unwelcome conclusion by supplying something which meets the needs propositions are supposed to satisfy without raising the problems they raise. His candidates for the role are the meanings of sentences. The reader may perhaps wonder, however, whether meanings are any less problematical than propositions. Furthermore, as Pitcher points out, the identification of propositions with meanings raises problems of its own. It seems that this identification not only fails to avoid the problems raised by Frege's entities but fails to meet the needs they satisfy as well. (For a notion of "statement" distinct both from "sentence" and from "proposition," the reader may refer to Strawson in Selection 20 and in the Suggestions for Further Reading for this group of selections, and to Selection 13 below.)

The issue here (which might be stated thus: "What are the entities which enter into logical relationships?") is also related to the questions dealt with in

3

Selections 10–13 below in that the arguments just referred to obviously depend on questions about the sense or senses of "existence" or "being" and about the circumstances under which we commit ourselves to the assertion that a certain kind of thing exists. In this it is also typical of its fellows, for philosophical issues can seldom be dealt with in isolation; the plausibility of an argument on one issue almost always depends on acceptance of a certain view on some other.

On the question of what account to give of the notion of logical truth, a question at least as old as Plato, all of the present selections begin with the view that there is such a thing, that is, that there is a difference between such propositions as "Caesar crossed the Rubicon," on the one hand, and "Either Caesar crossed the Rubicon or it's not the case that Caesar crossed the Rubicon," on the other, such that the latter, a typical logical truth, must be regarded differently from the former in that it is known in a different way, or it is not "about the world" in the same way, or it is somehow certain or indefeasible in a sense stronger than any we would apply to the former, or it is distinguishable from the former, a typical "factual truth," in some other similar way. For those who have doubts about the very existence of this contrast, the pieces by Mill and Quine in the Suggestions for Further Reading for this group of selections will be of interest as presenting views which appear to deny at least that the contrast is as sharp as often suggested, while the pieces by Nagel, Grice and Strawson, and Mates raise difficulties with these views.

Of the present selections, Russell's, which does not necessarily represent his views at other times during his long philosophical career, is to the current issue roughly what Frege's is to the issue about propositions. It is a Platonic view, "with merely such modifications as time has shown to be necessary." A "world of universals" is invoked, acquaintance with whose relations to one another accounts for our "certainty" regarding truths of logic and mathematics. (Notice that the question of "different kinds of being" is very much relevant here as well.)

Hahn attempts to provide an alternative account which will answer to the demands which Russell's view aims to satisfy without postulating any such mysterious entities as universals or any such puzzling faculty as would enable us to become acquainted with their relations to one another. The result is a statement of a view widely held over the past few decades, the view known as "linguistic conventionalism." The fact that logic is not in any obvious sense about *this* world is admitted, but it is not to be inferred that it is therefore about some *other* world, "it does not treat of objects at all but only about our way of speaking about objects." The necessity which impresses us as a feature of logical truth is simply the necessity which derives from our "prescribed methods of speaking." Here again, however, the question arises whether this account makes intelligible the facts which must be admitted on all sides. Pap argues that "the conventionalist cannot get around the admission that there is such a thing as a priori knowledge of logical truths, which is in no intelligible sense reducible to stipulation of, or acquaintance with, linguistic rules." (Observe also the connection he makes between this issue and the one discussed in the preceding group of selections.)

If, as Anderson and Belnap suggest, the notion "if . . . then" is "the heart of logic," it is not surprising that many controversies have arisen concerning attempts to develop formal systems which capture the relationship which holds between a set of propositions and some other (not necessarily different) proposition when the latter is validly deducible from the former. Quine carefully clarifies the claims which have been advanced on behalf of the relationship, usually called "material implication," which is usually defined in terms of the following truth table:

$$P \supset Q$$

$$
\begin{array}{ccc}
t & t & t \\
t & f & f \\
f & t & t \\
f & t & f \\
\end{array}
$$

Among other things, his argument makes it clear that the question whether this "horseshoe" relationship is adequate to any interesting sense of "if . . . then" is quite distinct from the question whether a satisfactory account of deductive validity can be given in terms of it. The fact that any material implication with a false antecedent is true is not the current problem. (Selections 16 and 17 below deal with that issue.) It is such theorems as "$p \supset (q \supset p)$," the "paradoxes of material implication," which raise difficulties when we are considering the latter question. The difficulty is that such a theorem, considered as involving a claim about deducibility, is thought to involve a commitment to the obviously false view that a true proposition is deducible from any proposition whatsoever. Here again, Quine's argument should enable us to see that, properly understood, the theorem involves no such claim.

Quine has in fact argued (see the Suggestions for Further Reading for this group of selections) that the project undertaken by Lewis in the selection included here is simply a result of the confusion between use and mention of which Whitehead and Russell were guilty and which he has exposed. Nonetheless, it is still possible to regard Lewis' aim as that of developing formally a relationship which holds between propositions if and only if a relation of valid deducibility holds between them, a claim which not even the most enthusiastic defender of the "horseshoe" would defend with regard to it. Since there is no difference between the inferences sanctioned by the theorems of Lewis' systems and by the tautologies of truth-functional logic, except those involving the "modal" notions, possibility, necessity, and so on, which Lewis finds it necessary to introduce, the reader may wonder whether the pursuit of Lewis' aim is worth the complications and difficulties which the introduction of modal operators on the analogue of the standard truth-functional connectives brings with it. (For a sample of these difficulties, many of which involve the combination of modal notions with quantifiers, and an idea of some ways of dealing with them, see the arguments of Quine and Marcus in the Suggestions for Further Reading for this group of selections.)

Given that both accounts of validity so far mentioned in the main countenance the same inferences, however, there are still some of these which raise difficulties. These difficulties cluster around the so-called "paradoxes of strict implication" in Lewis' system, of which "$\Box \sim p \dashv 3 (p \dashv 3 q)$" will serve as a sample. A theorem in truth-functional logic involving the same commitment is "$(p \& \sim p) \supset q$." These theorems quite clearly do involve the claim that any proposition whatsoever follows from a logically false proposition, and there are comparable theorems which involve the claim that a logically true proposition follows from anything whatsoever. Lewis argues that these principles are "unavoidable consequences of indispensable rules of inference," but Anderson and Belnap are convinced that the rules of which they are indeed unavoidable consequences are not so indispensable, and they set out to develop a formal system meeting the requirement, which is ignored in Lewis' system and which accounts for the paradoxical character of the paradoxes, that propositions which stand to one another in a relation of logical deducibility must be *relevant* to one another.

Propositions

1   Gottlob Frege: THE THOUGHT (1918)

Grammatically the word "true" appears as an adjective. Hence the desire arises to delimit more closely the sphere in which truth can be affirmed, in which truth comes into the question at all. One finds truth affirmed of pictures, ideas, statements, and thoughts. It is striking that visible and audible things occur here alongside things which cannot be perceived with the senses. This hints that shifts of meaning have taken place. Indeed! Is a picture, then, as a mere visible and tangible thing, really true, and a stone, a leaf, not true? . . .

When one ascribes truth to a picture one does not really want to ascribe a property which belongs to this picture altogether independently of other things, but one always has something quite different in mind and one wants to say that that picture corresponds in some way to this thing. "My idea corresponds to Cologne Cathedral" is a sentence and the question now arises of the truth of this sentence. So what is improperly called the truth of pictures and ideas is reduced to the truth of sentences. What does one call a sentence? A series of sounds; but only when it has a sense, by which is not meant that every series of sounds that has sense is a sentence. And when we call a sentence true we really mean its sense is. From which it follows that it is for the sense of a sentence that the question of truth arises in general. Now is the sense of a sentence an idea? In any case being true does not consist in the correspondence of this sense with something else, for otherwise the question of truth would reiterate itself to infinity.

Reprinted with the kind permission of the editor from *Mind*, n.s., Vol. LXV, July 1956, pp. 289–311. Translated by A. M. and Marcelle Quinton.

Without wishing to give a definition, I call a thought something for which the question of truth arises. So I ascribe what is false to a thought just as much as what is true.[1] So I can say: the thought is the sense of the sentence without wishing to say as well that the sense of every sentence is a thought. The thought, in itself immaterial, clothes itself in the material garment of a sentence and thereby becomes comprehensible to us. We say a sentence expresses a thought. . . .

In order to work out more precisely what I want to call thought, I shall distinguish various kinds of sentences.[2] One does not want to deny sense to an imperative sentence, but this sense is not such that the question of truth could arise for it. Therefore I shall not call the sense of an imperative sentence a thought. Sentences expressing desires or requests are ruled out in the same way. Only those sentences in which we communicate or state something come into the question. But I do not count among these exclamations in which one vents one's feelings, groaning, sighing, laughing, unless it has been decided by some agreement that they are to communicate something. But how about interrogative sentences? In a word-question we utter an incomplete sentence which only obtains a true sense through the completion for which we ask. Word-questions are accordingly left out of consideration here. Sentence-questions are a different matter. We expect to hear "yes" or "no." The answer "yes" means the same as an indicative sentence, for in it the thought that was already completely contained in the interrogative sentence is laid down as true. So a sentence-question can be formed from every indicative sentence. An exclamation cannot be regarded as a communication on this account, since no corresponding sentence-question can be formed. An interrogative sentence and an indicative one contain the same thought; but the indicative contains something else as well, namely, the assertion. The inter-

[1] In a similar way it has perhaps been said 'a judgment is something which is either true or false.' In fact I use the word 'thought' in approximately the sense which 'judgment' has in the writings of logicians. I hope it will become clear in what follows why I choose 'thought.' Such an explanation has been objected to on the ground that in it a distinction is drawn between true and false judgments which of all possible distinctions among judgments has perhaps the least significance. I cannot see that it is a logical deficiency that a distinction is given with the explanation. As far as significance is concerned, it should not by any means be judged as trifling if, as I have said, the word 'true' indicates the aim of logic.

[2] I am not using the word 'sentence' here in a purely grammatical sense where it also includes subordinate clauses. An isolated subordinate clause does not always have a sense about which the question of truth can arise, whereas the complex sentence to which it belongs has such a sense.

rogative sentence contains something more too, namely a request. Therefore two things must be distinguished in an indicative sentence: the content, which it has in common with the corresponding sentence-question, and the assertion. The former is the thought, or at least contains the thought. So it is possible to express the thought without laying it down as true. Both are so closely joined in an indicative sentence that it is easy to overlook their separability. Consequently we may distinguish:

(1) the apprehension of a thought — thinking,
(2) the recognition of the truth of a thought — judgment,[3]
(3) the manifestation of this judgment — assertion.

We perform the first act when we form a sentence-question. An advance in science usually takes place in this way: first a thought is apprehended, such as can perhaps be expressed in a sentence-question, and, after appropriate investigations, this thought is finally recognized to be true. We declare the recognition of truth in the form of an indicative sentence. We do not have to use the word "true" for this. And even when we do use it the real assertive force lies, not in it, but in the form of the indicative sentence and where this loses its assertive force the word "true" cannot put it back again. This happens when we do not speak seriously. As stage thunder is only apparent thunder and a stage fight only an apparent fight, so stage assertion is only apparent assertion. It is only acting, only fancy. In his part the actor asserts nothing, nor does he lie, even if he says something of whose falsehood he is convinced. In poetry we have the case of thoughts being expressed without being actually put forward as true in spite of the form of the indicative sentence, although it may be suggested to the hearer to make an assenting judgment himself. Therefore it must still always be asked, about what is presented in the form of an indicative sentence, whether it really contains an assertion. And this question must be answered in the negative if the requisite seriousness is lacking. It is

---

[3] It seems to me that thought and judgment have not hitherto been adequately distinguished. Perhaps language is misleading. For we have no particular clause in the indicative sentence which corresponds to the assertion, that something is being asserted lies rather in the form of the indicative. We have the advantage in German that main and subordinate clauses are distinguished by the word-order. In this connexion it is noticeable that a subordinate clause can also contain an assertion and that often neither main nor subordinate clause express a complete thought by themselves but only the complex sentence does.

irrelevant whether the word "true" is used here. This explains why it is that nothing seems to be added to a thought by attributing to it the property of truth.

An indicative sentence often contains, as well as a thought and the assertion, a third component over which the assertion does not extend. This is often said to act on the feelings, the mood of the hearer or to arouse his imagination. Words like "alas" and "thank God" belong here. Such constituents of sentences are more noticeably prominent in poetry, but are seldom wholly absent from prose. They occur more rarely in mathematical, physical, or chemical than in historical expositions. What are called the humanities are more closely connected with poetry and are therefore less scientific than the exact sciences which are drier the more exact they are, for exact science is directed toward truth and only the truth. Therefore all constituents of sentences to which the assertive force does not reach do not belong to scientific exposition but they are sometimes hard to avoid, even for one who sees the danger connected with them. Where the main thing is to approach what cannot be grasped in thought by means of guesswork these components have their justification. The more exactly scientific an exposition is the less will the nationality of its author be discernible and the easier will it be to translate. On the other hand, the constituents of language, to which I want to call attention here, make the translation of poetry very difficult, even make a complete translation almost always impossible, for it is in precisely that in which poetic value largely consists that languages differ most.

It makes no difference to the thought whether I use the word "horse" or "steed" or "cart-horse" or "mare." The assertive force does not extend over that in which these words differ. What is called mood, fragrance, illumination in a poem, what is portrayed by cadence and rhythm, does not belong to the thought.

Much of the language serves the purpose of aiding the hearer's understanding, for instance the stressing of part of a sentence by accentuation or word-order. One should remember words like "still" and "already" too. With the sentence "Alfred has still not come" one really says "Alfred has not come" and, at the same time, hints that his arrival is expected, but it is only hinted. It cannot be said that, since Alfred's arrival is not expected, the sense of the sentence is therefore false. The word "but" differs from "and" in that with it one intimates that what follows is in contrast with what would be expected from what preceded it. Such suggestions in speech make no difference to the thought. A sentence can be transformed by changing the verb from active to passive and making the object the subject at the same time. In the same way the dative may be changed into the nominative while "give" is replaced by "receive." Naturally such transformations are not indifferent in every respect; but they do not touch the thought, they do not touch what is true or false. If the inadmissibility of such transformations were generally admitted then all deeper logical investigation would be hindered. It is just as important to neglect distinctions that do not touch the heart of the matter as to make distinctions which concern what is essential. But what is essential depends on one's purpose. To a mind concerned with what is beautiful in language what is indifferent to the logician can appear as just what is important.

Thus the contents of a sentence often go beyond the thoughts expressed by it. But the opposite often happens too, that the mere wording, which can be grasped by writing or the gramophone does not suffice for the expression of the thought. The present tense is used in two ways: first, in order to give a date, second, in order to eliminate any temporal restriction where timelessness or eternity is part of the thought. Think, for instance, of the laws of mathematics. Which of the two cases occurs is not expressed but must be guessed. If a time indication is needed by the present tense one must know when the sentence was uttered to apprehend the thought correctly. Therefore the time of utterance is part of the expression of the thought. If someone wants to say the same today as he expressed yesterday using the word "today," he must replace this word with "yesterday." Although the thought is the same its verbal expression must be different so that the sense, which would otherwise be affected by the differing times of utterance, is readjusted. The case is the same with words like "here" and "there." In all such cases the mere wording, as it is given in writing, is not the complete expression of the thought, but the knowledge of certain accompanying conditions of utterance, which are used as means of expressing the thought, are needed for its correct apprehension. The pointing of fingers, hand movements, glances may belong here too. The same utterance containing the word "I" will express different thoughts in the mouths of different men, of which some may be true, others false. . . .

Yet there is a doubt. Is it at all the same thought which first that man expresses and now this one?

A person who is still untouched by philosophy knows first of all things which he can see and touch, in short, perceive with the senses, such as trees, stones and houses, and he is convinced that another person equally can see and touch the same tree and the same stone which he himself sees and touches. Obviously no thought belongs to these things. Now can he, nevertheless, stand in the same relation to a person as to a tree?

Even an unphilosophical person soon finds it necessary to recognize an inner world distinct from the outer world, a world of sense-impressions, of creations of his imagination, of sensations, of feelings and moods, a world of inclinations, wishes and decisions. For brevity I want to collect all these, with the exception of decisions, under the word "idea."

Now do thoughts belong to this inner world? Are they ideas? They are obviously not decisions. How are ideas distinct from the things of the outer world? First:

Ideas cannot be seen or touched, cannot be smelled, nor tasted, nor heard.

I go for a walk with a companion. I see a green field, I have a visual impression of the green as well. I have it but I do not see it.

Secondly: ideas are had. One has sensations, feelings, moods, inclinations, wishes. An idea which someone has belongs to the content of his consciousness.

The field and the frogs in it, the sun which shines on them are there no matter whether I look at them or not, but the sense-impression I have of green exists only because of me, I am its bearer. It seems absurd to us that a pain, a mood, a wish should rove about the world without a bearer, independently. An experience is impossible without an experient. The inner world presupposes the person whose inner world it is.

Thirdly: ideas need a bearer. Things of the outer world are however independent.

My companion and I are convinced that we both see the same field; but each of us has a particular sense-impression of green. I notice a strawberry among the green strawberry leaves. My companion does not notice it, he is colour-blind. The colour-impression, which he receives from the strawberry, is not noticeably different from the one he receives from the leaf. Now does my companion see the green leaf as red, or does he see the red berry as green, or does he see both as of one colour with which I am not acquainted at all? These are unanswerable, indeed really nonsensical, questions. For when the word "red" does not state a property of things but is supposed to characterize sense-impressions belonging to my consciousness, it is only applicable within the sphere of my consciousness. For it is impossible to compare my sense-impression with that of someone else. For that it would be necessary to bring together in one consciousness a sense-impression, belonging to one consciousness, with a sense-impression belonging to another consciousness. Now even if it were possible to make an idea disappear from one consciousness and, at the same time, to make an idea appear in another consciousness, the question whether it were the same idea in both would still remain unanswerable. It is so much of the essence of each of my ideas to be the content of my consciousness, that every idea of another person is, just as such, distinct from mine. But might it not be possible that my ideas, the entire content of my consciousness might be at the same time the content of a more embracing, perhaps divine, consciousness? Only if I were myself part of the divine consciousness. But then would they really be my ideas, would I be their bearer? This oversteps the limits of human understanding to such an extent that one must leave its possibility out of account. In any case it is impossible for us as men to compare another person's ideas with our own. I pick the strawberry, I hold it between my fingers. Now my companion sees it too, this very same strawberry; but each of us has his own idea. No other person has my idea but many people can see the same thing. No other person has my pain. Someone can have sympathy for me but still my pain always belongs to me and his sympathy to him. He does not have my pain and I do not have his sympathy.

Fourthly: every idea has only one bearer; no two men have the same idea.

For otherwise it would exist independently of this person and independently of that one. Is that lime-tree my idea? By using the expression "that lime-tree" in this question I have really already anticipated the answer, for with this expression I want to refer to what I see and to what other people can also look at and touch. There are now two possibilities. If my intention is realized when I refer to something with the expression "that lime-tree" then the thought expressed in the sentence "that lime-tree is my idea" must obviously be negated. But if my intention is not realized, if I only think I see without really seeing, if on that account the designation "that lime-tree" is empty, then I

have gone astray into the sphere of fiction without knowing it or want-
ing to. In that case neither the content of the sentence "that lime-tree
is my idea" nor the content of the sentence "that lime-tree is not my
idea" is true, for in both cases I have a statement which lacks an object.
So then one can only refuse to answer the question for the reason that
the content of the sentence "that lime-tree is my idea" is a piece of
fiction. I have, naturally, got an idea then, but I am not referring to
this with the words "that lime-tree." Now someone may really want to
refer to one of his ideas with the words "that lime-tree." He would
then be the bearer of that to which he wants to refer with those words,
but then he would not see that lime-tree and no one else would see it
or be its bearer.

I now return to the question: is a thought an idea? If the thought
I express in the Pythagorean theorem can be recognized by others
just as much as by me then it does not belong to the content of my
consciousness, I am not its bearer; yet I can, nevertheless, recognize it
to be true. However, if it is not the same thought at all which is taken
to be the content of the Pythagorean theorem by me and by another
person, one should not really say "the Pythagorean theorem" but "my
Pythagorean theorem," "his Pythagorean theorem" and these would
be different; for the sense belongs necessarily to the sentence. Then
my thought can be the content of my consciousness and his thought
the content of his. Could the sense of my Pythagorean theorem be true
while that of his was false? I said that the word "red" was applicable
only in the sphere of my consciousness if it did not state a property of
things but was supposed to characterize one of my sense-impressions.
Therefore the words "true" and "false," as I understand them, could
also be applicable only in the sphere of my consciousness, if they were
not supposed to be concerned with something of which I was not the
bearer, but were somehow appointed to characterize the content of my
consciousness. Then truth would be restricted to the content of my
consciousness and it would remain doubtful whether anything at all
comparable occurred in the consciousness of others.

If every thought requires a bearer, to the contents of whose consciousness it belongs, then it would be a thought of this bearer only and
there would be no science common to many, on which many could
work. But I, perhaps, have my science, namely, a whole of thought
whose bearer I am and another person has his. Each of us occupies
himself with the contents of his own consciousness. No contradiction

between the two sciences would then be possible and it would really be idle to dispute about truth, as idle, indeed almost ludicrous, as it would be for two people to dispute whether a hundred-mark note were genuine, where each meant the one he himself had in his pocket and understood the word "genuine" in his own particular sense. If some-one takes thoughts to be ideas, what he then recognizes to be true is, on his own view, the content of his consciousness and does not properly concern other people at all. If he were to hear from me the opinion that a thought is not an idea he could not dispute it, for, indeed, it would not now concern him.

So the result seems to be: thoughts are neither things of the outer world nor ideas.

A third realm must be recognized. What belongs to this corresponds with ideas, in that it cannot be perceived by the senses, but with things, in that it needs no bearer to the contents of whose consciousness to belong. Thus the thought, for example, which we expressed in the Pythagorean theorem is timelessly true, true independently of whether anyone takes it to be true. It needs no bearer. It is not true for the first time when it is discovered, but is like a planet which, already before anyone has seen it, has been in interaction with other planets.[4] . . .

We are not bearers of thoughts as we are bearers of our ideas. We do not have a thought as we have, say, a sense-impression, but we also do not see a thought as we see, say, a star. So it is advisable to choose a special expression and the word 'apprehend' offers itself for the pur-pose. A particular mental capacity, the power of thought, must corre-spond to the apprehension[5] of thought. In thinking we do not produce thoughts but we apprehend them. For what I have called thought stands in the closest relation to truth. What I recognize as true I judge to be true quite independently of my recognition of its truth and of my thinking about it. That someone thinks it has nothing to do with the truth of a thought. 'Facts, facts, facts' cries the scientist if he wants to emphasise the necessity of a firm foundation for science. What is a fact?

4 One sees a thing, one has an idea, one apprehends or thinks a thought. When one apprehends or thinks a thought one does not create it but only comes to stand in a certain relation, which is different from seeing a thing or having an idea, to what already existed beforehand.

5 The expression 'apprehend' is as metaphorical as 'content of consciousness.' The nature of language does not permit anything else. What I hold in my hand can certainly be regarded as the content of my hand but is all the same the content of my hand in quite a different way from the bones and muscles of which it is made and their tensions, and is much more extraneous to it than they are.

A fact is a thought that is true. But the scientist will surely not recognise something which depends on men's varying states of mind to be the firm foundation of science. The work of science does not consist of creation but of the discovery of true thoughts. The astronomer can apply a mathematical truth in the investigation of long past events which took place when on earth at least no one had yet recognized that truth. He can do this because the truth of a thought is timeless. Therefore that truth cannot have come into existence with its discovery.

Not everything is an idea. Otherwise psychology would contain all the sciences within it or at least it would be the highest judge over all the sciences. Otherwise psychology would rule over logic and mathematics. But nothing would be a greater misunderstanding of mathematics than its subordination to psychology. Neither logic nor mathematics has the task of investigating minds and the contents of consciousness whose bearer is a single person. Perhaps their task could be represented rather as the investigation of the mind, of the mind not of minds.

The apprehension of a thought presupposes someone who apprehends it, who thinks. He is the bearer of the thinking but not of the thought. Although the thought does not belong to the contents of the thinker's consciousness yet something in his consciousness must be aimed at the thought. But this should not be confused with the thought itself. Similarly Algol itself is different from the idea someone has of Algol.

The thought belongs neither to my inner world as an idea nor yet to the outer world of material, perceptible things.

This consequence, however cogently it may follow from the exposition, will nevertheless not perhaps be accepted without opposition. It will, I think, seem impossible to some people to obtain information about something not belonging to the inner world except by sense-perception. Sense-perception indeed is often thought to be the most certain, even to be the sole, source of knowledge about everything that does not belong to the inner world. But with what right? For sense-impressions are necessary constituents of sense-perceptions and are a part of the inner world. In any case two men do not have the same, though they may have similar, sense-impressions. These alone do not disclose the outer world to us. Perhaps there is a being that has only sense-impressions without seeing or touching things. To have visual impressions is not to see things. How does it happen that I see the tree just there where I do see it? Obviously it depends on the visual impressions I have and on the particular type which occur because I see with two eyes. A particular image arises, physically speaking, on each of the two retinas. Another person sees the tree in the same place. He also has two retinal images but they differ from mine. We must assume that these retinal images correspond to our impressions. Consequently we have visual impressions, not only not the same, but markedly different from each other. And yet we move about in the same outer world. Having visual impressions is certainly necessary for seeing things but not sufficient. What must still be added is non-sensible. And yet this is just what opens up the outer world for us; for without this non-sensible something everyone would remain shut up in his inner world. So since the answer lies in the non-sensible, perhaps something non-sensible could also lead us out of the inner world and enable us to grasp thoughts where no sense-impressions were involved. Outside one's inner world one would have to distinguish the proper outer world of sensible, perceptible things from the realm of the nonsensibly perceptible. We should need something non-sensible for the recognition of both realms but for the sensible perception of things we should need sense-impressions as well and these belong entirely to the inner world. So that in which the distinction between the way in which a thing and a thought is given mainly consists is something which is attributable, not to both realms, but to the inner world. Thus I cannot find this distinction to be so great that on its account it would be impossible for a thought to be given that did not belong to the inner world.

The thought, admittedly, is not something which it is usual to call real. The world of the real is a world in which this acts on that, changes it and again experiences reactions itself and is changed by them. All this is a process in time. We will hardly recognize what is timeless and unchangeable as real. Now is the thought changeable or is it timeless? The thought we express by the Pythagorean theorem is surely timeless, eternal, unchangeable. But are there not thoughts which are true today but false in six months time? The thought, for example, that the tree there is covered with green leaves, will surely be false in six months time. No, for it is not the same thought at all. The words 'this tree is covered with green leaves' are not sufficient by themselves for the utterance, the time of utterance is involved as well. Without the time-indication this gives we have no complete thought, i.e. no thought at all. Only a sentence supplemented by a time-indication and complete in every respect expresses a thought. But this, if it is true, is true not only today or tomorrow but timelessly. Thus the present tense in 'is true' does not refer to the speaker's present but is, if the expression be permitted, a tense of timelessness. If we use the mere form of the indicative sentence, avoiding the word 'true,' two things must be distinguished, the expression of the thought and the assertion. The time-indication that may be contained in the sentence belongs only to the expression of the thought, while the truth, whose recognition lies in the form of the indicative sentence, is timeless. Yet the same words, on account of the variability of language with time, take on another sense, express another thought; this change, however, concerns only the linguistic aspect of the matter.

And yet! What value could there be for us in the eternally unchangeable which could neither undergo effects nor have effect on us? Something entirely and in every respect inactive would be unreal and non-existent for us. Even the timeless, if it is to be anything for us, must somehow be implicated with the temporal. What would a thought be for me that was never apprehended by me? But by apprehending a thought I come into a relation to it and it to me. It is possible that the same thought that is thought by me today was not thought by me yesterday. In this way the strict timelessness is of course annulled. But one is inclined to distinguish between essential and inessential properties and to regard something as timeless if the changes it undergoes involve only its inessential properties. A property of a thought will be called inessential which consists in, or follows from the fact that, it is apprehended by a thinker.

How does a thought act? By being apprehended and taken to be true. This is a process in the inner world of a thinker which can have further consequences in this inner world and which, encroaching on the sphere of the will, can also make itself noticeable in the outer world. If, for example, I grasp the thought which we express by the theorem of Pythagoras, the consequence may be that I recognise it to be true and, further, that I apply it, making a decision which brings about the acceleration of masses. Thus our actions are usually prepared by thinking and judgment. And so thought can have an indirect influence on the motion of masses. The influence of one person on another is brought about for the most part by thoughts. One communicates a thought. How does this happen? One brings about changes in the common outside world which, perceived by another person, are supposed to induce him to apprehend a thought and take it to be true. Could the great events of world history have come about without the communication of thoughts? And yet we are inclined to regard thoughts as unreal because they appear to be without influence on events, while thinking, judging, stating, understanding and the like are facts of human life. How much more real a hammer appears compared with a thought. How different the process of handing over a hammer is from the communication of a thought. The hammer passes from one control to another, it is gripped, it undergoes pressure and on account of this its density, the disposition of its parts, is changed in places. There is nothing of all this with a thought. It does not leave the control of the communicator by being communicated, for after all a person has no control over it. When a thought is apprehended, it at first only brings about changes in the inner world of the apprehender, yet it remains untouched in its true essence, since the changes it undergoes involve only inessential properties. There is lacking here something we observe throughout the order of nature: reciprocal action. Thoughts are by no means unreal but their reality is of quite a different kind from that of things. And their effect is brought about by an act of the thinker without which they would be ineffective, at least as far as we can see. And yet the thinker does not create them but must take them as they are. They can be true without being apprehended by a thinker and are not wholly unreal even then, at least if they could be apprehended and by this means be brought into operation.

2   A. D. Woozley: JUDGEMENT (1949)

DIFFICULTIES IN THE PROPOSITION THEORY

So much, then, for the case that what the mind has before it in judging are not facts but independent objects called propositions. The arguments in the theory's favour which we have outlined indicate a number of conditions which a satisfactory theory of judgement must fulfil, and purport to show how this theory does fulfil them. We do

Reprinted with the kind permission of the publisher from A. D. Woozley, *Theory of Knowledge* (London, Hutchinson University Library, 1949).

suppose that universal truths, such as those of mathematics and logic, have an objectivity independent of anyone's happening to think them. It must be possible for men to think the same things as each other, to communicate their thoughts in conversation, to think the same things irrespective of nationality or language, to think today what they thought yesterday, to reject or to accept what previously they believed or doubted, and finally to disagree with each other in a manner such that at least one of the disputants must be wrong.

All these things must be possible, because they actually occur, and we are all perfectly familiar with all of them. Consequently, no account of the nature of judgement can be accepted which is not consistent with them all; and the arguments for the propositional theory have consisted in giving a catalogue of the requirements and showing that each in turn is satisfied by the theory. Nevertheless, despite all these points in its favour, I am unable to accept it. For that a theory satisfies the required conditions does not conclusively establish its rightness; there may be other theories which also satisfy the same conditions; and there may be other conditions, not yet specified, which it fails to fulfil.

WHAT WOULD A PROPOSITION BE?

The attractiveness of the propositional theory lay in its supplying *some thing* required by each of the conditions in the catalogue. A thing was needed which could be objectively true, which could be neutral (or public) as between minds, languages, dates, etc.; and the required thing was offered by the theory in the form of a proposition. But now what kind of a thing is such a proposition? So far, nothing whatever has been learned about it except that it is the missing piece which completes certain conditions. When we ask what a proposition is, according to the theory, we are offered a somewhat thin and cheerless answer. First, what kind of existence does it have? Clearly, it does not exist as a physical object does. To say that a physical object, e.g. this book, exists either means or involves that it is here for anyone who likes to pick up, to read, to throw away, that if I leave it lying on this table the next person to come across it will find it on this table rather than on that bookshelf, that unless it is burned by fire or damaged by water it will probably look much as it does now for a good many years yet, and so on. In short, we have to talk of a physical object's existence in terms of possible perceptions, of spatial locations, of dates, and periods in time.

If the distinction which is commonly drawn in theories of perception . . . between sense data and physical objects, is a sound distinction, the existence to be ascribed to the former is probably different from the existence to be ascribed to the latter. Putting it in a conveniently graphic if not wholly accurate way, a sense datum may be thought of as a very small slice of the history of a physical object. The elliptical appearance we are given as we look at the penny certainly exists; but we do not mean the same thing by saying that it exists as we mean when we say of the penny that it exists. Of the elliptical appearance we mean that it *occurs*, and we do not suppose that it continues when we look away, or when we change position, so as to see a somewhat different ellipse. However, whatever the differences of existence which we ascribe to physical objects and to their sensible appearances respectively, both seem totally unlike the existence that a proposition may be supposed to have according to the theory. Existence for physical objects and for sense data involves both time and space, but existence for propositions must involve neither. To ask where a proposition is is clearly a silly question, for a proposition is just not a thing of the sort that can be seen or touched, or that can have any spatial relations at all.

Similarly, temporal questions about propositions are silly, for one of the great points about them, according to the theory, was that they were timeless. If a critic objects that we obviously do ask temporal questions about a proposition, such as asking when it will become true, the answer is that we are asking the question, not about the proposition, but about whatever it is that the proposition itself is a proposition about. Certainly, in an ordinary and legitimate sense of 'become true' a proposition can become true if, for instance, it is a proposition about the future, and when events turn out as predicted: "It will rain tomorrow" becomes true tomorrow when it does rain. But that is only a shorthand way of saying that whether the proposition is true or not depends on what happens tomorrow. If it is going to rain tomorrow, then the proposition asserting that it will is true now; although we may not know until tomorrow's rain comes that it is true, our knowing that it is true is not to be confused with its being true.

We must distinguish between a proposition's having spatial or temporal reference and its being itself a spatial or temporal object, i.e.

standing in spatial or temporal relations to other objects. Many propositions have some spatial reference or other (e.g. when I say that my house is on the north side of the street), and most have some temporal reference or other (e.g. when I say that my headache hurts less now than it did), but none is itself spatial or temporal. Nobody may have thought of the proposition that material bodies attract each other before Newton thought of it, but the proposition did not come into existence on the day on which he first thought of it.

If the existence of propositions is not the same as that of physical objects or their appearances, neither is it the same as that of mental states, and for one of the same pair of reasons, viz. that mental states belong to the temporal order. As regards space, it is almost as silly (*pace* the thoroughgoing materialist) to ask where is a given mental state as to ask where is a given proposition — not quite as silly, because my present desire to go to the movies is related to my body in a special way: it may have among its causes some condition of my body, it certainly can only be fulfilled if my body is taken to a cinema, and in any case it belongs to me rather than to anyone else. Nevertheless, we never do ask of a specifically mental state "Where is it?" as we do ask it of a bodily state, or a sensation. We say, "Show me where it hurts," or "Whereabouts do you feel the pain?" but we do not say, "Where is this desire of yours for a cigarette?" or "Whereabouts is your belief that you've got a flat tyre?" [1] Nevertheless, mental states are things which occur in time and have dates, which come, go, and reappear. My desire to go to the cinema started I am not exactly sure when, but about ten minutes ago; I first believed that the earth's surface was curved when I saw ships at sea disappear below the horizon; I felt alarmed by the sight of the policeman who called at our house until he said he was collecting for the Discharged Prisoners' Fund; and so on.

When the theory says that propositions exist, or have existence independent of any particular mind, it is saying something quite unlike what we mean when we say of a person that he exists, or of a mental state or a physical object that it exists. It has being, but it is outside space and time. It is a queer substantial entity, totally unlike anything else one ever comes across. Here, at the risk of exposing my pedestrianism, I confess myself completely baffled: the metaphysical

---

[1] There are, of course, idiomatic metaphors, such as "Where is your resolution gone?" But they *are* metaphors, and the spatial words are not taken literally. The badly behaved child who is asked, "Where are your manners?" would be ill advised to answer that they could not be anywhere.

status which we are asked to recognize these propositions as having seems to be the same as that which Plato's Ideas have, and is to me equally unintelligible. Incomprehensibility may be due to a defect either in the theory or in the capacity of the person trying to understand it. I can only record that I do find the theory incomprehensible on this question of existence, and pass on to other difficulties. Fortunately, incomprehensibility can be a matter of degrees; for, if it were not, the difficulty of its incomprehensibility would prevent one from even thinking of other difficulties; and as long as one leaves the question of propositions' metaphysical status shadowy one can see other difficulties.

THE HYPOTHESIS OF PROPOSITIONS IS UNVERIFIABLE

The next difficulty is perhaps a variation of the first, but seems worth emphasizing, for it brings out a new point. According to the theory, we assert the existence of these substantial propositions, not because we discover by some form of inspection that they exist, although we had never noticed them before, but because they are required as a condition of the possibility of making judgements, false as well as true. Now, such a method of argument *appears* unobjectionable in itself and to be an argument of the sort on which the natural sciences mainly rely. The scientist wants to account for a number and variety of observed happenings, and proceeds to do it by formulating an hypothesis, such that if the hypothesis is true things will happen in the way he has already observed them to happen.

That is only the first stage of scientific procedure, and would have little reliance placed on it by any worthwhile scientist until various further steps had been taken; he would want to find out whether there was more than one hypothesis that would cover his observed facts, i.e. whether they were susceptible of any possible alternative explanations; he would want to verify his hypothesis, either directly (where that could be done), or, more commonly, indirectly, by working out what other occurrences would have to take place under a specified set of conditions if the hypothesis were true, and then by carrying out an experiment under that set of conditions to determine whether the predicted occurrences do take place. If they do not, and if he is satisfied that the experiment has been properly carried out under the correct conditions and that his deductions from the hypothesis have been accurate, then he will reject the hypothesis; if he originally formulated two or more hypotheses that would cover his first set of observations, he will want to discriminate between them by following out the experimental method for each in turn, eliminating every alternative that yields predictions which the subsequent experiments fail to bear out; thus, by outright rejection or modification of hypotheses, he proceeds until he is left with the simplest and most general hypothesis that both will account for the previous observations and will be successfully borne out by subsequent experiments.

Reverting to the proposition theory, we find that the existence of these propositions is the hypothesis formulated to account for the facts of judgement. Is it put forward *as the only possible* hypothesis, as that which is necessarily entailed by the facts of judgement being what they are? If it is, then the secondary stage of scientific procedure is not required, and can serve no purpose. For if the facts of judgement are what they are, and if they cannot be what they are unless there are substantial propositions, then the theory of substantial propositions can need no further verification. But if the existence of substantial propositions really is entailed by the facts of judgement, i.e. if it really is the only possible hypothesis, then it is very odd that so many philosophers, men not without intellectual perspicacity or honesty, should have been unable to accept it.

Is it, then, on the other hand, a more modest claimant, *as at least one possible* explanation of the facts of judgement? The difficulty here is twofold. First, there seems to be no further way of verifying the hypothesis, i.e. no further set of possible facts which can be deduced from it, and which can then be checked by subsequent observation; in short, the theory is not in this way empirically verifiable or fruitful. Secondly, it is hard to avoid the suspicion that to postulate the existence of propositions is only in appearance and not in fact to suggest a hypothesis that will account for the facts of judgement. To explain: we should not suppose that a scientist had accounted for the solidification of water at freezing point if he said that it was because water became ice at that point, or because there was a certain property about water which caused it to solidify at that point. His first alleged reason is no reason at all, for it merely states that water solidifies at freezing point because it solidifies at freezing point. And his alternative explanation is no better because, although it does not repeat itself as the first does, it simply says that there is something or other about water that makes it solidify, without telling us what that something or other is. He has not accounted in any way for the occurrence, but has merely declared that there must be something to account for it; we are none the wiser. But if he tells us that the cause of water solidifying is the reduction of the random motion of molecules to a point at which it is overcome by the attraction forces between them, so that they change from the irregular pattern of a liquid or gas to the regular pattern of ice, then he has given us a scientific explanation; and if we are capable of following his explanation, we shall have obtained an answer to our question.

Now, does the postulation of substantial propositions do any more to account for the facts of judgement than (a) to say that there must be something or other to account for them; and (b) to suggest that the name to be given to this something should be 'proposition'? We are none the wiser, as medieval inquirers were none the wiser when they offered the sort of explanation which Moliére parodies in *Le Malade Imaginaire*, when the would-be doctor says that opium induces sleep because it possesses a *virtus dormitiva*. Such qualities were commonly called "occult qualities," and were very properly exploded by Descartes. I find it difficult to believe that substantial propositions are not correspondingly "occult substances," and that we are not being asked to solve a problem in the theory of knowledge by taking refuge in a myth. If a proposition is a something-I-know-not-what required for judgement, we are deluding ourselves if we suppose that by postulating propositions we are solving any problem at all.

AN INFINITY OF PROPOSITIONS WOULD BE NEEDED

Finally (not that there are not other objections, mostly connected with time, too elaborate to expound here), the thought of the number of such propositions that there will have to be may give us pause. If to make a judgement or to believe something requires a proposition before the mind to be judged or believed, then the realm of propositions will have to contain a vast array of propositions, to provide for every judgement that may be made. There will have to be a proposition corresponding to every different judgement that ever has been made, is being made, or will be made in the history of the universe; and unless every judgement is determined in accordance with a rigidly causal scheme, it would look as if the realm would have to include not only a proposition for each actual different judgement, but also a proposition for every *possible* different judgement. Not only will there be every possible true proposition, but also every possible false proposition — if, indeed, to say that means anything at all.

To every slight difference in judgement a correspondingly different proposition will be required; and there will be more or less vague propositions corresponding with the more or less vague judgements which we make. For instance, I may want to tell somebody the size of a full-grown foxhound; but it will not be enough that there should be one proposition recording it. For there is any number of descriptions which I may give, starting with the less exact and gradually approaching the more exact. Quite ignoring the false descriptions I might give, all of which have to be provided for, I might start by saying that a full-grown foxhound was somewhere in size between a guinea pig and a camel, and then go on, substituting for a guinea pig rabbit, cat, cocker spaniel, etc., and substituting for camel lion, foal, Great Dane, etc.; for every one of these more exact formulations another proposition will be required.

Again, we all know how easy it is, when two men are talking, especially on a fairly abstract subject, for one to say something which the other will understand in a slightly different way from what the speaker intended, not very different, perhaps, not enough to send the conversation off the rails, but enough to justify us in saying that the same sentence did not mean quite the same thing for each of them. Are we, then, to suppose that to each minute difference in interpretation there corresponds a minutely different proposition available in the realm of substantial propositions? Hitler's cries for *Lebensraum* would seem a farce compared with the needs of propositions. One more queer class might be mentioned, which would have to be admitted — logically impossible propositions: they must be allowed, because they are made use of in judgements, e.g. in the judgements that they are logically impossible, and because they are used as the premises in *reductio ad absurdum* arguments. Not only then should we have to provide for propositions which are in fact false, but also for propositions which could in no conceivable circumstances be true. Such a world seems to threaten not merely the understanding, but even sanity.

PROPOSITION AS THE MEANING OF A SENTENCE

Turning now to consider what better alternatives we can find in place of the previous theory, I find it necessary to continue speaking in terms of propositions, although in a different sense. If this seems confusing, I can only reply that there is no other word in common philosophical usage which will serve as a substitute, and that hereafter I propose to stick consistently to this second, more common, and less tendentious usage. Hitherto we have considered whether there are mind-independent substances available as objects of judgement; and the name given to these putative entities was 'propositions.' We have seen reason to believe them difficult to accept. In future I shall mean by a proposition 'the meaning of a sentence.'

The question, "Are there propositions?" which, according to the previous usage, seemed to be an important metaphysical question asking about existence, now is very easily disposed of. For it is the same as the question, "Do sentences have meanings?" to which the answer quite obviously is that they do. Not that they *all* do, for plenty of arrangements of words can be constructed into sentences according to the rules of grammar and syntax, which yet possess no descriptive meaning at all: e.g. the sentences, "The square root of 3 is blue," "Monkeys multiplied by grass snakes equal tuxedos," and other linguistically correct but gibberish sentences of that sort. But most of the sentences which most of the time most of us use have descriptive meaning of some sort; and that is what I now mean by 'proposition.'

It is convenient to have propositions in this sense because we do often, as philosophers, want to make two distinctions. First, we want to distinguish between a sentence and what it means: a sentence is a linguistically correct (correctness admittedly being a matter both of convention and of degree) form of words written or spoken, read or heard, but something is usually understood by the sentence, and that something is its meaning; as we have already seen, different sentences in the same or in different languages can possess the same meaning; and the same sentence in different contexts or to different people can possess different meanings, either because the sentence is vague or because it is ambiguous — e.g. "The 9:50 is hardly late today" may not mean the same to a stranger as it does to one painfully familiar with that particular railway's habits; and because the same word (i.e. the same shape or sound) often has two quite unrelated meanings puns are possible (e.g. "Bear right in the middle of the town"). It is convenient to indicate the form of words or linguistic pattern by calling it a sentence, and to indicate what the sentence signifies or means by calling it a proposition.

Secondly, we want to distinguish between what a sentence means and the fact which makes it true or false. This may not be an ultimately tenable distinction — as we shall see later it is not — if it leads us to treat a proposition as a *thing* of one sort and a fact as a *thing* of another sort. But it is a common enough working distinction of reason, which has its uses, as long as we do not allow it to mislead us. We do not, on the whole, talk of a sentence being true or false, but rather of its being correct or incorrect, and of what the sentence asserts as being true or false. And we commonly use expressions such as, "It is one thing to discover what he means, but quite another to discover whether what he means is true."

PROPOSITIONS NOT INDEPENDENT ENTITIES

If a proposition is what we mean when we talk or write, then a proposition is present to the mind when we think or judge. We may speak of entertaining a proposition — i.e. of considering a meaning as preliminary to accepting or rejecting it, to judging affirmatively or negatively. This is not to say that thinking must be done in sentences, although my own experience suggests to me that it is all done in symbols of some sort or other. But clearly thinking and judging are done with meanings, that is, with what will be meanings of sentences, or bits of sentences, if they are put into words at all.

The exact relation of thought to speech raises a number of difficult and interesting questions which we cannot pursue here. But they do seem to be very intimately connected, to such an extent that it is very hard to see how an animal having no power of speech could, for instance, wish that it could be moved from this field to the next in four days' time. In our present sense, then, propositions are necessary to judgement; and what we require to do is to give a satisfactory account of judgement, without introducing the hydra-headed entities of the previous theory. If we can produce an account by which propositions are mind-dependent although the elements of which they are composed are independent of mind, we may hope to avoid both the extravagant multiplication of entities of the substantial theory and the difficulties of simple dualism.

Such an account would be quite consistent with the conditions listed earlier. The need for objective truths does not in fact require objective propositions. For while it is true that the proposition "$3 \times 4 = 7 + 5$" was true before anyone thought of it and does not cease to be true if at any time nobody happens to be thinking it, its objectivity is satisfied provided that if anybody at any time thinks it, then what he thinks is true. To say that it is an objective truth would be to say that, although the proposition itself is mind-dependent, i.e. requires some mind or other, yet its character of being true is not in any additional sense mind-dependent. I may choose whether or not to think the proposition, but if I do, then I think a proposition the truth of which is independent of me or of anybody else who may happen to think it; nothing that anyone can do will affect its character of being true.

Whether I make the radio program on the Home Service audible or not does depend on me, for I shall not hear it unless I switch it on; what I hear when I switch it on does not depend on me, and there is nothing I can do to alter its character; I can switch off again, but that is all. In other words, although a thing may depend for its existence on something else, what character it will have if it exists does not necessarily depend on that other thing. A proposition may require a mind in order to be a proposition, but its truth-value need not depend on that or any other mind. Now, surely that is all that is required for objective truths, viz. that their truth should be independent of this, that, or the other mind. Similarly with the other conditions: a proposition could be mind-dependent and still neutral or public as between different minds, sentences, languages, dates, and mental attitudes; and two propositions do not have to be substantial entities in order to be logically incompatible with each other.

3 George Pitcher: PROPOSITIONS AND MEANINGS (1964)

The correspondence theory says: truth is a relation — that of correspondence — between what is said or thought and a fact or state of affairs in the world. Difficulties and perplexities arise concerning the nature of this relation and the nature of both its terms. Consider the first term of the relation, that to which the predicate 'true' is applied — namely, what is said or thought. I have been using the

George Pitcher, Editor, *Truth*, © 1964. Reprinted by permission of Prentice-Hall, Inc., Englewood Cliffs, New Jersey.

vague and ambiguous locution 'what is said or thought' mainly because it *is* vague and ambiguous enough to get by if it is not too carefully examined. But what exactly is meant by 'what is said or thought'? Suppose someone said truly "It is raining," so that what he said was true. He spoke or uttered the English sentence 'It is raining,' but *that* is not what we want to call true. If instead of "It is raining" he had said "Il pleut" or "Es regnet," then in the sense of 'said' in which what he said was true, he would still have said the same thing, for these are just three ways of saying the same thing; but he would have uttered a different sentence. Therefore what he said, in the relevant sense — i.e., in the sense according to which what he said is *true* — is not the English sentence 'It is raining.' If one person says "It is raining," another "Il pleut," and a third "Es regnet," a correct answer to the question "What did he say?" would in each case be "He said that it is raining" — for each would have said *the same thing*. And it is this element which all three utterances have in common — this same thing that is said in all three cases — that is the real bearer of truth, not the different sentences which the speakers happen to utter.

But what *is* this common element? It is, evidently, the common idea behind each of the separate utterances, the common thought which each of the different sentences is used to express. Not, mind you, the thoughts qua individual acts of thinking that occur at certain definite times and in certain particular minds, for those are different individual events and what we want is some *one* thing which is common to them all. What we want is the identical *content* of these different acts of thinking, that *of which* they are all acts of thinking. This content of any number of possible individual thoughts has been called a *proposition*: and it has been held that propositions are the real bearers of truth (and falsity).

It seems sometimes to have been assumed as obvious that propositions must be objective *entities*, on the ground that if two or more sentences all express the same thing, then of course there must be a thing which they all express. The same conviction was also reached as follows. When a person thinks or believes something, it is always a proposition that he thinks or believes. Hence, a proposition is an entity; for whenever a person thinks or believes something, there must *be* a thing that he thinks or believes.[1]

[1] See Plato, *Theaetetus* 189A, and L. Wittgenstein, *Philosophical Investigations* (Oxford: Basil Blackwell & Mott, Ltd., 1953), Part I, Sec. 518.

Propositions were thus often conceived to be timeless nonlinguistic entities capable of being apprehended, and of being believed or disbelieved, by any number of different minds. This conception of propositions encounters numerous difficulties, of which I shall discuss two kinds.

(a) We may begin by noting that there is a strong temptation to strip a proposition of any assertive force. Consider the following utterances: (i) The door is shut, (ii) Shut the door!, (iii) Is the door shut?, (iv) Oh, if the door were only shut!, (v) If the door is shut, then the picnic is off, (vi) The door is not shut, (vii) Either the door is shut or I've lost my mind. It is obvious that there is something in common to all these utterances, namely the idea, as we might put it, of the door's being shut. If we have no special prejudices in favor of categorical assertions and thus give no logical priority to utterances like (i), as against any of the other possible kinds, then we might naturally view the mere idea of the door's being shut as a kind of intelligible content or matter which minds can coolly contemplate and which utterances can embody with various different forms imposed upon it. Thus in (i), it is asserted that the content (the door's being shut) describes an actual state of affairs — the content is *asserted*; in (ii) the order is given that the content describe, in the near future, an actual state of affairs — the content is ordered; and so on. The intelligible content looks like our old friend the proposition, only stripped now of its assertive force.[2]

This way of regarding propositions seems right on at least one count: it makes asserting, ordering, questioning, and so on, actions which *people* perform by saying something, rather than actions which are mysteriously embodied, without any agent to perform them, in a wordless abstract entity that exists independently of human or other agents. Notice, however, that this new nonassertorial entity is *not*, although it may appear to be, the same thing as the proposition we began with. Propositions were introduced as the common ideas or thoughts which several different sentences may express. Such an idea or thought, however, contained an assertive element: in our example, it was the thought that it is raining — not the mere nonassertorial thought of its raining, but the assertorial thought that it *is* raining.

This new nonassertorial way of regarding propositions engenders difficulties. One could argue as follows, for example: (i) A mere intelligible content, such as "the door's being shut," cannot be true or false, since it makes no claim; it *asserts* (or *denies*) nothing. If someone were to assert (or deny) the content, by saying "The door is (or is not) shut," then his remark would indeed be true or false, but the content itself is neither. *Comment*: This plausible line of argument deprives the proposition of the very role for which it was invented — namely, that of being the sole bearer of truth (and falsity).[3]

To avoid this trouble, one might argue instead in the following way: (ii) Of course remarks, assertions, statements, and so on, can be true, but so can propositions. Propositions, on the present nonassertorial view, are the intelligible contents of remarks and hence, it may be said, are used to make true remarks; but both the propositions and the remarks are true. Consider this analogy: a die can be used to form star-shaped cookies, but both the cookie and the die are star-shaped:[4] why, then, should not a proposition and the remarks, statements, etc. it is used to make both be capable of truth? A true proposition will not be a true *assertion*, of course (just as the die is not a star-shaped cookie); it will be more like a true picture or representation of reality. *Comment*: For the present nonassertorial view of propositions, this line of reasoning is more satisfactory than the first, but it does introduce a kind of schizophrenia into the theory of truth, for it makes two radically different kinds of things the bearers of truth. Moreover, the sense in which remarks, assertions, and so on, are true seems to be somewhat different from that in which nonassertorial propositions are, if the latter are at all like pictures or representations. This dualistic result may not be fatal to the view under consideration, but it does make it untidy, at least.

(b) Whether propositions retain their assertive force or not, however, the very notion of a proposition as a timeless, wordless entity is fraught with well-known difficulties. How are we to conceive of this sort of entity? What, for example, are its constituents? The answer that immediately suggests itself, and indeed seems to be the only possible one, is that a proposition is composed of the meanings of the individual words or phrases making up the various different sentences which may be used to express it. The reasoning which lends support

---

[3] Hereafter I shall avoid the needless and annoying repetition of such expressions as 'and falsity,' 'or falsehood,' 'and false,' and so on; they should, however, be understood, wherever appropriate.

[4] This analogy was suggested to me by Richard Rorty.

to this answer is the following: (i) Propositions were introduced in the first place as being what two or more sentences *with the same meaning* (e.g., 'It is raining,' 'Il pleut,' and 'Es regnet') have in common. Evidently, then, (ii) a proposition is the common meaning of all the sentences that can be used to express it. And so, (iii) a proposition must be composed of the meanings of the individual words or phrases which make up those sentences.

Let us accept this argument for the moment. Let us even swallow the camel of admitting the existence of Platonic meanings corresponding to each word. Still, there are some troublesome gnats to be strained at. First, if a proposition is to be formed, it is not enough that there simply *be* the Platonic meanings of the relevant individual words: the meanings must also be combined with one another. But what are the rules of combination, how is the combination supposed to be brought about, and what sort of complex entity is the result? Consider the corresponding problem at the level of words. In order to have a sentence, a group of individual words must be combined. But here we have a reasonably clear idea of how this is done: a person does it by writing (or speaking) the words one after another in accordance with the rules of syntax for the language, and the resulting complex entity is of a familiar sort. But it is not at all clear that we understand what is supposed to go on at the higher level of Platonic meanings. For example, are there rules of meaning-combination as there are rules of word-combination — rules of conceptual syntax? If so, what are they? When one tries to discover what they are, he sees either nothing or mere pale reflections of ordinary syntactical rules — and that ought to make us suspicious. And suppose there were such things as rules of conceptual syntax: what would it be to *combine* the individual Platonic meanings in accordance with the rules? Not writing them down next to each other or speaking them one after another; for one cannot write down or speak a meaning (in this sense of 'a meaning'). Are they then just eternally combined with each other in all the possible ways — thus constituting immutable conceptual facts in Plato's heaven — and does the mind, when it entertains a proposition, simply pick out for consideration one of these everlasting possible combinations? But then this account does not differ, except verbally, from saying that the individual Platonic meanings are *not* combined in themselves at all, and that the mind combines them by thinking them together in some as yet unexplained way, when it entertains propositions.

The foregoing difficulties need not, however, exercise us unduly, for the argument (i)-(iii) (of the last paragraph but one) which gave rise to them is not acceptable. Plausible as it may have seemed, it cannot be accepted, for both (i) and (ii) are false. (i) is false: propositions were introduced as the common content of what is said or asserted when, in a number of utterances, the same thing is said or asserted. In the particular example I gave earlier, three sentences having the same meaning happened to be used: but this was not essential, for the same thing is often said or asserted by using sentences with different meanings. Sam Jones' brother says "My brother is sick"; the same Sam Jones' mother says, at the same time, "My son is sick"; and his son, at the same time, says "My father is sick." It is plausible to suppose that all three people asserted the same thing — i.e., expressed the same proposition — and yet no one could reasonably maintain that the three sentences they used all have the same meaning. And (ii) is false: if a proposition is the bearer of truth (and falsity), then it cannot be the meaning of a class of sentences, for, as Austin points out, "We never say 'The meaning (or sense) of this sentence (or of these words) is true.'" Again, although we can say of a proposition that it was asserted or denied, it makes no sense to say this of the meaning of a sentence.[5]

I conclude that the argument does not establish (iii). And, since the initial plausibility of (iii) derives entirely from (ii), which is false, I conclude also that (iii) is false. But if the meanings of words are not the constituents of propositions, what are? What *are* the constituents of what-a-person-asserts, the *content* of what he says? It seems difficult, or impossible, to answer. But this must surely be a great embarrassment to those who hold that propositions are real entities: if we cannot even begin to say what their constituents are, we hardly have a clear idea of what *they* are.

[5] I owe this point to R. Cartwright. See his "Propositions," in *Analytical Philosophy*, R. J. Butler, ed. (Oxford: Basil Blackwell & Mott, Ltd., 1962), p. 101. In this article, the points here under discussion, and related ones, are treated perceptively and thoroughly.

Logical Truth

4 Bertrand Russell: A PRIORI KNOWLEDGE AND UNIVERSALS (1912)

It is very common among philosophers to regard what is a priori as in some sense mental, as concerned rather with the way we must think than with any fact of the outer world. We noted in the preceding chapter the three principles commonly called 'laws of thought.' The view which led to their being so named is a natural one, but there are strong reasons for thinking that it is erroneous. Let us take as an illustration the law of contradiction. This is commonly stated in the form 'Nothing can both be and not be,' which is intended to express the fact that nothing can at once have and not have a given quality. Thus, for example, if a tree is a beech it cannot also be not a beech; if my table is rectangular it cannot also be not rectangular, and so on.

Now what makes it natural to call this principle a law of *thought* is that it is by thought rather than by outward observation that we persuade ourselves of its necessary truth. When we have seen that a tree is a beech, we do not need to look again in order to ascertain whether it is also not a beech; thought alone makes us know that this is impossible. But the conclusion that the law of contradiction is a law of *thought* is nevertheless erroneous. What we believe, when we believe the law of contradiction, is not that the mind is so made that it must believe the law of contradiction. *This* belief is a subsequent result of psychological

From Bertrand Russell, *The Problems of Philosophy*, Oxford University Press, Inc., New York, 1912, 1959. Reprinted through the permission of the publishers.

reflection, which presupposes the belief in the law of contradiction. The belief in the law of contradiction is a belief about things, not only about thoughts. It is not, e.g., the belief that if we *think* a certain tree is a beech, we cannot at the same time *think* that it is not a beech; it is the belief that if the tree *is* a beech, it cannot at the same time *be* not a beech. Thus the law of contradiction is about things, and not merely about thoughts; and although belief in the law of contradiction is a thought, the law of contradiction itself is not a thought, but a fact concerning the things in the world. If this, which we believe when we believe the law of contradiction, were not true of the things in the world, the fact that we were compelled to *think* it true would not save the law of contradiction from being false; and this shows that the law is not a law of *thought*.

A similar argument applies to any other a priori judgment. When we judge that two and two are four, we are not making a judgment about our thoughts, but about all actual or possible couples. The fact that our minds are so constituted as to believe that two and two are four, though it is true, is emphatically not what we assert when we assert that two and two are four. And no fact about the constitution of our minds could make it *true* that two and two are four. Thus our a priori knowledge, if it is not erroneous, is not merely knowledge about the constitution of our minds, but is applicable to whatever the world may contain, both what is mental and what is non-mental.

The fact seems to be that all our a priori knowledge is concerned with entities which do not, properly speaking, *exist*, either in the mental or in the physical world. These entities are such as can be named by parts of speech which are not substantives; they are such entities as qualities and relations. Suppose, for instance, that I am in my room. I exist, and my room exists; but does 'in' exist? Yet obviously the word 'in' has a meaning; it denotes a relation which holds between me and my room. This relation is something, although we cannot say that it exists *in the same sense* in which I and my room exist. The relation 'in' is something which we can think about and understand, for, if we could not understand it, we could not understand the sentence 'I am in my room.' Many philosophers, following Kant, have maintained that relations are the work of the mind, that things in themselves have no relations, but that the mind brings them together in one act of thought and thus produces the relations which it judges them to have.

This view, however, seems open to objections similar to those which we urged before against Kant. It seems plain that it is not thought which produces the truth of the proposition 'I am in my room.' It may be true that an earwig is in my room, even if neither I nor the earwig nor any one else is aware of this truth; for this truth concerns only the earwig and the room, and does not depend upon anything else. Thus relations, as we shall see more fully in the next chapter, must be placed in a world which is neither mental nor physical. This world is of great importance to philosophy, and in particular to the problems of a priori knowledge. In the next chapter we shall proceed to develop its nature and its bearing upon the questions with which we have been dealing. . . .

The problem with which we are now concerned is a very old one, since it was brought into philosophy by Plato. Plato's 'theory of ideas' is an attempt to solve this very problem, and in my opinion it is one of the most successful attempts hitherto made. The theory to be advocated in what follows is largely Plato's, with merely such modifications as time has shown to be necessary.

The way the problem arose for Plato was more or less as follows. Let us consider, say, such a notion as *justice*. If we ask ourselves what justice is, it is natural to proceed by considering this, that, and the other just act, with a view to discovering what they have in common. They must all, in some sense, partake of a common nature, which will be found in whatever is just and in nothing else. This common nature, in virtue of which they are all just, will be justice itself, the pure essence the admixture of which with facts of ordinary life produces the multiplicity of just acts. Similarly with any other word which may be applicable to common facts, such as 'whiteness' for example. The word will be applicable to a number of particular things because they all participate in a common nature or essence. This pure essence is what Plato calls an 'idea' or 'form.' (It must not be supposed that 'ideas,' in his sense, exist in minds, though they may be apprehended by minds.) The 'idea' *justice* is not identical with anything that is just: it is something other than particular things, which particular things partake of. Not being particular, it cannot itself exist in the world of sense. Moreover it is not fleeting or changeable like the things of sense: it is eternally itself, immutable and indestructible.

Thus Plato is led to a supra-sensible world, more real than the common world of sense, the unchangeable world of ideas, which alone gives to the world of sense whatever pale reflection of reality may belong to it. The truly real world, for Plato, is the world of ideas; for whatever we may attempt to say about things in the world of sense, we can only succeed in saying that they participate in such and such ideas, which, therefore, constitute all their character. Hence it is easy to pass on into a mysticism. We may hope, in a mystic illumination, to *see* the ideas as we see objects of sense; and we may imagine that the ideas exist in heaven. These mystical developments are very natural, but the basis of the theory is in logic, and it is as based in logic that we have to consider it.

The word 'idea' has acquired, in the course of time, many associations which are quite misleading when applied to Plato's 'ideas.' We shall therefore use the word 'universal' instead of the word 'idea,' to describe what Plato meant. The essence of the sort of entity that Plato meant is that it is opposed to the particular things that are given in sensation. We speak of whatever is given in sensation, or is of the same nature as things given in sensation, as a *particular*; by opposition to this, a *universal* will be anything which may be shared by many particulars, and has those characteristics which, as we saw, distinguish justice and whiteness from just acts and white things.

When we examine common words, we find that, broadly speaking, proper names stand for particulars, while other substantives, adjectives, prepositions, and verbs stand for universals. Pronouns stand for particulars, but are ambiguous: it is only by the context or the circumstances that we know what particulars they stand for. The word 'now' stands for a particular, namely the present moment; but like pronouns, it stands for an ambiguous particular, because the present is always changing.

It will be seen that no sentence can be made up without at least one word which denotes a universal. The nearest approach would be some such statement as 'I like this.' But even here the word 'like' denotes a universal, for I may like other things, and other people may like things. Thus all truths involve universals, and all knowledge of truths involves acquaintance with universals.

Seeing that nearly all the words to be found in the dictionary stand for universals, it is strange that hardly anybody except students of philosophy ever realizes that there are such entities as universals. We do not naturally dwell upon those words in a sentence which do not stand for particulars; and if we are forced to dwell upon a word which stands for a universal, we naturally think of it as standing for some one of the particulars that come under the universal. When, for example, we hear the sentence, 'Charles I's head was cut off,' we may naturally enough think of Charles I, of Charles I's head, and of the operation of cutting off *his* head, which are all particulars; but we do not naturally dwell upon what is meant by the word 'head' or the word 'cut,' which is a universal. We feel such words to be incomplete and insubstantial; they seem to demand a context before anything can be done with them. Hence we succeed in avoiding all notice of universals as such, until the study of philosophy forces them upon our attention.

Even among philosophers, we may say, broadly, that only those universals which are named by adjectives or substantives have been much or often recognized, while those named by verbs and prepositions have been usually overlooked. This omission has had a very great effect upon philosophy; it is hardly too much to say that most metaphysics, since Spinoza, has been largely determined by it. The way this has occurred is, in outline, as follows: Speaking generally, adjectives and common nouns express qualities or properties of single things, whereas prepositions and verbs tend to express relations between two or more things. Thus the neglect of prepositions and verbs led to the belief that every proposition can be regarded as attributing a property to a single thing, rather than as expressing a relation between two or more things. Hence it was supposed that, ultimately, there can be no such entities as relations between things. Hence either there can be only one thing in the universe, or, if there are many things, they cannot possibly interact in any way, since any interaction would be a relation, and relations are impossible.

The first of these views, advocated by Spinoza and held in our own day by Bradley and many other philosophers, is called *monism*; the second, advocated by Leibniz but not very common nowadays, is called *monadism*, because each of the isolated things is called a *monad*. Both these opposing philosophies, interesting as they are, result, in my opinion, from an undue attention to one sort of universals, namely the sort represented by adjectives and substantives rather than by verbs and prepositions.

As a matter of fact, if any one were anxious to deny altogether that there are such things as universals, we should find that we cannot strictly prove that there are such entities as *qualities*, i.e., the universals represented by adjectives and substantives, whereas we can prove that there must be *relations*, i.e. the sort of universals generally represented by verbs and prepositions. Let us take in illustration the universal *whiteness*. If we believe that there is such a universal, we shall say that things are white because they have the quality of whiteness. This view, however, was strenuously denied by Berkeley and Hume, who have been followed in this by later empiricists. The form which their denial took was to deny that there are such things as 'abstract ideas.' When we want to think of whiteness, they said, we form an image of some particular white thing, and reason concerning this particular, taking care not to deduce anything concerning it which we cannot see to be equally true of any other white thing. As an account of our actual mental processes, this is no doubt largely true. In geometry, for example, when we wish to prove something about all triangles, we draw a particular triangle and reason about it, taking care not to use any characteristic which it does not share with other triangles. The beginner, in order to avoid error, often finds it useful to draw several triangles, as unlike each other as possible, in order to make sure that his reasoning is equally applicable to all of them. But a difficulty emerges as soon as we ask ourselves how we know that a thing is white or a triangle. If we wish to avoid the universals *whiteness* and *triangularity*, we shall choose some particular patch of white or some particular triangle, and say that anything is white or a triangle if it has the right sort of resemblance to our chosen particular. But then the resemblance required will have to be a universal. Since there are many white things, the resemblance must hold between many pairs of particular white things; and this is the characteristic of a universal. It will be useless to say that there is a different resemblance for each pair, for then we shall have to say that these resemblances resemble each other, and thus at last we shall be forced to admit resemblance as a universal. The relation of resemblance, therefore, must be a true universal. And having been forced to admit this universal, we find that it is no longer worthwhile to invent difficult and unplausible theories to avoid the admission of such universals as whiteness and triangularity.

Berkeley and Hume failed to perceive this refutation of their rejection of 'abstract ideas,' because, like their adversaries, they only thought of *qualities*, and altogether ignored *relations* as universals. We have therefore here another respect in which the rationalists appear to have been in the right as against the empiricists, although, owing to the neglect or denial of relations, the deductions made by rationalists were, if anything, more apt to be mistaken than those made by empiricists.

Having now seen that there must be such entities as universals, the next point to be proved is that their being is not merely mental. By this is meant that whatever being belongs to them is independent of their being thought of or in any way apprehended by minds. We have already touched on this subject at the end of the preceding chapter, but we must now consider more fully what sort of being it is that belongs to universals.

Consider such a proposition as 'Edinburgh is north of London.' Here we have a relation between two places, and it seems plain that the relation subsists independently of our knowledge of it. When we come to know that Edinburgh is north of London, we come to know something which has to do only with Edinburgh and London: we do not cause the truth of the proposition by coming to know it, on the contrary we merely apprehend a fact which was there before we knew it. The part of the earth's surface where Edinburgh stands would be north of the part where London stands, even if there were no human being to know about north and south, and even if there were no minds at all in the universe. This is, of course, denied by many philosophers, either for Berkeley's reasons or for Kant's. But we have already considered these reasons, and decided that they are inadequate. We may therefore now assume it to be true that nothing mental is presupposed in the fact that Edinburgh is north of London. But this fact involves the relation 'north of,' which is a universal; and it would be impossible for the whole fact to involve nothing mental if the relation 'north of,' which is a constituent part of the fact, did involve anything mental. Hence we must admit that the relation, like the terms it relates, is not dependent upon thought, but belongs to the independent world which thought apprehends but does not create.

This conclusion, however, is met by the difficulty that the relation 'north of' does not seem to *exist* in the same sense in which Edinburgh and London exist. If we ask 'Where and when does this relation exist?' the answer must be 'Nowhere and nowhen.' There is no place or time where we can find the relation 'north of.' It does not exist in Edinburgh any more than in London, for it relates the two and is neutral as between them. Nor can we say that it exists at any particular time. Now everything that can be apprehended by the senses or by introspection exists at some particular time. Hence the relation 'north of' is radically different from such things. It is neither in space nor in time, neither material nor mental; yet it is something.

It is largely the very peculiar kind of being that belongs to universals which has led many people to suppose that they are really mental. We can think *of* a universal, and our thinking then exists in a perfectly ordinary sense, like any other mental act. Suppose, for example, that we are thinking of whiteness. Then *in one sense* it may be said that whiteness is 'in our mind.' We have here the same ambiguity as we noted in discussing Berkeley in Chapter IV. In the strict sense, it is not whiteness that is in our mind, but the act of thinking of whiteness. The connected ambiguity in the word 'idea,' which we noted at the same time, also causes confusion here. In one sense of this word, namely the sense in which it denotes the *object* of an act of thought, whiteness is an 'idea.' Hence, if the ambiguity is not guarded against, we may come to think that whiteness is an 'idea' in the other sense, i.e. an act of thought; and thus we come to think that whiteness is mental. But in so thinking, we rob it of its essential quality of universality. One man's act of thought is necessarily a different thing from another man's; one man's act of thought at one time is necessarily a different thing from the same man's act of thought at another time. Hence, if whiteness were the thought as opposed to its object, no two different men could think of it, and no one man could think of it twice. That which many different thoughts of whiteness have in common is their *object*, and this object is different from all of them. Thus universals are not thoughts, though when known they are the objects of thoughts.

We shall find it convenient only to speak of things *existing* when they are in time, that is to say, when we can point to some time *at* which they exist (not excluding the possibility of their existing at all times). Thus thoughts and feelings, minds and physical objects *exist*. But universals do not exist in this sense; we shall say that they *subsist* or *have being*, where 'being' is opposed to 'existence' as being timeless. The world of universals, therefore, may also be described as the world of being. The world of being is unchangeable, rigid, exact, delightful to the mathematician, the logician, the builder of metaphysical systems, and all who love perfection more than life. The world of existence is fleeting, vague, without sharp boundaries, without any clear plan or arrangement, but it contains all thoughts and feelings, all the data of sense, and all physical objects, everything that can do either good or harm, everything that makes any difference to the value of life and the world. According to our temperaments, we shall prefer the contemplation of the one or of the other. The one we do not prefer will probably seem to us a pale shadow of the one we prefer, and hardly worthy to be regarded as in any sense real. But the truth is that both have the same claim on our impartial attention, both are real, and both are important to the metaphysician. . . .

Returning now to the problem of a priori knowledge, which we left unsolved when we began the consideration of universals, we find ourselves in a position to deal with it in a much more satisfactory manner than was possible before. Let us revert to the proposition 'two and two are four.' It is fairly obvious, in view of what has been said, that this proposition states a relation between the universal 'two' and the universal 'four.' This suggests a proposition which we shall now endeavour to establish: namely, *All a priori knowledge deals exclusively with the relations of universals.* This proposition is of great importance, and goes a long way towards solving our previous difficulties concerning a priori knowledge.

The only case in which it might seem, at first sight, as if our proposition were untrue, is the case in which an a priori proposition states that *all* of one class of particulars belong to some other class, or (what comes to the same thing) that *all* particulars having some one property also have some other. In this case it might seem as though we were dealing with the particulars that have the property rather than with the property. The proposition 'two and two are four' is really a case in point, for this may be stated in the form 'any two and any other two are four,' or 'any collection formed of two twos is a collection of four.' If we can show that such statements as this really deal only with universals, our proposition may be regarded as proved.

One way of discovering what a proposition deals with is to ask ourselves what words we must understand — in other words, what objects we must be acquainted with — in order to see what the proposition means. As soon as we see what the proposition means, even if we do not yet know whether it is true or false, it is evident that we must have acquaintance with whatever is really dealt with by the proposition. By applying this test, it appears that many propositions which might seem to be concerned with particulars are really concerned only with universals. In the special case of 'two and two are four,' even when we interpret it as meaning 'any collection formed of two twos is a collection of four,' it is plain that we can *understand* the proposition, i.e. we can see what it is that it asserts, as soon as we know what is meant by 'collection' and 'two' and 'four.' It is quite unnecessary to know all the couples in the world: if it were necessary, obviously we could never understand the proposition, since the couples are infinitely numerous and therefore cannot all be known to us. Thus although our general statement *implies* statements about particular couples, *as soon as we know that there are such particular couples*, yet it does not itself assert or imply that there are such particular couples, and thus fails to make any statement whatever about any actual particular couple. The statement made is about 'couple,' the universal, and not about this or that couple.

Thus the statement 'two and two are four' deals exclusively with universals, and therefore may be known by anybody who is acquainted with the universals concerned and can perceive the relation between them which the statement asserts. It must be taken as a fact, discovered by reflecting upon our knowledge, that we have the power of sometimes perceiving such relations between universals, and therefore of sometimes knowing general a priori propositions such as those of arithmetic and logic. The thing that seemed mysterious, when we formerly considered such knowledge, was that it seemed to anticipate and control experience. This, however, we can now see to have been an error. *No* fact concerning anything capable of being experienced can be known independently of experience. We know a priori that two things and two other things together make four things, but we do *not* know a priori that if Brown and Jones are two, and Robinson and Smith are two, then Brown and Jones and Robinson and Smith are four. The reason is that this proposition cannot be understood at all unless we know that there are such people as Brown and Jones and Robinson and Smith, and this we can only know by experience. Hence, although our general proposition is a priori, all its applications to actual particulars involve experience and therefore contain an empirical element. In this way what seemed mysterious in our a priori knowledge is seen to have been based upon an error.

It will serve to make the point clearer if we contrast our genuine a priori judgement with an empirical generalization, such as 'all men are mortals.' Here as before, we can *understand* what the proposition means as soon as we understand the universals involved, namely *man* and *mortal*. It is obviously unnecessary to have an individual acquaintance with the whole human race in order to understand what our proposition means. Thus the difference between an a priori general proposition and an empirical generalization does not come in the *meaning* of the proposition; it comes in the nature of the *evidence* for it. In the empirical case, the evidence consists in the particular instances. We believe that all men are mortal because we know that there are innumerable instances of men dying, and no instances of their living beyond a certain age. We do not believe it because we see a connexion between the universal *man* and the universal *mortal*. It is true that if physiology can prove, assuming the general laws that govern living bodies, that no living organism can last for ever, that gives a connexion between *man* and *mortality* which would enable us to assert our proposition without appealing to the special evidence of *men* dying. But that only means that our generalization has been subsumed under a wider generalization, for which the evidence is still of the same kind, though more extensive. The progress of science is constantly producing such subsumptions, and therefore giving a constantly wider inductive basis for scientific generalizations. But although this gives a greater *degree* of certainty, it does not give a different *kind*: the ultimate ground remains inductive, i.e. derived from instances, and not an a priori connexion of universals such as we have in logic and arithmetic.

5   Hans Hahn: CONVENTIONALISM (1933)

The old conception of logic is approximately as follows: logic is the account of the most universal properties of things, the account of those properties which are common to all things; just as ornithology is the science of birds, zoology the science of all animals, biology the science of all living beings, so logic is the science of *all* things, the science of being as such. If this were the case, it would remain wholly unintelligible whence logic derives its certainty. For we surely do not know all things. We have not observed everything and hence we cannot know how everything behaves.

Our thesis, on the contrary, asserts: logic does not by any means treat of the totality of things, it does not treat of objects at all but

Reprinted from the pamphlet *Logik, Mathematik und Naturerkennen*, published in Vienna in 1933 as the second volume of the series entitled *Einheitswissenschaft*, with the kind permission of Mrs. Lily Hahn, Gerold & Co., Vienna, and Professor Rudolf Carnap, co-editor of *Einheitswissenschaft*. Translated by Arthur Pap.

only of our way of speaking about objects; logic is first generated by language. The certainty and universal validity, or better, the irrefutability of a proposition of logic derives just from the fact that it says nothing about objects of any kind.

Let us clarify the point by an example. I talk about a well-known plant: I describe it, as is done in botanical reference books, in terms of the number, color and form of its blossom leaves, its calyx leaves, its stamina, the shape of its leaves, its stem, its root, etc., and I make the stipulation: let us call any plant of this kind "snow rose," but let us also call it "helleborus niger." Thereupon I can pronounce with absolute certainty the universally valid proposition: "every snow rose is a helleborus niger." It is certainly valid, always and everywhere; it is not refutable by any sort of observation; but it says nothing at all about facts. I learn nothing from it about the plant in question, when it is in bloom, where it may be found, whether it is common or rare. It tells me nothing about the plant; it cannot be disconfirmed by any observation. This is the basis of its certainty and universal validity. The statement merely expresses a convention concerning the way we wish to talk about the plant in question.

Similar considerations apply to the principles of logic. Let us make the point with reference to the two most famous laws of logic: the law of contradiction and the law of the excluded middle. Take, for example, colored objects. We learn, by training as I am tempted to say, to apply the designation "red" to some of these objects, and we stipulate that the designation "not red" be applied to all other objects. On the basis of this stipulation we now can assert with absolute certainty the proposition that there is no object to which both the designation "red" and the designation "not red" are applied. It is customary to formulate this briefly by saying that nothing is both red and not red. This is the law of contradiction. And since we have stipulated that the designation "red" is to be applied to some objects and the designation "not red" to *all* other objects, we can likewise pronounce with absolute certainty the proposition: everything is either designated as "red" or as "not red," which it is customary to formulate briefly by saying that everything is either red or not red. This is the law of the excluded middle. These two propositions, the law of contradiction and the law of the excluded middle, say nothing at all about objects of any kind. They do not tell me of any of them whether they are red or not red, which color they have, or anything else. They merely stipulate a method for applying the designations "red" and "not red" to objects, i.e. they prescribe a *method of speaking about things*. And their universal validity and certainty, their irrefutability, just derives from the fact that they say nothing at all about objects.

The same is to be said of all the other principles of logic. We shall presently return to this point. But first let us insert another consideration. We have previously maintained that there can be no material a priori, i.e. no a priori knowledge about matters of fact. For we cannot know the outcome of an observation before the latter takes place. We have made clear to ourselves that no material a priori is contained in the laws of contradiction and of excluded middle, since they say nothing about facts. There are those, however, who would perhaps admit that the nature of the laws of logic is as described, yet would insist that there is a material a priori elsewhere, e.g. in the statement "nothing is both red and blue" (of course what is meant is: at the same time and place) which is alleged to express real a priori knowledge about the nature of things. Even before having made any observation, they say, one can predict with absolute certainty that it will not disclose a thing which is both blue and red; and it is maintained that such a priori knowledge is obtained by "eidetic insight" or an intuitive grasp of the essence of colors. If one desires to adhere to our thesis that there is no kind of material a priori, one must somehow face statements like "nothing is both blue and red." I want to attempt this in a few suggestive words, though they cannot by any means do full justice to this problem which is not easy. It surely is correct that we can say with complete certainty before having made any observations: the latter will not show that a thing is both blue and red — just as we can say with complete certainty that no observation will yield the result that a thing is both red and not red, or that a snow rose is not a helleborus niger. The first statement, however, is not a case of a material a priori any more than the second and third. Like the statements "every snow rose is a helleborus niger": and "nothing is both red and not red," the statement "nothing is both blue and red" says nothing at all about the nature of things; it likewise refers only to our proposed manner of speaking about objects, of applying designations to them. Earlier we said: there are some objects that we call "red," every other object we call "not red," and from this we derive the laws of contradiction and excluded middle. Now we say: some objects we call "red," some *other* objects we call "blue," and *other* objects again we call "green," etc. But if it is in this way that we ascribe color designations to objects, then we can say with certainty in advance: in this procedure no object is designated both as "red" and as "blue," or more briefly: no object is both red and blue. The reason why we can say this with certainty is that we have regulated the ascription of color designations to objects in just this way.

We see, then, that there are two totally different kinds of statements: those which really say something about objects, and those which do not say anything about objects but only stipulate rules for speaking about objects. If I ask "what is the color of Miss Erna's new dress?" and get the answer "Miss Erna's new dress is not both red and blue (all over)," then no information about this dress has been given to me at all. I have been made no wiser by it. But if I get the answer "Miss Erna's new dress is red," then I have received some genuine information about the dress.

Let us clarify this distinction in terms of one more example. A statement which really says something about the objects which it mentions, is the following: "If you heat this piece of iron up to 800°, it will turn red, if you heat it up to 1300°, it will turn white." What makes the difference between this statement and the statements cited above, which say nothing about facts? The application of temperature designations to objects is *independent* of the application of color designations, whereas the color designations "red" and "not red," or "red" and "blue" are applied to objects in *mutual dependence*. The statements "Miss Erna's new dress is either red or not red" and "Miss Erna's new dress is not both red and blue" merely express this dependence, hence make no assertion about that dress, and are for that reason absolutely certain and irrefutable. The above statement about the piece of iron, on the other hand, relates independently given designations, and therefore really says something about that piece of iron and is for just that reason not certain nor irrefutable by observation.

The following example may make the difference between these two kinds of statements particularly clear. If someone were to tell me: "I raised the temperature of this piece of iron to 800° but it did not turn red," then I would test his assertion; the result of the test may be that he was lying, or that he was the victim of an illusion, but perhaps it would turn out that — contrary to my previous beliefs — there are cases where a piece of iron heated to 800° does not become red-hot, and in that case I would just change my opinion about the reaction of iron to heating. But if someone tells me "I raised the temperature of this piece of iron to 800°, and this made it turn both red and not red" or "it became both red and white," then I will certainly make no test whatever. Nor will I say "he has told me a lie," or "he has become the victim of an illusion" and it is quite certain that I would not change my beliefs about the reaction of iron to heating. The point is — it is best to express it in language which any card player is familiar with — that the man has revoked: he has violated the rules in accordance with which we want to speak, and I shall refuse to speak with him any longer. It is as though one attempted in a game of chess to move the bishop orthogonally. In this case too, I would not make any tests, I would not change my beliefs about the behavior of things, but I would refuse to play chess with him any longer.

To sum up: we must distinguish two kinds of statements: those which say something about facts and those which merely express the way in which the rules which govern the application of words to facts depend upon each other. Let us call statements of the latter kind *tautologies*: they say nothing about objects and are for this very reason certain, universally valid, irrefutable by observation; whereas the statements of the former kind are not certain and are refutable by observation. The logical laws of contradiction and of the excluded middle are tautologies, likewise, e.g., the statement "nothing is both red and blue."

And now we maintain that in the same way all the other laws of logic are tautologies. Let us, therefore, return to logic once more in order to clarify the matter by an example. As we said, the designation "red" is applied to certain objects and the convention is adopted of applying the designation "not red" to any other object. It is this convention about the use of negation which is expressed by the laws of contradiction and of the excluded middle. Now we add the convention — still taking our examples from the domain of colors — that any object which is called "red" is also to be called "red or blue," "blue or red," "red or yellow," "yellow or red," etc., that every object which is called "blue," is also called "blue or red," "red or blue," "blue or yellow," "yellow or blue," etc., and so on. On the basis of this convention, we can again assert with complete certainty the proposition: "every red object is either red or blue." This is again a tautology. We do not speak about the objects, but only about our manner of talking about them.

If once more we remind ourselves of the way in which the desig-

nations "red," "not red," "blue," "red or blue," etc. are applied to
objects, we can moreover assert with complete certainty and irrefutability: everything to which both designations "red or blue" and "not
red" are applied, is also designated as "blue" — which is usually put
more briefly: if a thing is red or blue and not red, then it is blue. Which
is again a tautology. No information about the nature of things is
contained in it, it only expresses the sense in which the logical words
"not" and "or" are used.

Thus we have arrived at something fundamental: our conventions
regarding the use of the words "not" and "or" is such that in asserting
the two propositions "object A is either red or blue" and "object A is
not red," I have implicitly already asserted "object A is blue." This
is the essence of so-called *logical deduction*. It is not, then, in any way
based on real connections between states of affairs, which we apprehend
in thought. On the contrary, it has nothing at all to do with the nature
of things, but derives from our manner of speaking about things. A
person who refused to recognize logical deduction would not thereby
manifest a different belief from mine about the behavior of things,
but he would refuse to speak about things according to the same rules
as I do. I could not convince him, but I would have to refuse to speak
with him any longer, just as I should refuse to play chess with a partner
who insisted on moving the bishop orthogonally.

What logical deduction accomplishes, then, is this: it makes us
aware of all that we have implicitly asserted — on the basis of conventions regarding the use of language — in asserting a system of
propositions, just as, in the above example, "object A is blue" is implicitly asserted by the assertion of the two propositions "object A is red
or blue" and "object A is not red."

In saying this we have already suggested the answer to the question, which naturally must have forced itself on the mind of every
reader who has followed our argument: if it is really the case that the
propositions of logic are tautologies, that they say nothing about
objects, what purpose does logic serve?

The logical propositions which were used as illustrations derived
from conventions about the use of the words "not" and "or" (and
it can be shown that the same holds for all the propositions of so-called
propositional logic). Let us, then, first ask for what purpose the words
"not" and "or" are introduced into language. Presumably the reason
is that we are not omniscient. If I am asked about the color of the dress

worn by Miss Erna yesterday, I may not be able to remember its color. I cannot say whether it was red or blue or green; but perhaps I will be able to say at least "it was not yellow." Were I omniscient, I should know its color. There would be no need to say "it was not yellow": I could say "it was red." Or again: my daughter has written to me that she received a cocker-spaniel as a present. As I have not seen it yet, I do not know its color; I cannot say "it is black" nor "it is brown"; but I *am* able to say "it is black or brown." Were I omniscient, I could do without this "or" and could say immediately "it is brown."

Thus logical propositions, though being purely tautologous, and logical deductions, though being nothing but tautological transformations, have significance for us because we are not omniscient. Our language is so constituted that in asserting such and such propositions we implicitly assert such and such other propositions — but we do not see immediately all that we have implicitly asserted in this manner. It is only logical deduction that makes us conscious of it. I assert, e.g., the propositions "the flower which Mr. Smith wears in his buttonhole, is either a rose or a carnation," "if Mr. Smith wears a carnation in his buttonhole, then it is white," "the flower which Mr. Smith wears in his buttonhole is not white." Perhaps I am not consciously aware that I have implicitly asserted also "the flower which Mr. Smith wears in his buttonhole is a rose"; but logical deduction brings it to my consciousness. To be sure, this does not mean that I know whether the flower which Mr. Smith wears in his buttonhole really is a rose; if I notice that it is not a rose, then I must not maintain my previous assertions — otherwise I sin against the rules of speaking, I revoke. . . .

And now let us be clear what a world-wide difference there is between our conception and the traditional — perhaps one may say: platonizing — conception, according to which the world is made in accordance with the laws of logic and mathematics ("God is perennially doing mathematics"), and our thinking, a feeble reflection of God's omniscience, is an instrument given to us for comprehending the eternal laws of the world. No! Our thinking cannot give insight into any sort of reality. It cannot bring us information of any fact in the world. It only refers to the manner in which we speak about the world. All it can do is to transform tautologically what has been said. There is no possibility of piercing through the sensible world disclosed by observation to a "world of true being": any metaphysics is impossible! Impossible, not because the task is too difficult for our human thinking, but because it is meaningless, because every attempt to do metaphysics is an attempt to speak in a way that contravenes the agreement as to how we wish to speak, comparable to the attempt to capture the queen (in a game of chess) by means of an orthogonal move of the bishop.

6   Arthur Pap: LAWS OF LOGIC (1959)

The philosophers of science who have contributed the lion's share to the clarification of mathematics, logic, and the relation of these formal sciences to experience, are the logical positivists. And it is one of their characteristic tenets that the laws or truths of logic are tautologies and thus have no "factual content"; another terminology often used to make the same claim is that they are "analytic," in contrast to the synthetic propositions established by the factual sciences. It is also not uncommon to pass from this assertion to the conclusion that the allegedly inexorable necessity of the laws of logic is somehow reducible to linguistic conventions. The latter thesis is sometimes called *logical conventionalism.* . . .

Why did this seem to have great philosophical significance to the logical positivists, as well as to some of their critics? Because it was believed that a tautology owes its *necessity* to the force of linguistic conventions, and that therefore such a reduction would *explain* logical necessity without any metaphysical assumptions. Consider again the prototype of tautology, "*p* or not-*p*," which corresponds to the law of the excluded middle: For any proposition *p*, either *p* or the negation of *p* is true. That any statement of this form must be true follows from the definitions of "or" and "not," given in the form of statements of the truth-conditions of disjunctions and negations. Similarly, the principle of deductive inference, that whatever proposition is implied by true propositions is itself true, would seem to owe its validity to the very rule governing the use of "implies": to say that *p* implies *q* though *p* is true and *q* false, is just as self-contradictory as to say that *X* is a bachelor and married at the same time. If so, it looks as though the compulsion we feel to assent to these laws of logic is simply the ingrained

Reprinted with permission of The Macmillan Company from *An Introduction to the Philosophy of Science* by Arthur Pap. © The Free Press of Glencoe 1962.

habit of abiding by the linguistic conventions we were educated to conform to when we were taught the language. But linguistic conventions, after all, *may* be changed. Therefore, say the logical conventionalists, systems of logic may be changed; there is no absolute logical necessity; the logical necessity of a proposition is entirely relative to linguistic conventions, which it is possible to change. . . .

If by saying that no law of logic has *absolute* validity we mean that whether or not a given formula or sentence expresses a law of logic (in either the narrower sense, viz. truth-functional tautology, or the broader sense of "formal truth") depends on the interpretation of the logical constants, the claim is undoubtedly correct. But once it is clearly understood that the truth or falsehood of *any* sentence depends on its interpretation, such a "relativism" appears to be quite innocuous. At any rate, in this light the controversy between the conventionalist and the rationalist regarding the necessity of the laws of logic appears rather futile. What one ascribes truth to, be it formal or empirical truth, is never a bare sentence (string of marks, or sequence of noises), but a statement that is made by means of a given sentence, and what that statement is depends on the *meanings* that are assigned to the constituent symbols. Clearly the truth of a statement I am making by the use of a sentence *p* cannot be converted into falsehood by putting upon some symbol contained in *p* an interpretation different from the one I intended. And this is the case whether the statement be necessary or contingent. What I mean by saying "There are no squares that are not equilateral" is necessarily true and will remain so even if the word "square" should come to be used in the sense in which "triangle" is used at present. If at such a later time, at which we are supposing the relevant linguistic conventions to be different, the same words were used in accordance with what were then the linguistic conventions, they would be used to make a false statement. But that does not mean that the statement I am *now* making by means of that sentence would have been falsified.

It is hard to believe that the conventionalist interpretation of the laws of logic, which has been advocated by acute, sophisticated philosophers, amounts to just a gross failure to distinguish between a bare sentence (a certain kind of sequence of linguistic signs) and an assertion made by means of a sentence. Some conventionalists have meant to say, indeed have said explicitly, that the rationalists err in regarding the traditional laws of logic as necessary truths apprehended by reason, because they are "laws" in a prescriptive rather than a descriptive sense. When we speak of the laws of nature, such as the law of freely falling bodies, the law of gravitation, the laws of chemistry, we mean universal statements that *describe* the world, the course of nature as it happens to be. Now, the laws of logic do not describe any contingent features of the world that can be conceived to be different. They do not even describe mental phenomena, e.g., men's habits of drawing such and such conclusions from such and such premises. For if we find a man reasoning fallaciously, i.e., inferring from propositions assumed to be true a proposition that just does not follow from them, we do not say that the relevant law of logic has been refuted. We are prepared to describe conceivable observations that would refute certain presumed laws of nature, including laws of mental association, but it would be even absurd to suppose that any observations, whether of physical or of psychological facts, might ever refute a law such as "If a thing has either property P or property Q, and it does not have P, then it has Q." According to the conventionalist's diagnosis of rationalism, the rationalist has been led to postulate a mysterious realm of necessary truths apprehended by reason because, while realizing that the valid sentences of logic do not describe empirical facts, he makes the mistaken assumption that they do describe facts of some kind. But, says the conventionalist, they are not descriptive sentences at all, they are *rules*. In particular, they are rules for the use of logical constants. Naturally, a rule cannot be refuted by any facts, because it does not make sense to speak of "refuting" a rule; a rule can only be violated.

In order to understand this conception of laws of logic as linguistic rules, we should reflect on the method of specifying the meanings of logical constants, i.e., such expressions as "and," "or," "not," "if, then," "all," which are involved in scientific discourse about any subject-matter. The validity of a statement of logic depends only on the meanings of logical constants, but how are the latter to be specified? Explicit definition is not possible. Some logical constants, on the other hand, can be contextually defined in terms of others. Examples:

all things have property P = *not-*(*some* things do *not* have P)
$$p \ and \ q = not\text{-}(not\text{-}p \ or \ not\text{-}q)$$
$$p \ or \ q = if \ not\text{-}p, \ then \ q$$

Let us assume that in our logical system the logical constants here used to define contextually "all," "and," and "or," viz. "some," "not," and "if, then," occur as primitives. How are we to explain their meanings, their rules of usage? Superficially it seems that this can easily be done (at least for "not" and "if, then") by means of truth tables which stipulate the conditions under which statements of the forms "not-p" and "if p, then q" are true. The truth table for "not" is very simple:

p	not-p
T	F
F	T

Here "T" means true, and "F" false, and the table is to be read from left to right as follows: if p is true, then not-p is false, and if p is false, then not-p is true. But as a definition this is circular if "p is false" is in turn defined as "p is not true." More obviously still, it would be circular to attempt to explain the meaning of "if, then" by means of a truth table. Quite apart from the consideration that the truth of a conditional statement (i.e., statement of the form "If p, then q") does not just depend on the truth-values of the component statements, but rather on their meanings (technically this is expressed by saying that "if, then" is, in most uses, not a truth-functional connective), it is clear that we use "if, then" in interpreting any truth table. For a truth table says that a given kind of compound statement, such as conjunction, disjunction, negation, is true *if* the combinations of truth-values of the component statements are such and such. We must have recourse, then, to another method of formulating the rules of use of the primitive logical constants. The method in question differs fundamentally from *definition* in the usual sense, i.e., formulation of rules of substitution or translation by virtue of which the defined expression is theoretically eliminable. It is the method of *postulates*.

Thus we might explain "if, then" by stipulating that all statements of the following forms are to be true (note that this is different from *asserting* that all such statements *are* true, for according to ordinary usage of "assert," "I assert that p is true" makes sense only if it makes sense to doubt whether p is true, but such doubt is senseless if "p" just serves to specify, partially, the meanings of constituent terms):[1] if

[1] Readers who are untrained in formal logic will find it easier to grasp the sense of these postulates if they occasionally replace "if p, then q" by "p implies q" — though this is technically inaccurate inasmuch as grammar requires "p" and "q" to be quoted when they are connected by "implies." The first postulate, for example, is then recognizable as the principle of the hypothetical syllogism in the form: if "p" implies "q," then, if "q" implies "r," then "p" implies "r."

(if p, then q), then, if (if q, then r), then (if p, then r); if p, then, if (if p, then q), then q. Then we might add postulates introducing "not" along with "if, then": if p, then not-(not-p); if not-q, then, if (if p, then q), then not-p; if p, then (if not-p, then q). We have postulated, then, that all statements derivable from these schemas by substituting statements for the statement variables (in such a way that the same statement replaces the same variable within a given schema, though the same statement may be substituted for different variables) are to be true. The schemas correspond to the following principles of logic: the principle of the hypothetical syllogism (corresponding to *barbara* in the theory of categorical syllogisms); a statement implied by a true statement is true (*modus ponens*); the principle of noncontradiction; a statement that implies a false statement is false (*modus tollens*); from a contradiction any proposition follows.

The conventionalist, now, maintains that it is senseless to speak, in the manner of rationalists, of insight into the necessary truth of such principles, because they are nothing but conventional assignments of meanings to the logical constants "if, then" and "not." It does not make sense to ask how we know, indeed know for certain, that every substitution instance of these schemas is true, because no cognitive claim is involved in stipulations of rules of usage. You can say, "I do not wish to use 'if, then' in such a way that every substitution instance of this schema is true," but it would be nonsense to say, "I do not believe that all substitution instances of this schema are true." In the same way, if one were to stipulate, " 'Green' is to be used to designate the color of these objects," he might be opposed by one who, for whatever reason, did not wish to use the word "green" that way. But one cannot sensibly counter: "Before accepting your rule I want to make sure that those objects really are green."

To be sure, if the expression for which a rule of usage is laid down already has a prior use, one can sensibly ask whether the rule conforms to that prior use. In the case of our logical schemata, it is clear that if any logician were to "postulate" them (in the explained sense), he would be guided by his familiarity with the already existing rules of usage of the logical constants. He would not, for example, postulate that all substitution instances of "If q, then (if p, then q), then p" are to be true, because if he did, he would require us to use "if, then" differently from the way it is in fact used. In other words, according to the actual use of "if, then" in English not all substitution instances of this schema are true. Whether or not the stipulations accord with actual linguistic usage is a question of empirical fact. But what the conventionalist is out to refute is the view that our knowledge of logical truths amounts to a priori knowledge of necessary propositions. Our knowledge that, say, the logical constants "if, then" and "not" are so used by English-speaking people that all substitution instances of, say, "If p, then not-(not-p)" are true, is just plain empirical knowledge. It is, of course, conceivable that a man might deny a statement of that form, but in that case we would just have to conclude that his speech habits are different: perhaps he uses "if, then" the way "either-or" is ordinarily used, for example. But to tell him "You cannot deny it, *because it is necessarily true*" is, according to the conventionalist, like saying "You must speak the way we speak, because you have to speak that way."

Yet, the conventionalist cannot get around the admission that there is such a thing as a priori knowledge of logical truths, which is in no intelligible sense reducible to stipulation of, or acquaintance with, linguistic rules. In the first place, it is a meaningful question to ask whether it is possible, say, to define "if, then" on the basis of "not" and "or" in such a way that (*a*) the definition accords approximately with ordinary usage, (*b*) our postulates are transformed into truth-functional tautologies if "not" and "or" are defined as truth-functional connectives in the usual way. The definition that fulfills these requirements is: If p, then q = not-p or q. We know, for example, on the basis of truth-table analysis, that any statement of the form "not-p or not-(not-p or q) or q" (the transform into primitive notation of "if p, then, if (if p, then q), then q") is a tautology. Surely it does not make sense to say *it is a linguistic rule* that in a language containing the mentioned rules for the use of "not" and "or" any statement of the above form is a tautology. Indeed, this metastatement is a necessary statement, not a contingent statement about linguistic usage. That is, it is inconceivable that, while the rules for the use of "not" and "or" remain the same, a statement of the above form should fail to be a tautology.

Secondly, logicians usually lay down their postulates, not in order to prescribe a usage for logical constants or to describe how they are in fact used, but in order to construct a system, and this means that they intend to deduce a lot of theorems from the postulates. These deductions are, of course, guided by rules of deduction. Two of the most important rules of deduction (whether or not they be absolutely indispensable) are the rule of substitution and the rule of detachment (or "modus ponens"). The rule of substitution says with reference to our postulates: any formula obtainable from a postulate by substituting for a statement variable another statement variable or a truth-function of a statement variable, the same substitution being made for each occurrence of a given variable, is a theorem (and any formula derivable from a theorem in the same manner is also a theorem). The rule of detachment says: if A and (if A, then B) are postulates or theorems, then B is a theorem (here A and B are syntactic variables ranging over formulae of the system). Without raising the question of the justification of these rules of deductive proof, we wish to insist on the following simple point: a metastatement to the effect that such and such a formula is a theorem in the system that is characterized by such and such postulates and such and such rules of deduction is not a "rule" of any kind. It is, if true, *necessarily true*. It is a fact that cannot be altered by changing rules, that in a deductive system with specified formation rules, postulates, and rules of deduction, such and such a formula is a theorem whose proof involves such and such a minimal number of elementary steps. That the discovery of such "facts" by mathematicians and logicians involves the manipulation of symbols in accordance with rules is entirely consistent with its being an intellectual discovery — even if it is a proposition about symbols and not about intangible and invisible abstract entities. Even if algebra were construed as a science whose subject matter consists of symbols, not of abstract entities such as numbers, it would be a meaningful question whether, say, Fermat's "last theorem" (for $n > 2$, there are no solutions for the equation: $x^n + y^n = z^n$) is really a theorem in such and such a system of algebra. Mathematicians have not found the answer yet, but most of them regard it as a serious and meaningful question. And the proposition in question is either necessary or impossible; it is not an empirical proposition. It would be silly to say that the question here is whether such and such rules ought to be adopted. The question is not like the question whether there is a number that satisfies the equation "$x^2 = 2$"; it is rather like the question whether there is a rational number that satisfies that equation. It was, indeed, no discovery that there is an irrational number that satisfies it. This was a matter of decision, of deciding to broaden, by fiat, the extension of the term "number," whatever the reasons motivating the decision may have been. But Euclid did not *stipulate* that the equation has no rational solution; he *discovered* it by a well-known indirect proof.

We conclude that though logical conventionalists have rendered a valuable service in focusing attention on the role played by linguistic conventions in the acquisition of logical and mathematical knowledge, they have not shown that there is no such thing as a priori knowledge of necessary propositions and that the necessity of the laws of logic "depends" in some intelligible sense on linguistic conventions. In particular, to say of a certain complicated statement that it is a tautology, is not to deny that it is necessarily true nor that it makes sense to speak of "discovering" its truth; it is rather to explicate what the necessity and its discovery consist in. The thesis of Whitehead and Russell that all mathematical propositions are tautologies is still acutely controversial; and the thesis that all necessary propositions are tautologies is certainly false. But whether it be true or false has no bearing whatever on the question whether there is such a thing as purely intellectual discovery of necessary truths. Of course there is such discovery. And the discovery by means of some mechanical decision procedure (such as the use of "truth tables") that a certain complicated form of deductive argument is valid because the corresponding implication is a tautology is not the least useful and respectable among such intellectual discoveries.

Entailment

7   Willard Van Orman Quine: IMPLICATION AND THE CONDITIONAL (1940)

To say that a city or a word has a given property, e.g. populousness or disyllabism, we attach the appropriate predicate to a name of the city or word in question. To say that a statement has a given property, e.g. the phonetic property of being a hexameter or the semantic property of truth or falsehood, we attach the appropriate predicate to a name of the statement in question — not to the statement itself. Thus, to attribute truth to:

> (1) Jones is ill

we write:

> (2) 'Jones is ill' is true,

and to attribute falsehood we write:

> (3) 'Jones is ill' is false.

Equivalently, we may write:

> (4) (1) is true,
> (5) (1) is false;

but never:

(6) Jones is ill is true,

(7) Jones is ill is false,

on the analogy of:

(8) $\sim$ Jones is ill.

(2)–(5) are about the statement (1), but (8) is not; it, like (1), is about Jones. 'Is true' and 'is false' attach to names of statements precisely because, unlike '$\sim$', they are predicates by means of which we speak *about* statements. Whereas statement connectives ('$\sim$', '$\cdot$', '$\vee$', '$\supset$', '$\equiv$') attach to statements to form statements, a predicate is an expression which attaches to names to form statements. Grammar alone is enough to condemn (6) and (7), since each occurrence of 'is' should have a noun as subject. Confusion over this matter results in the view that the suffix 'is true' is vacuous, and that the suffix 'is false' is the English translation of the prefix '$\sim$'; the view, in other words, that (6) is equivalent to (1) and (7) to (8).

In order to say that two objects stand in a given relation, e.g. hate, or remoteness, one puts an appropriate binary predicate (transitive verb) between names of the objects thus: 'Roosevelt hates Hitler,' 'Berlin is far from Washington.' To say that two statements stand in a given relation, whether the phonetic relation of rhyming or the semantic relation of implication, we put the appropriate binary predicate between names of the statements — not between the statements themselves. We may write:

(9) 'All men are mortal' implies 'all white men are mortal,'

(10) The third statement of the book implies the seventh,

but never:

(11) All men are mortal implies all white men are mortal

on the analogy of:

(12) If all men are mortal then all white men are mortal,

(13) All men are mortal $\supset$ all white men are mortal.

The verb 'implies' belongs between names of statements precisely because, unlike '$\supset$' or 'if-then,' it expresses a relation between statements; it is a binary predicate by means of which we talk *about* statements. (9) and (10) are about statements, while (12) and (13) are about men.

The relation of implication in one fairly natural sense of the term, VIZ. *logical implication*, is readily described with help of the auxiliary notion of *logical truth*. A statement is logically true if it is not only true but remains true when all but its logical skeleton is varied at will; in other words, if it is true and contains only logical expressions essentially, any others vacuously. Now one statement may be said logically to imply another when the truth-functional conditional which has the one statement as antecedent and the other as consequent is logically true. Thus (9), so construed, is equivalent to: (13) is logically true.

A trivial analogue, *material implication*, may be said to hold whenever the truth-functional conditional which has the one statement as antecedent and the other as consequent is true. Thus one statement materially implies another provided merely that the first is false or the second true. This relation is so broad as not to deserve the name of implication at all except by analogy. But — and this is the point usually missed — 'materially implies' is still a binary predicate, not a binary statement connective. It stands to '⊃' precisely as 'is false' stands to '∼'. Insertion of the connective '⊃' between statements as in (13) amounts to inserting the verb 'materially implies,' not between the statements themselves as in (11), but between their names as in (9).

With a few trivial exceptions such as material implication, any relation between statements will depend on something more than the truth values of the statements related. Such is the case, e.g. with the phonetic relation of rhyming. The same holds for the semantic relation of logical implication described above, and for any other relation which has (unlike material implication) a serious claim to the name of implication. Such relations are quite consonant with a policy of shunning non-truth-functional modes of statement composition, since a relation of statements is not a mode of statement composition. On this account, the policy of admitting none but truth-functional modes of statement composition is not so restrictive as might have at first appeared; what could be accomplished by a subjunctive conditional or other non-truth-functional mode of statement composition can commonly be accomplished just as well by talking *about* the statements in question, thus using an implication relation or some other strong relation of statements instead of the strong mode of statement composition. Instead of saying:

If Perth were 400 miles from Omaha then Perth would be in America one might say:

'Perth is 400 miles from Omaha' implies 'Perth is in America,'

in some appropriate sense of implication.

Much of what has been said regarding implication applies equally to other semantic relations of statements, e.g. *equivalence* and *compatibility*. Statements are logically equivalent when they logically imply each other, and logically compatible when one does not imply the other's denial. Or, what comes to the same thing, statements are logically equivalent when the biconditional formed from them is logically true, and they are logically compatible except when the conjunction formed from them is logically false, i.e. except when the denial of the conjunction is logically true. Trivial analogues, material equivalence and compatibility, are similarly determined: statements are materially equivalent when they materially imply each other, and materially compatible when one does not materially imply the other's denial. Or, what comes to the same thing, statements are materially equivalent whenever their biconditional is true, and materially compatible except when their conjunction is false, hence whenever their conjunction is true. Material equivalence is agreement in truth value, and material compatibility is joint truth. Equivalence and compatibility, even in this degenerate sense, must be distinguished from the biconditional and conjunction; insertion of '≡' or '·' between statements amounts to inserting 'is materially equivalent to' or 'is materially compatible with,' not between the statements themselves, but between their names.

Note that 'is true,' 'is false,' 'implies,' 'is equivalent to,' etc. do not admit of iterated application as do the statement connectives. The expressions which '∼', '·,' '⊃,' etc. govern and the expressions which they produce are homogeneously statements; the expressions produced can hence be so governed in turn, and thus we obtain statements of the forms:

$$\sim\sim-, \quad -\supset(-\supset-), \quad (\sim-\cdot-)\supset\sim-,$$

etc. But 'is false,' 'implies,' etc. govern names and produce statements; hence the expressions produced cannot be so governed in turn. Formally the predicates 'is false' and 'implies' resemble the predicates 'is negative' and '≤' of arithmetic rather than the statement connectives '∼' and '⊃'. Just as it is true for all numbers x, y, z that

$$(x \leqslant y \cdot y \leqslant z) \supset x \leqslant z$$

and   (v is negative $\cdot x \leqslant y$) $\supset x$ is negative,

so it is true for all statements ϕ, ψ, χ that

$$(\phi \text{ implies } \psi \cdot \psi \text{ implies } \chi) \supset \phi \text{ implies } \chi$$

and   (ψ is false $\cdot \phi$ implies ψ) $\supset \phi$ is false;

on the other hand the contexts:

$$(\phi \text{ implies } \psi \cdot \psi \text{ implies } \chi) \text{ implies } (\phi \text{ implies } \chi)$$

and: (ψ is false $\cdot \phi$ implies ψ) implies (ϕ is false)

make no more sense than:

$$(x \leqslant y \cdot y \leqslant z) \leqslant (x \leqslant z),$$
$$(v \text{ is negative} \cdot x \leqslant y) \leqslant (x \text{ is negative}).$$

In Whitehead and Russell's exposition and terminology the distinction between predicate and statement connective is blurred. The notation '— $\supset$ —' is explained indiscriminately in the sense of the truth-functional conditional and in the sense of material implication. It is translated not only thus:

(14) If — then —

but also thus:

(15) If — is true then — is true,
(16) — is false or — is true,
(17) — implies —.

Similarly '$\equiv$' is explained both in the sense of the truth-functional biconditional and in the sense of material equivalence, and '$\sim$' is explained both in the sense of denial and in the sense of falsehood. The authors even adopt 'implication' or 'material implication' as their regular terminology in connection with '$\supset$', and 'equivalence' in connection with '$\equiv$'. Actually, as we have seen, the blanks in (14) admit only statements whereas those in (15)–(17) admit only names of statements. In the construction of examples, indeed, grammatical sense leads Whitehead and Russell to fill the blanks of '— is true,' '— is false,' and '— implies —' with quotations rather than statements;[1] but the distinction is straightway obliterated in the discussion.

Once having noted the discrepancy between (14) and the other

[1] " 'x wrote Waverly' is true" (*Principia Mathematica*, vol. 1, p. 68); " 'the author ... was a poet' is false" (*ibid.*); " 'Socrates is a man' implies 'Socrates is mortal' " (*ibid.*, pp. 20, 138).

proposed translations of '— ⊃ —,' one need not delay in making his choice. In all technical developments the expressions which Whitehead and Russell adjoin to the sign '⊃' have the form of statements rather than names. The mere fact of its iteration indeed, e.g. in the manner

$$— ⊃ (— ⊃ —),$$

is enough to determine the sign as a statement connective rather than a predicate about statements. In short, the versions (15)–(17) do not operate in Whitehead and Russell's work beyond the level of unfortunate exposition and nomenclature. The English idion which '— ⊃ —' supplants in practice is not (15), (16), or (17), but (14). The case is similar with '≡' and '∼'.

On the topic of implication Whitehead and Russell have many critics, who rightly object that the trivial relation of material implication expressed in (16) is too weak to constitute a satisfactory version of (17). But it is seldom observed that this objection does not condemn the truth-functional conditional '— ⊃ —' as a version of 'if — then —'. Lewis, Smith, and others have undertaken systematic revision of '⊃' with a view to preserving just the properties appropriate to a satisfactory relation of implication; but what the resulting systems describe are actually modes of statement composition — revised conditionals of a non-truth-functional sort — rather than implication relations between statements.

If we were willing to reconstrue statements as names of some sort of entities, we might take implication as a relation between those entities rather than between the statements themselves; and correspondingly for equivalence, compatibility, etc. This procedure would dissolve the distinction between material implication and the truth-functional conditional, and likewise between other sorts of implication and other sorts of conditionals. 'Implies' would come to enjoy simultaneously the status of a binary predicate and the status of a binary statement connective. Expressions such as (11) would be legitimized; and so also would the iterated use of implication, characteristic of Lewis and Smith. For thus construing statements as names some slight support can be adduced, indeed, by appeal to substantive clauses. The statement 'All men are mortal' might be held to designate that abstract entity, whatever it is, which we ordinarily designate by the substantive 'that all men are mortal.' A deterring consideration, however, is the obscurity of these alleged entities. What are they like? and

under what circumstances may the entities designated by two statements be said to be the same or different entities? Certain entities
which are perhaps less obscure than these but no less abstract will
indeed be countenanced at a later point, viz. classes or properties, if
only through ignorance of how to get on without them; but entities
designated by statements are happily dispensable.[2] It thus seems well
to adhere to the common-sense view that statements are not names at
all, though they may contain names along with verbs and adverbs and
the rest. A statement remains meaningful, but meaningful by virtue
of its structure together with the meanings of the constituent names and
other words; its meaningfulness does not consist in its being a name of
something.

Conceding that 'implies' belongs between names of statements as
in (9), rather than between statements, one might still urge that such a
relation of implication produces a derivative mode of composition of
the statements themselves — namely, a mode which consists notation-
ally of compounding the statements by means of 'implies' *and* the two
pairs of quotation marks.[3] If implication is construed as going beyond
questions of truth value, this derivative mode of statement composition will not be truth-functional. Implication thus construed would
then seem, after all, to interfere with a policy of admitting none but
truth-functional modes of statement composition. By the same argument, indeed, a purely morphological or phonetic relation such as
containing or rhyming would interfere similarly. Actually, however,
derivation of modes of statement composition from relations in the
suggested fashion involves abuse of quotation. The statements buried
in the quotations in (9) cannot be treated in turn as constituents of
(9), for a quotation figures as a single irreducible word. Similar abuse
of quotation was seen in §4 to lead from ' "Cicero" has six letters' to
' "Tully" has six letters.'[4]

These latter remarks serve only to show that we can construe
implication as going beyond questions of truth value without *thereby*
committing ourselves to any form of conditional which goes beyond

[2] See my "Ontological Remarks on the Propositional Calculus," *Mind* (1934);
"Logistical Approach to the Ontological Problem," *Journal of Unified Science* (1940);
and "Designation and Existence," *Journal of Philosophy* (1939).

[3] Analogous reasoning appears in Huntington's "Note on a Recent Set of
Postulates for the Calculus of Propositions," *Journal of Symbolic Logic* (1939), p. 11.

[4] See also Tarski, "Der Wahrheitsbegriff in dem formalisierten Sprachen,"
Studia Phil. (1936), §1.

questions of truth value. The need for some such strong form of conditional might still be urged on other grounds. Certainly not all uses of the subjunctive conditional submit to the easy method of paraphrase illustrated in the case of Perth and America. When this fails we may look to other devices, e.g. Carnap's method of reduction sentences ("Testability and Meaning," *Philosophy of Science* (1936), pp. 439–453); but if any really useful cases prove to resist all such methods of analysis, then we shall perhaps have to choose pragmatically between the usefulness of those cases and the convenience and clarity of the truth-functional kind of statement composition. Mathematics itself gives rise to no such recalcitrant cases; and any which seem to arise beyond the bounds of mathematics should be critically regarded.[5]

8   Clarence Irving Lewis: STRICT IMPLICATION (1932)

The chief business of a canon of deduction is to delineate correctly the properties of that relation which holds between any premise, or set of premises, and a conclusion which can validly be inferred. Commonly this relation is called 'implication.' But as the preceding chapter has shown, there is more than one relation which can be made the basis of inference. If we conceive that the distinguishing mark of an implication-relation, pIq, is that if p is a true premise and pIq holds, q also will be true, then, as we have seen, the number of relations having this property, but distinguished one from another in other respects and answering to different laws, is indefinitely large. . . .

Now in some sense or other there must be a truth about deducibility which is not relative to this variety and difference of systems and their relations. Either a given proposition q is genuinely deducible from another, p, or it is not. Either, then, there is some one system which alone is true when pIq is translated "q is deducible from p," or none of

[5] For further discussion and references see Carnap, *The Logical Syntax of Language*, §§ 67–71.

From C. I. Lewis and C. H. Langford, *Symbolic Logic*, Dover Publications, Inc., New York, 1932, 1959. Reprinted through the permission of the publisher.

them states the truth of logic in that sense. On the other hand, there is a certain kind of consistency and rigor which characterizes truth-value systems, as well as systems of other than the truth-value type. There appears to be a sense in which any law of any such system represents an undeniable truth. The systems themselves are developed by a procedure which evidently possesses some kind of logical compulsion. Inference, based on any one of these truth-implications, may be used to derive the laws of the system from postulates or previously established theorems. And that such inference does not lead us astray is evidenced by the fact that all principles thus derived are verifiable by the matrix method. If the 'truth about deducibility' does not somehow include and account for this fact, then we shall have an unsolved puzzle left on our hands.

Any two implication-relations will be such that one of them holds in some class of cases in which the other does not. They cannot, then, each of them hold when and only when the consequent in the relation is genuinely deducible from the antecedent — if the truth about deducibility is unambiguous and fixed. Yet any one of them may genuinely give rise to inference; if the antecedent is a proposition known to be true, then the consequent will not be false. It becomes a problem, then, in what sense, if any, there can be a single relation answering to laws which are unambiguously determined, which holds when and only when q is deducible from p.

Let us first inquire what, if anything, is common to all the relations which can give rise to inference. All of them have the property that when the antecedent p in any such relation pIq is assertable as true, the consequent q cannot fail to have this status also. This property must belong not only to truth-implications but also to any relation, whether of the truth-value type or not, which could give rise to inference. The very meaning of inferring or deducing, and the purpose for which we perform any such operation, require that it should never be the case that a proposition which is true should imply one which is not.

All *truth* implications have the *additional* property in common that if p and q are both assertable as true, then pIq holds, regardless of any further consideration. That is, for any meaning of 'implies' which is definable in any truth-value system, it must be the case that, of any pair of true propositions (those having the value 1), each implies the other. The reason for this is simple: any relation whatever, of the truth-value type, must either hold always when the terms it relates are both true, or it must always fail to hold when both are true. For by the very nature of a truth-value function, given the fact that p and q are both true, any truth-relation must, by that fact alone, be categorically determined to hold between these terms, or it must be categorically determined not to hold. Hence, for any truth implication, either *every* true proposition must imply *every* true proposition, or *no* true proposition will imply *any* true proposition. This latter alternative would mean that the relation could never give rise to inference, since either true propositions would imply only those which are not true, or no true proposition would imply anything.

Thus any truth-implication, appearing in any truth-value system whatever, will be such that not only does no true proposition imply any which is not true, but also every true proposition implies every other which is true. This second property of such relations leads to a very important consequence: if we should take any such truth-implication, pIq, to be equivalent to "q is deducible from p," then every pair of true propositions must be such that each can validly be deduced from the other. Thus, in terms of any truth-implication, two propositions could be independent (one not deducible from the other) only if one of them be true and the other false.

As a statement about deducibility, this is quite surely an absurdity. Otherwise, any mathematical system which, for any conceivable interpretation, could represent the truth about something or other, would be deducible *in toto* from any single proposition of it taken as a postulate. It seems to us that the falsity of the assertion "Every true proposition is deducible from every other" hardly requires proof. But if this *is* false, then we have the unavoidable consequence that there can be no relation of truth-implication, pIq, which holds whenever q is deducible from p, and *fails* to hold when q is *not* deducible from p. Since all such truth-implications hold whenever p and q are both true, every such relation is *too inclusive* in its meaning to be equivalent to "q is deducible from p."

This conclusion is inescapable. But in that case, how can a truth-implication validly give rise to inference? . . .

We find a very simple answer to the question how an implication-relation which is rather 'queer,' and not at all equivalent to the relation of deducibility, may nevertheless give rise to completely valid inference. Define this relation — in English or any other terms which make its meaning really clear — and choose an instance in which the relation actually holds and the antecedent is actually true. The consequent also will then be true; for if the antecedent were true but the consequent false, the relation would not hold. Moreover, if for the relation pIg its meaning as defined be substituted, it will be found that from the two premises (1) "p is true" and (2) "pIq (read in English) holds," the truth of q can validly be deduced, by the commonly accepted principles of deduction. And yet if one takes pIq to express "q is deducible from p," the relation may not hold at all: it may be as absurd as it would be to say, "From 'Vinegar tastes sour,' we deduce 'Some men have beards.'"

We see further that if we wish to elicit that relation which holds whenever, in terms of any one of the variety of possible implication-relations, a deduction can validly be made, it is required that we should be able to distinguish between "pIq is true" and "pIq is a *tautology*." When pIq is true but not tautological, q can be deduced from the two premises, p and pIq; but only because "(p and pIq)Iq" is a tautology. When pIq is a *tautology*, q can be deduced from p.

This is precisely the logical significance of the relation $p \prec q$ in the system of Strict Implication. The one requirement of all implication-relations is that pIq must *not* hold when p is true and q false. Thus in order to express "pIq is a tautology," what is needed is to elicit a relation R such that pRq will mean "p true and q false, is a logically impossible combination," or "It is necessarily true — true under all conceivable circumstances — that it is not the case that p is true and q false." This is exactly the meaning of Strict Implication, as is evidenced by the equivalences:

$$p \prec q \cdot = \cdot \sim \Diamond (p \sim q) \cdot = \cdot \sim \Diamond \sim [\sim (p \sim q)].$$

Whenever any truth-implication, pIq, expresses a tautology (is necessarily true) the relation $p \prec q$ holds: when pIq is true but does not express a tautology, $p \prec q$ does not hold. So far, then, $p \prec q$ has the property requisite to that relation which holds when q is deducible from p, and does *not* hold when q is *not* deducible from p.

The same fact is evidenced, in more striking fashion, by the relation which exists between strict implication and any truth-implication, of any truth-value calculus. Let any relation of truth-implication be introduced into the system of Strict Implication, by suitable definition. (This can always be done: if in no other way, by explicit introduction of the truth-values and definition in terms of these.) The laws of this relation of truth-implication will then be provable theorems in the system of Strict Implication. And in these laws, in any case in which this truth-implication, I, is tautological, it will be possible to replace it by $\dashv3$; but in any case in which pIq is true but is not tautological, the relation I will *not* be replaceable by $\dashv3$. Every instance in which this truth-implication I gives rise to *inference*, in the truth-value system in which it occurs, will be a case in which I can be replaced by $\dashv3$. For example, we introduced the relation of Material Implication into the system of Strict Implication, in Chapter VI, by definition of $p \supset q$. From this definition, it was possible (using the propositions of Strict Implication as principles of deduction) to deduce every theorem of the system of Material Implication. This was demonstrated by deducing the postulates for Material Implication, as given in *Principia Mathematica*. In such theorems, as deduced in the system of Strict Implication, in every case in which the relation $\supset$ is assertable in a law (i.e., is tautological), $\supset$ can be replaced by $\dashv3$. But when an unasserted (non-tautological) relation $\supset$ appears in a theorem, it cannot, in general, be replaced by $\dashv3$.

We set down below two columns for comparison. Under (1), is given a proposition in the form in which it appears in the system of Material Implication. Each of the theorems cited can be proved in that form, from the definition of $p \supset q$, in the system of Strict Implication. But also it can be proved in the form given under (2), where any relation $\supset$ which is tautological is replaced by $\dashv3$. Where the relation $\supset$ appears under (2), it is not tautological in the theorem; and if $\supset$ were here replaced by $\dashv3$, the theorem would be false. (Reference numbers are, of course, those of the theorems in Chapter VI, where proof is given.)

(1)		(2)	
15.21	$p . \supset . q \supset p.$	15.2	$p . \dashv3 . q \supset p.$
15.23	$\sim p . \supset . p \supset q.$	15.22	$\sim p . \dashv3 . p \supset q.$
15.31	$\sim (p \supset q) . \supset . p \supset \sim q.$	15.3	$\sim (p \supset q) . \dashv3 . p \supset \sim q.$
15.41	$\sim (p \supset q) . \supset . q \supset p.$	15.4	$\sim (p \supset q) . \dashv3 . q \supset p.$

Of special interest is 14.29, $p . p \supset q : \dashv3 . q.$ Let us presume, for the moment, that $p \dashv3 q$ is precisely equivalent to "q is deducible from p." Then 14.29 means "q is deducible from the two premises, 'p' and 'p materially implies q.'" It does *not* mean that when $p \supset q$ holds, q is deducible from p. Inability to distinguish between (1) "If p is true and $p \supset q$ holds, then q is true" and (2) "When $p \supset q$ holds, q is deducible from p" is responsible for most of the confusion about material implication and deducibility. This distinction may be subtle, and the confusion understandable; but remembering our illustration, p = "Vinegar tastes sour" and q = "Some men have beards," we should see clearly that (1) is true but (2) is false.

Let us now turn back, briefly, to what we have said is a special case in which truth-implications give rise to inference, namely, the case in which such a relation is used in deducing one law of the system in which it occurs from another which has been assumed or already established. In that special case, the antecedent p in the relation will be a tautology (since it is a law of the system); pIq will also express a tautology; and the q which is deduced must also be a tautology. We have seen that in any case in which a truth-implication pIq gives rise to inference, "$(p$ and $pIq)Iq$" will be a tautology. Where the truth-implication in question is the relation of material implication, this principle is what is expressed by 14.29,

$$p.p \supset q: \dashv .q.$$

The further fact that if p is a tautology, or necessary truth, and $p \supset q$ is a tautology, then q is a tautological or necessary truth, is what is stated by 18.53:

$$p \dashv q. \sim\Diamond\sim p: \dashv .\sim\Diamond\sim q.$$

Since $p \dashv q. = .\sim\Diamond\sim[\sim(p \sim q)]. = .\sim\Diamond\sim(p \supset q)$, this may be transformed into

$$\sim\Diamond\sim p.\sim\Diamond\sim(p \supset q): \dashv .\sim\Diamond\sim q.$$

That is, if q is deducible from p (as it is when pIq is a tautology), then from this and the fact that p is a tautological or necessary truth we can deduce that q is a tautology also. Thus not only may a relation of truth-implication give rise to inference, but also it gives rise to inference in such a manner that when the premise is a law of the system, the consequent also will be a law of the system. The principles of Strict Implication express the facts about any such deduction in an explicit manner in which they cannot be expressed within the truth-value system itself, for the reason that, in Strict Implication, what is tautological is distinguishable from what is merely true, whereas this difference does not ordinarily appear in the symbols of a truth-value system.

In the light of all these facts, it appears that the relation of strict implication expresses precisely that relation which holds when valid deduction is possible, and fails to hold when valid deduction is not possible. In that sense, the system of Strict Implication may be said to provide that canon and critique of deductive inference which is the desideratum of logical investigation. All the facts about those cases in which any other implication-relation may genuinely give rise to inference are incorporated in and explained by the laws of this system — or they may be so incorporated by introducing the implication-relation in question into the system by definition. Also Strict Implication explains the paradoxes incident to truth-implications, such as

$$15.2 \quad p . \dashv . q \supset p \quad \text{and} \quad 15.21 \quad p . \supset . q \supset p,$$

"If p is true, then any proposition q implies p"; and

$$15.22 \quad \sim p . \dashv . p \supset q \quad \text{and} \quad 15.23 \quad \sim p . \supset . p \supset q,$$

"If p is false, then p implies any proposition q." It explains these by making it clear that "p implies q" in these cases is not equivalent to "q is deducible from p," but is a relation which may hold when p and q are independent propositions.

The one serious doubt which can arise concerning the equivalence of $p \dashv q$ to the relation of deducibility and concerning the adequacy of Strict Implication to the problems of deduction in general arises from the fact that strict implication has its corresponding paradoxes:

$$19.74 \quad \sim \Diamond p . \dashv p \dashv q,$$

"If p is impossible, then p strictly implies any proposition q"; and

$$19.75 \quad \sim \Diamond \sim p . \dashv . q \dashv p,$$

"If q is necessary, then any proposition p strictly implies q." If $p \dashv q$ is equivalent to "q is deducible from p," then to satisfy these theorems it must be the case that, from any proposition which negates a necessary or tautological truth, anything whatever can be deduced; and that any proposition whose truth is necessary or tautological can be deduced from anything whatever.

We wish to show that this is indeed the case, and that these theorems, as well as others in the system of Strict Implication which may be subject to a similar doubt, are paradoxical only in the sense of expressing logical truths which are easily overlooked.

But there are certain ambiguities which may cloud the issue. First, it must be understood that 'deducible' here means 'deducible by some mode of inference which is valid.' It might seem that this meaning is the obvious one which could not be missed, but, as we shall see, it might easily be confused with another which is of quite different import.

Second, we must observe the meaning of 'necessary' and 'impossible' here. By definition,

$$18.14 \quad \sim \Diamond \sim p . = . \sim p \dashv p . = . \sim (\sim p \circ \sim p);$$

To say "p is necessary" means "p is implied by its own denial" or "The denial of p is not self-consistent."

$$18.12 \quad \sim \Diamond p . = . p \dashv \sim p . = . \sim (p \circ p);$$

To say "p is impossible" means "p implies its own negation" or "p is not self-consistent." Necessary truths, so defined, coincide with the class of tautologies, or truths which can be certified by logic alone; and impossible propositions coincide with the class of those which deny some tautology.

Every tautology is expressible as some proposition of the general form $p \lor \sim p$. . . .

We may now indicate the manner in which, from a proposition whose truth is impossible, anything whatever may be deduced. The negation of any proposition which is of the form $\sim p \lor p$ is a corresponding proposition of the form $p \sim p$:

$$\sim p \lor p . = . \sim (p \sim p).$$

From any proposition of the form $p \sim p$, any proposition whatever, q, may be deduced as follows:

Assume $p \sim p$.	(1)
(1) $\dashv p$	(2)

If p is true and p is false, then p is true.

(1) $\dashv \sim p$	(3)

If p is true and p is false, then p is false.

(2) . $\dashv$:$p \lor q$	(4)

If, by (2), p is true, then at least one of the two, p and q, is true.

$$(3) . (4) : \dashv . q$$

If, by (3), p is false; and, by (4), at least one of the two, p and q, is true; then q must be true.

This demonstration is a paradigm, in which p may be any proposition so chosen that $\sim p \lor p$ will express the tautology which is in question; and q may be any proposition whatever. Thus any proposition one chooses may be deduced from the denial of a tautological or necessary truth: the theorem

$-p \cup p = -(p \& -p)$

$p \& -p$

etc.

$$\sim\!\Diamond p. \ \exists \ .p \ \exists \ q$$

states a fact about deducibility.

Similarly, from any proposition whatever, p, every proposition of the form $\sim\!q \lor q$ may be deduced, as follows:

$$\text{Assume } p. \tag{1}$$

$$(1). \ \exists \ :p \sim\!q. \ \lor \ .pq \tag{2}$$

If p is true, then either p is true and q false or p and q are both true.

$$(2) \ . = \ :p. \ \sim\!q \lor q \tag{3}$$

"Either p is true and q false or p and q are both true" is equivalent to "p is true, and either q is false or q is true."

$$(3). \ \exists \ .\sim\!q \lor q$$

If p is true, and either q is false or q is true, then either q is false or q is true.

This demonstration, likewise, is a paradigm, in which p may be any proposition whatever, and q may be so chosen as to give any desired tautology, $\sim\!q \lor q$. Thus tautologies in general are deducible from any premise we please: the theorem

$$\sim\!\Diamond\!\sim\!q. \ \exists \ .p \ \exists \ q$$

states a fact about deducibility.

Hence the two paradoxical theorems cited are no ground of objection to the supposition that strict implication, $p \ \exists \ q$, coincides in its properties with the relation "q is deducible from p." . . .

For the validity of the trains of reasoning in these proofs we must, of course, appeal to intuition. A point of logic being in question, no other course is possible. But let the reader ask himself whether they involve any mode of inference which he is willing to be deprived of — for instance, in making deductions in geometry. The proofs have the air of clumsy legerdemain, not because they are sophistical, but because they are 'so unnecessary.' They merely emphasize the fact that the logical division of any proposition p with respect to any exhaustive set of other alternatives, $\sim\!q \lor q$, does not alter the logical force of the assertion p. That is to say, the tautological character of tautologies is something which ordinary logical procedures assume; and in that sense, all tautologies are presumed as already given. This merely reflects the inevitable fact that, when deductions are to be made, logical principles themselves are already implicit. . . .

Strict Implication, defining $p \dashv 3\ q$ as a statement which holds when and only when the conjoint statement $p \sim q$, which asserts the premise and denies the conclusion, is self-inconsistent, is put forward with the intent to satisfy the requirement that $p \dashv 3\ q$ hold when and only when q is a consequence validly deducible from the premise p. On account of the paradoxes, there are many who doubt that it does so satisfy this requirement. And some amongst them have put forward alternative developments of a calculus of propositions designed to eliminate the paradoxes. It is especially regrettable to omit consideration of such proposals. But these have been too numerous and various to allow adequate report and discussion of them here. I shall, however, venture the conviction — recognizing my hazard in so doing — that without sacrifice or plain omission of some intuitively acceptable, analytically certifiable, and time-honored principle of inference, or the introduction of some assumption which fails of accord with such perduring logical principles, the paradoxes of Strict Implication are inescapable. They are unavoidable consequences of indispensable rules of inference.

9   Alan Ross Anderson and Nuel D. Belnap: ENTAILMENT (1962)

1. Paradoxes. Intuitionistic implication. Although there are many candidates for "logical connectives," such as conjunction, disjunction, negation, and for some writers even identity of individuals, we take the heart of logic to be the notion "if . . . then —"; we therefore devote the first chapter to this topic, commencing with some familiar remarks about the paradoxes.

1.1. Paradoxes. The "implicational paradoxes" are treated by most contemporary logicians somewhat as follows:

Reprinted in revised and shortened form with the kind permission of the authors and editors from "The Pure Calculus of Entailment," *Journal of Symbolic Logic*, Vol. 21, No. 1, March 1962, pp. 19–52, and "Tautological Entailments," *Philosophical Studies*, Vol. XIII, January–February 1962, Nos. 1–2, pp. 9–24.

The two-valued propositional calculus sanctions as valid many of the obvious and satisfactory principles which we recognize intuitively as valid, such as

$$(A \rightarrow (B \rightarrow C)) \rightarrow ((A \rightarrow B) \rightarrow (A \rightarrow C))$$

and

$$(A \rightarrow B) \rightarrow ((B \rightarrow C) \rightarrow (A \rightarrow C));$$

it consequently suggests itself as a candidate for a formal analysis of "if . . . then—." To be sure, there are certain odd theorems such as

$$A \rightarrow (B \rightarrow A)$$

and

$$A \rightarrow (B \rightarrow B)$$

which might offend the naive, and indeed these have been referred to in the literature as "paradoxes of implication." But this terminology reflects a misunderstanding. "If A, then if B then A" really means no more than "Either not-A, or else not-B or A," and the latter is clearly a logical truth; hence so is the former. Properly understood, there are no "paradoxes" of implication.

Of course this is a rather weak sense of "implication," and one may for certain purposes be interested in a stronger sense of the word. We find a formalization of a stronger sense in semantics, where "A implies B" means that there is no assignment of values to variables which makes A true and B false, or in modal logics, where we consider strict implication, taking "if A then B" to mean "It is impossible that (A and not-B)." And, *mutatis mutandis*, some rather odd things happen here too. But again nothing "paradoxical" is going on; the matter just needs to be understood properly—that's all.

And the weak sense of "if . . . then—" can be given formal clothing, after Tarski-Bernays as in Łukasiewicz 1929 (see bibliography), as follows:

$$A \rightarrow (B \rightarrow A),$$
$$(A \rightarrow B) \rightarrow ((B \rightarrow C) \rightarrow (A \rightarrow C)),$$
$$((A \rightarrow B) \rightarrow A) \rightarrow A,$$

with a rule of *modus ponens*.

The position just outlined will be found stated in many places and by many people; we shall refer to it as the Official view. We agree with the Official view that there are no paradoxes of implication, but for reasons which are quite different from those ordinarily given. To be sure there is a misunderstanding involved, but it does not consist in the fact that the strict and material "implication" relations are "odd kinds" of implication, but rather in the claim that material and strict "implication" are "kinds" of implication at all. In what follows, we will defend in detail the view that material "implication" is *not* an implication relation. Since our reasons for this view are *logical* (and not the usual grammatical pettifoggery), it might help at the outset to give an example which will indicate the sort of criticism we plan to lodge.

Let us imagine a logician who offers the following formalization as an explication or reconstruction of implication in formal terms. In addition to the rule of *modus ponens* he takes as primitive the following three axioms:

$$A \rightarrow A,$$
$$(A \rightarrow B) \rightarrow ((B \rightarrow C) \rightarrow (A \rightarrow C)), \quad \text{and}$$
$$(A \rightarrow B) \rightarrow (B \rightarrow A).$$

One might find those who would object that "if . . . then —" doesn't seem to be symmetrical, and that the third axiom is objectionable. But our logician has an answer to that.

There is nothing paradoxical about the third axiom; it is just a matter of understanding the formulas properly. "If A then B" means simply "Either A and B are both true, or else they are both false," and if we understand the arrow in that way, then our rule will never allow us to infer a false proposition from a true one, and moreover all the axioms are evidently logical truths. The implication relations of this system may not *exactly* coincide with the intuitions of naive, untutored folk, but it is quite adequate for my needs, and for the rest of us who are reasonably sophisticated. And it has the important property, common to all kinds of implication, of *never leading from truth to falsehood*.

There are of course some differences between the situation just sketched and the Official view outlined above, but in point of perversity, muddleheadedness, and downright error, they seem to us entirely on a par. Of course proponents of the view that material and strict "implication" have something to do with implication have frequently apologized by saying that the name "material implication" is "somewhat misleading," since it suggests a closer relation with implication than actually obtains. But we can think of lots of no more "misleading" names for the relation: "material conjunction," for example, or "material disjunction," or "immaterial negation." Material implication is *not* a "kind" of implication, or so we hold; it is no more a kind of implication than a blunderbuss is a kind of buss.

1.2. Program. This brief polemical blast will serve to set the tone for our subsequent investigations, which will concern the matter of trying to give a formal analysis of the notion of logical implication, variously referred to also as "entailment," or "the converse of deducibility" (Moore 1920), expressed in such logical locutions as "if ... then —," "implies," "entails," etc., and answering to such conclusion-signalling logical phrases as "therefore," "it follows that," "hence," "consequently," and the like.

We proceed to the formal analysis as follows:

In the remainder of this section, we use the especially perspicuous variant of natural deduction (due originally, and independently, to Gentzen 1934 and Jaskowski 1934) of Fitch 1952 in order to motivate the choice of formal rules for "→" (taking the arrow as the formal analogue of the connective "that ... entails that —"). The resulting system, equivalent to the pure implicational part H_I of Heyting's intuitionistic logic, is seen to have some of the properties associated with the notion of entailment.

In the next two sections we argue that, in spite of this partial agreement, H_I is deficient in two distinguishable respects. First, it ignores considerations of *necessity* associated with entailment; in **2**, modifications of H_I are introduced to take necessity into account, and these are shown to lead to the pure implicational fragment of the system S4 of strict implication (Lewis and Langford 1932). Second, H_I is equally blind to considerations of *relevance*; modifications of H_I in **3**, designed to accommodate this important feature of entailment, yield a calculus R_I, equivalent to the implicational part of the system of relevant implication first considered by Moh 1950 and Church 1951.

With **4** we are (for the first time) home: combining necessity and relevance leads naturally and plausibly to the pure calculus E_I of entailment. **5** proves that E_I really does capture the concepts of necessity and relevance in certain mathematically definite senses, and with this we complete the main argument of the chapter.

We remind the reader that we are in this chapter considering only pure implicational systems, leaving connections between entailment and other logical notions until later. For the purposes of the present discussion we use the arrow ambiguously, in order to compare various proposed formalizations of entailment; the context will indicate which of the various sorts of implication is under consideration. We shall use A, B, C, D, ..., A_i, ... as metalinguistic variables ranging over wffs (well-formed formulas) which are to be taken as specified in the usual way. Dots replace parentheses in accordance with conventions of Church 1956: outermost parentheses are omitted; a dot may replace a left-handed parenthesis, the mate of which is to be restored at the end of the parenthetical part in which the dot occurs (otherwise at the end of the formula); otherwise parentheses are to be restored by association to the left. Example: each of $(A \rightarrow \cdot B \rightarrow C) \rightarrow \cdot A \rightarrow B \rightarrow \cdot A \rightarrow C$ and $A \rightarrow (B \rightarrow C) \rightarrow \cdot A \rightarrow B \rightarrow \cdot A \rightarrow C$ abbreviates $((A \rightarrow (B \rightarrow C)) \rightarrow ((A \rightarrow B) \rightarrow (A \rightarrow C)))$.

1.3. Natural deduction. Since we wish to interpret "$A \rightarrow B$" as "A entails B," or "B is deducible from A," we clearly want to be able to *assert* $A \rightarrow B$ whenever there exists a deduction of B from A; i.e., we will want a rule of "Entailment Introduction" (hereafter "$\rightarrow$ I") having the property that if

A	hypothesis (hereafter "hyp")
·	
·	
·	
B	[conclusion]

is a valid deduction of B from A, then $A \rightarrow B$ shall follow from that deduction.

Moreover, the fact that such a deduction exists, or correspondingly that an entailment $A \rightarrow B$ holds, warrants the *inference* of B from A. That is, we expect also that an Elimination Rule (henceforth "$\rightarrow$ E") will obtain for $\rightarrow$, in the sense that whenever $A \rightarrow B$ is asserted, we shall be entitled to infer B from A.

So much is simple and obvious, and presumably not open to question. Problems arise, however, when we ask what constitutes a "valid deduction" of B from A. How may we fill in the dots in the proof scheme above?

At least one rule seems as simple and obvious as the foregoing. Certainly the supposition that A warrants the (trivial) inference that B; and if B has been deduced from A, we are entitled to infer B on the supposition A. That is, we may *repeat* ourselves:

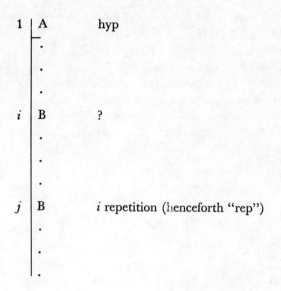

This rule leads immediately to the following theorem, the *law of identity*:

$$
\begin{array}{lll}
1 & \quad A & \text{hyp} \\
2 & \quad A & 1 \text{ rep} \\
3 & A \to A & 1\text{--}2 \to I
\end{array}
$$

We take the law of identity to be a truth about entailment; $A \to A$ represents the archetypal form of inference, the trivial foundation of all reasoning, in spite of those who would call it "merely a case of stuttering." Strawson 1952, (p. 15) says that "a man who repeats himself does not reason. But it is inconsistent to assert and deny the same thing. So a logician will say that a statement has to itself the relationship [entailment] he is interested in." Strawson has got the cart before the horse: the reason that A and $\overline{A}$ are inconsistent is precisely because A follows from itself, rather than conversely. (The difference emerges below in the full system E of Anderson and Belnap 1962 where we have $A \rightarrow A \rightarrow \overline{A\&\overline{A}}$ but not $\overline{A\&\overline{A}} \rightarrow \cdot A \rightarrow A$, just as we have $A \rightarrow B \rightarrow \overline{A\&\overline{B}}$ but not $\overline{A\&\overline{B}} \rightarrow \cdot A \rightarrow B$.)

But obviously more than the law of identity is required if a theory of entailment is to be developed, and we therefore consider initially a device contained in the variant of natural deduction due to Fitch 1952, which allows us to construct *within* proofs of entailment, further proofs of entailment called "subordinate proofs," or "subproofs." In the course of a deduction, under the supposition that A (say), we may begin a new deduction, with a new hypothesis:

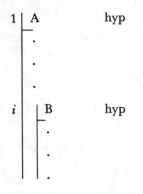

The new subproof is to be conceived of as an "item" of the proof of which A is the hypothesis, just like A or any other formula occurring in that proof. And the subproof of which B is hypothesis might itself have a consequence (by $\rightarrow$ I) occurring in the proof of which A is the hypothesis.

We next ask whether or not the hypothesis A holds also under the assumption B. In the system of Fitch 1952, the rules are so arranged that (for example) the hypothesis A may also be repeated under the assumption that B, such a repetition being called a "reiteration" to distinguish it from repetitions within the same proof or subproof:

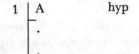

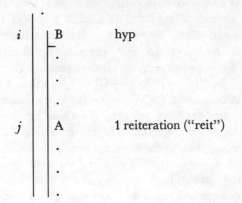

We designate as $H_I{}^*$ the system defined by the five rules, $\rightarrow I$, $\rightarrow E$, hyp, rep, and reit. A proof is *categorical* if all hypotheses in the proof have been discharged by use of $\rightarrow I$; and A is a *theorem* if A is the last step of a categorical proof. These rules lead naturally and easily to proofs of intuitively satisfactory theorems about entailment, such as the following *law of transitivity*.

1	$A \rightarrow B$	hyp
2	$B \rightarrow C$	hyp
3	$A \rightarrow B$	1 reit
4	A	hyp
5	$A \rightarrow B$	3 reit
6	B	$4\ 5 \rightarrow E$
7	$B \rightarrow C$	2 reit
8	C	$6\ 7 \rightarrow E$
9	$A \rightarrow C$	$4\text{-}8 \rightarrow I$
10	$B \rightarrow C \rightarrow \cdot A \rightarrow C$	$2\text{-}9 \rightarrow I$
11	$A \rightarrow B \rightarrow (B \rightarrow C) \rightarrow (A \rightarrow C)$	$1\text{-}10 \rightarrow I$

Lewis (Lewis and Langford 1932, p. 496) doubts whether "this proposition should be regarded as a valid principle of deduction: it would never lead to any inference $A \rightarrow C$ which would be questionable when $A \rightarrow B$ and $B \rightarrow C$ are given premises; but it gives the inference $B \rightarrow C \rightarrow \cdot A \rightarrow C$ whenever $A \rightarrow B$ is a premise. Except as an elliptical statement for "$(A \rightarrow B)\&(B \rightarrow C) \rightarrow \cdot A \rightarrow C$ and $A \rightarrow B$ is true," this inference is dubious." On the contrary, Ackermann 1956 is surely right that "unter der Voraussetzung $A \rightarrow B$ ist der Schluss von $B \rightarrow C$ auf $A \rightarrow C$ logisch zwingend." The mathematician is involved in no ellipsis in arguing that "if the lemma is deducible from the axioms, then this entails that the deducibility of the theorem from the axioms is entailed by the deducibility of the theorem from the lemma."

The proof method sketched above has the advantage, in common with other systems of natural deduction, of motivating proofs: in order to prove $A \rightarrow B$, (perhaps under some hypothesis or hypotheses) we follow the simple and obvious strategy of playing both ends against the middle: breaking up the conclusion to be proved, and setting up subproofs by hyp until we find one with a variable as last step. Only then do we begin applying reit, rep, and $\rightarrow$ E.

As a short cut we allow reiterations directly into subproofs, subsubproofs, etc., with the understanding that a complete proof requires that reiterations be performed always from one proof into another proof immediately subordinate to it. As an example (step 6 below), we prove the *self-distributive law* (H_I2, below):

1	$A \rightarrow \cdot B \rightarrow C$	hyp
2	$A \rightarrow B$	hyp
3	A	hyp
4	$A \rightarrow B$	2 reit
5	B	3 4 $\rightarrow$ E
6	$A \rightarrow \cdot B \rightarrow C$	1 reit
7	$B \rightarrow C$	3 6 $\rightarrow$ E
8	C	5 7 $\rightarrow$ E
9	$A \rightarrow C$	3–8 $\rightarrow$ I
10	$A \rightarrow B \rightarrow \cdot A \rightarrow C$	2–9 $\rightarrow$ I
11	$(A \rightarrow \cdot B \rightarrow C) \rightarrow \cdot A \rightarrow B \rightarrow \cdot A \rightarrow C$	1–10 $\rightarrow$ I

1.4. Intuitionistic implication. Fitch 1952 shows (essentially) that the set of theorems of H_I^* stemming from these rules is identical with the pure implicational fragment H_I of the intuitionist propositional calculus of Heyting 1930, which consists of the following two axioms, with $\to$ E as the sole rule:

$H_I1.$ $A \to \cdot B \to A$
$H_I2.$ $(A \to \cdot B \to C) \to \cdot A \to B \to \cdot A \to C$

H_I1 is proved in H_I^* as follows:

1	A	hyp
2	B	hyp
3	A	1 reit
4	$B \to A$	2–3 $\to$ I
5	$A \to \cdot B \to A$	1–4 $\to$ I

Thus far the theorems proved by the subordinate proof method have all seemed natural and obvious truths about our intuitive idea of *entailment*. But here we come upon a theorem which shocks our intuitions (at least our untutored intuitions), for the theorem seems to say that anything whatever has A as a logical consequence, provided only that A is true; if the formal machinery is offered as an analysis or reconstruction of the notion of entailment, or formal deducibility, the principle seems outrageous, — such at least is almost certain to be the initial reaction to the theorem, as anyone who has taught elementary logic very well knows. Formulas like $A \to \cdot B \to A$ and $A \to \cdot B \to B$ are of course familiar, and much discussed under the heading of "implicational paradoxes."

Those whose views concerning the philosophy of logic commit them to accept such principles are usually quick to point out that the freshman's objections are founded on confusion. E.g., Quine 1950 (p. 37) says that a confusion of use and mention is involved, and that (in effect) although

A implies (B implies A)

may be objectionable,

if A then if B then A

is not. But it is worth remarking that even if Quine and his followers are correct in maintaining that this feature of the grammar of English (or any other natural language) is absolutely essential to the logical point at issue, it is still true that the naive freshman objects as much to the second of the two formulations as the first. So do we.

Why does $A \rightarrow \cdot B \rightarrow A$ seem so queer? We believe that its oddness is due to two isolable features of the principle, which we consider forthwith.

2. Necessity: strict implication. For more than two millennia logicians have taught that logic is a *formal* matter, and that the validity of an inference depends not on material considerations, but on formal considerations alone. The companion view that the validity of a valid inference is no accident of nature, but rather a property a valid inference has necessarily, has had an equally illustrious history. But both of these conditions are violated if we take the arrow of H_I to express entailment. For if A is contingent, then $A \rightarrow \cdot B \rightarrow A$ says that an entailment $B \rightarrow A$ follows from or is deducible from a contingent proposition — in defiance of the condition that formal considerations *alone* validate valid inferences. And if A should be a true contingent proposition, then $B \rightarrow A$ is also contingently true, and an entailment is established as holding because of an accident of nature.

It might be said in defense of $A \rightarrow \cdot B \rightarrow A$ as an entailment that at least it is "safe," in the sense that if A is true, then it is always safe to infer A from an arbitrary B, since we run no risk of uttering a falsehood in doing so; this thought ("Safety First") seems to be behind attempts, in a number of elementary logic texts, to justify the claim that $A \rightarrow \cdot B \rightarrow A$ has something to do with implication. In reply we of course admit that if A is true than it is "safe" to say so (i.e., $A \rightarrow A$). But saying that A is true on the irrelevant assumption that B, is *not* to deduce A from B, nor to establish that B implies A, in *any* sensible sense of "implies." Of course we *can* say "Assume that snow is puce. Seven is a prime number." But if we say "Assume that snow is puce. *It follows that* (or *consequently*, or *therefore*, or *it may validly be inferred that*) seven is a prime number," then we have simply spoken falsely. A man who assumes the continuum hypothesis, and then remarks that it is a nice day, is not inferring the latter from the former, — even if he keeps his supposition fixed firmly in mind while noting the weather. And since a (true) A does not follow from an (arbitrary) B, we reject $A \rightarrow \cdot B \rightarrow A$ as expressing a truth of entailment or implication, a rejection which is in line with the view (shared even by those who hold that

$A \rightarrow \cdot B \rightarrow A$ expresses a fact about "if . . . then —") that entailments, if true at all are necessarily true.

How can we modify the formulation of H_I in such a way as to
guarantee that the logical truths expressible in it shall be necessary,
rather than contingent? As a start, we might reflect that in our usual
mathematical or logical proofs, we demand that all the conditions
required for the conclusion be stated in the hypothesis of a theorem.
After the word *"Proof:"* in a mathematical treatise, mathematical
writers seem to feel that no more hypotheses may be introduced —
and it is regarded as a criticism of a proof if not all the required hypotheses are stated explicitly at the outset. Of course additional machinery
may be invoked in the proof, but this must be of a logical character, i.e.,
in addition to the hypotheses, we may use only logically necessary
propositions in the argument. These considerations suggest that we
should be allowed to import into a deduction (i.e., into a subproof by
reiteration) only propositions which, if true at all, are necessarily true:
i.e., we should reiterate only entailments. And indeed such a restriction on reiteration would immediately rule out $A \rightarrow \cdot B \rightarrow A$ as a
theorem, while countenancing all the other theorems we have proved
thus far. We call the system with reiteration so restricted $S4_I$*. It can
be shown to be equivalent to the following axiomatic formulation,
which we call $S4_I$, since it is the pure strict "implicational" fragment of
Lewis' S4 (see Hacking 1963).

$S4_I1.$ $A \rightarrow A$
$S4_I2.$ $(A \rightarrow \cdot B \rightarrow C) \rightarrow \cdot A \rightarrow B \rightarrow \cdot A \rightarrow C$
$S4_I3.$ $A \rightarrow B \rightarrow \cdot C \rightarrow \cdot A \rightarrow B$

The restriction on reiteration suffices to remove one objectionable
feature of H_I, since it is now no longer possible to establish an entailment $B \rightarrow A$ on the (perhaps contingent) ground that A is simply true.
But of course it is well known that the "implication" relation of S4 is
also paradoxical, since we can easily establish that an arbitrary irrelevant proposition B "implies" A, provided A is a necessary truth.
$A \rightarrow A$ is necessarily true, and from it and $S4_I3$ follows $B \rightarrow \cdot A \rightarrow A$,
where B may be totally irrelevant to $A \rightarrow A$. This defect leads us to
consider an alternative restriction on H_I, designed to exclude such
fallacies of relevance.

3. Relevance: relevant implication. For more than two millennia logicians have taught that a necessary condition for the validity of an inference from A to B is that A be relevant to B. Virtually every logic book up to the present century has a chapter on fallacies of relevance, and many contemporary elementary texts have followed the same plan. Notice that contemporary writers, in the later and more formal chapters of their books, seem explicitly to contradict the earlier chapters, when they try desperately to con the students into accepting strict "implication" as a "kind" of implication relation, in spite of the fact that this relation countenances fallacies of relevance. But the denial that relevance is essential to valid argument, a denial which is implicit even in the view that "formal deducibility," in the sense of Montague and Henkin 1956, and others, is an implication relation, seems to us flatly in error.

Imagine, if you can, a situation as follows. A mathematician writes a paper on Banach spaces, and after proving a couple of theorems he concludes with a conjecture. As a footnote to the conjecture, he writes: "In addition to its intrinsic interest, this conjecture has connections with other parts of mathematics which might not immediately occur to the reader. For example, if the conjecture is true, then the first order functional calculus is complete; whereas if it is false, then it implies that Fermat's last conjecture is correct." The editor replies that the paper is obviously acceptable, but he finds the final footnote perplexing; he can see no connection whatever between the conjecture and the "other parts of mathematics," and none is indicated in the footnote. So the mathematician replies, "Well, I was using 'if . . . then —' and 'implies' in the way that logicians have claimed I was: the first order functional calculus *is* complete, and necessarily so, so anything implies that fact — and if the conjecture is false it is presumably impossible, and hence implies anything. And if you object to this usage, it is simply because you have not understood the technical sense of 'if . . . then —' worked out so nicely for us by logicians." And to this the editor counters: "I *understand* the technical bit all right, but it is simply not correct. In spite of what most logicians say about us, the standards maintained by this journal require that the antecedent of an 'if . . . then —' statement must be *relevant* to the conclusion drawn. And you have given no evidence that your conjecture about Banach spaces is relevant either to the completeness theorem or to Fermat's conjecture."

Now it might be thought that our mathematician's footnote should be regarded as true, "if . . . then —" being taken materially — but simply uninteresting because of its triviality. But notice that the editor's reaction was *not* "But heavens, that's trivial" (as the contention that the mathematical "if . . . then —" is the same as material "implication" would require); any such reaction on the part of an editor would properly be judged insane. His thought was rather, "I can't see any reason for thinking that this is *true*."

(In this connection we cite the case of an eminent logician of our acquaintance, who, on considering that Stone's representation theorem is equivalent to Post's completeness theorem, found the result interesting. He would have found it trivial, if he really believed, as he said he does, that he uses "equivalent" to mean "materially equivalent." He already knew they were both true. Nor would it have helped if he meant "strictly equivalent"; he also thought they were both necessarily true.)

No, the editor's point is that though the technical meaning is clear, it is simply not the same as the meaning ascribed to "if . . . then —" in the pages of his journal. Furthermore, he has put his finger precisely on the difficulty: to argue from the necessary truth of A to *if B then A* is simply to commit a fallacy of relevance. The fancy that relevance is irrelevant to validity strikes us as ludicrous, and we therefore make an attempt to explicate the notion of relevance of A to B.

For this we return to the notion of proof from hypotheses, the leading idea being that we want to infer $A \rightarrow B$ from "a proof of B from the hypothesis A." In the usual axiomatic formulations of propositional calculuses the matter is handled as follows. We say that $A_1, \ldots, A_n$ is a proof of B from the hypothesis A, if $A = A_1$, $B = A_n$, and each $A_i (i \geq 1)$ is either an axiom or else a consequence of predecessors among $A_1, \ldots, A_n$ by one of the rules. But in the presence of a deduction theorem of the form: from a proof of B on the hypothesis A, to infer $A \rightarrow B$, this definition leads immediately to fallacies of relevance; for if B is a theorem independently of A, then we have $A \rightarrow B$ where A may be irrelevant to B. For example, in a system with $A \rightarrow A$ as an axiom, we have:

$$
\begin{array}{lll}
1 & B & \text{hyp} \\
2 & A \rightarrow A & \text{axiom} \\
3 & B \rightarrow \cdot A \rightarrow A & 1\text{–}2, \rightarrow I
\end{array}
$$

In this example we indeed proved A → A, but though our eyes tell us that we proved it *under* the hypothesis B, it is crashingly obvious that we did not prove it *from* B: the defect lies in the definition, which fails to take seriously the word "from" in "proof *from* hypotheses." And this fact suggests a solution to the problem: we should devise a technique for keeping track of the steps used, and then allow application of the introduction rule only when A is relevant to B in the sense that A is *used* in arriving at B.

As a start in this direction, we suggest affixing a star (say) to the hypothesis of a deduction, and also to the conclusion of an application of → E just in case at least one premise has a star, steps introduced as axioms being unstarred. Restriction of → I to cases where in accordance with these rules both A and B are starred would then exclude theorems of the form A → B, where B is proved independently of A.

In other words, what is wanted is a system for which there is provable a deduction theorem, to the effect that there exists a proof of B *from* the hypothesis A if and only if A → B is provable. A system can be found in Church 1951 which can be shown to be such that A → B is a theorem just in case there is a proof B *from* the hypothesis A in the starred sense. (See also Moh Shaw-Kwei 1950 and Kripke 1960.) Church calls this system the "weak positive implicational propositional calculus," and uses the following axioms:

$R_I 1.$ $A \rightarrow A$ (*identity*)
$R_I 2.$ $A \rightarrow B \rightarrow \cdot C \rightarrow A \rightarrow \cdot C \rightarrow B$ (*transitivity*)
$R_I 3.$ $(A \rightarrow \cdot B \rightarrow C) \rightarrow \cdot B \rightarrow \cdot A \rightarrow C$ (*permutation*)
$R_I 4.$ $(A \rightarrow \cdot A \rightarrow B) \rightarrow \cdot A \rightarrow B$ (*contraction*)

Following a suggestion which John B. Bacon made to us in 1962, we think of this as a system of "relevant implication" (hence the name "R_I"), since relevance of antecedent to consequent, in a sense to be explained later, is secured thereby. The same suggestion was also made by Prawitz; first in a mimeographed version of Prawitz 1964 distributed to those attending the meeting at which the abstracted paper was read, and then in the more extended discussion in Prawitz 1965.

A deduction theorem was proved by both Moh 1950 and Church 1951; modified to suit present purposes, it may be stated as follows:

THEOREM.   If there exists a proof of B on the hypotheses $A_1, \ldots,$

A_n, in which all of $A_1, \ldots, A_n$ are used in arriving at B, then there is a proof of $A_n \rightarrow B$ from $A_1, \ldots, A_{n-1}$ satisfying the same condition.

So put, the result acquires a rather peculiar appearance: it seems odd that we should have to use *all* the hypotheses. One would have thought that for a group of hypotheses to be relevant to a conclusion, it would suffice if *some* of the hypotheses were used — at least if we think of the hypotheses as taken conjointly (cf. the *entailment theorem* of Belnap 1960). The peculiarity arises because of a tendency (thus far not commented on) to confound

$$(A_1 \& \ldots \& A_n) \rightarrow B$$

with

$$A_1 \rightarrow (A_2 \rightarrow (\ldots (A_n \rightarrow B) \ldots))$$

We would not expect to require that *all* the A_i be relevant to B in order for the first formula to be true, but we shall give reasons presently, deriving from another formulation of R_I, for thinking it sensible that the truth of the nested implication requires each of the A_i to be relevant to B; a feature of the situation which leads us to make a sharp distinction between the two formulas. It is presumably the failure to make this distinction which leads Curry 1959 (p. 13) to say of the relation considered in Moh's and Church's theorem above that it is one "which is not ordinarily considered in deductive methodology at all."

We feel that the star formulation of the deduction theorem makes clearer what is at stake in R_I. On the other hand Moh's and Church's deduction theorem has the merit of allowing for proof of multiply nested entailments in a more direct way than is available in the star formulation. Our next task therefore is to try to combine these approaches so as to obtain the advantages of both.

Returning now to a consideration of subordinate proofs, it seems natural to try to extend the star treatment, using some other symbol for deductions carried out in a subproof, but retaining the same rules for carrying this symbol along. We might consider a proof of contraction in which the inner hypothesis is distinguished by a dagger rather than a star:

$$
\begin{array}{lll}
1 & A \rightarrow \cdot A \rightarrow B \quad * & \text{hyp} \\
2 & A \quad \dagger & \text{hyp}
\end{array}
$$

(the different relevance marks reflecting the initial assumption that the two formulas, as hypotheses, are irrelevant to each other). Then generalizing the starring rules, we might require that in application of $\rightarrow$ E, the conclusion B must carry all the relevance marks of both premises A and A $\rightarrow$ B, thus:

1	A $\rightarrow$ ·A $\rightarrow$ B	*	hyp
2	A	†	hyp
3	A $\rightarrow$ ·A $\rightarrow$ B	*	1 reit
4	A $\rightarrow$ B	*†	2 3 $\rightarrow$ E
5	B	*†	2 4 $\rightarrow$ E

To motivate the restriction on $\rightarrow$ I, we recall that in proofs involving only stars, it was required that both A and B have stars, and that the star was discharged on A $\rightarrow$ B in the conclusion of a deduction. This suggests the following generalization: that in drawing the conclusion A $\rightarrow$ B by $\rightarrow$ I, we require that the relevance symbol on A also be present among those of B, and that in the conclusion A $\rightarrow$ B the relevance symbol of A (like the hypothesis A itself) be discharged. Two applications of this rule then lead from the proof above to

| 6 | A $\rightarrow$ B | * | 2–5 $\rightarrow$ I |
| 7 | (A $\rightarrow$ ·A $\rightarrow$ B) $\rightarrow$ ·A $\rightarrow$ B | | 1–6 $\rightarrow$ I |

But of course the easiest way of handling the matter is to use classes of numerals to mark the relevance conditions, since then we may have as many nested subproofs as we wish, each with a distinct numeral (which we shall write as a subscript) for its hypothesis. More precisely we allow that: (1) one may introduce a new hypothesis $A_{\{k\}}$, where k should be different from all subscripts on hypotheses of proofs to which the new proof is subordinate; (2) from A_a and $A \rightarrow B_b$ we may infer $B_{a \cup b}$; (3) from a proof of B_a from the hypothesis $A_{\{k\}}$, where k is in a, we may infer $A \rightarrow B_{a-\{k\}}$, and reit and rep retain subscripts (where a, b, c, range over classes of numerals).

As an example we prove the *law of assertion*.

1	$A_{\{1\}}$	hyp
2	$A \rightarrow B_{\{2\}}$	hyp
3	$A_{\{1\}}$	1 reit
4	$B_{\{1,2\}}$	2 3 $\rightarrow$ E
5	$A \rightarrow B \rightarrow B_{\{1\}}$	2–4 $\rightarrow$ I
6	$A \rightarrow \cdot A \rightarrow B \rightarrow B$	1–5 $\rightarrow$ I

This generalization $R_I{}^*$ can be shown to be equivalent to R_I.

If the subscripting device is taken as an explication of relevance, then it is seen that Church's R_I does secure relevance, since $A \rightarrow B$ is provable in R_I only if A is relevant to B. But if R_I is taken as an explication of entailment, then the requirement of necessity for a valid inference is lost. Consider the following special case of the law of assertion, just proved:

$$A \rightarrow \cdot A \rightarrow A \rightarrow A.$$

This says that if A is true, then it follows from $A \rightarrow A$. But it seems reasonable to suppose that any logical consequence of $A \rightarrow A$ should be necessarily true. (Note that in the familiar systems of modal logic, consequences of necessary truths are necessary.) We certainly do in practice recognize that there are truths which do not follow from a law of logic — but R_I obliterates this distinction. It seems evident, therefore, that a satisfactory theory of implication will require both relevance (like R_I) *and* necessity (like $S4_I$).

4. Necessity and relevance: entailment. We therefore consider the system which arises when we recognize that valid inferences require both necessity and relevance. Since the restrictions are most transparent as applied to the subproof format, we begin by considering the system $E_I{}^*$ which results from imposing the restriction on reiteration (of $S4_I{}^*$) together with the subscript requirements (of $R_I{}^*$). We summarize the rules of $E_I{}^*$ as follows:

(1) Hyp. A step may be introduced as the hypothesis of a new subproof, and each new hypothesis receives a unit class $\{k\}$ of numerical subscripts, where k is new.
(2) Rep. A_a may be repeated, retaining the relevance indices a.
(3) Reit. $(A \rightarrow B)_a$ may be reiterated, retaining a.

    (4) $\to$ E. From A$_a$ and (A $\to$ B)$_b$ to infer B$_{a\cup b}$.

    (5) $\to$ I. From a proof of B$_a$ on hypothesis $A_{\{k\}}$ to infer (A $\to$ B)$_{a\,-\{k\}}$, provided k is in a.

It develops that an axiomatic counterpart of E$_I$* has also been considered in the literature, E$_I$* in fact being equivalent to a pure implicational calculus derived from Ackermann 1956. One version of that system, to be called E$_I$, which can be shown to be equivalent to E$_I$*, is given by the following axioms:

E1.	A $\to$ A	*(identity)*
E2.	A $\to$ B $\to$ $\cdot$B $\to$ C $\to$ $\cdot$A $\to$ C	*(transitivity)*
E3.	A $\to$ B $\to$ $\cdot$A $\to$ B $\to$ C $\to$ C	*(restricted assertion)*
E4.	(A $\to$ $\cdot$B $\to$ C) $\to$ $\cdot$A $\to$ B $\to$ $\cdot$A $\to$ C	*(self-distribution)*

The equivalence of E$_I$* with E$_I$ gives us an easy proof technique for E$_I$, and we now state a summary list of laws of entailment, proofs of which will be left to the reader.

identity: A $\to$ A

transitivity: (suffixing)   A $\to$ B $\to$ $\cdot$B $\to$ C $\to$ $\cdot$A $\to$ C

             (prefixing)   A $\to$ B $\to$ $\cdot$C $\to$ A $\to$ $\cdot$C $\to$ B

contraction: (A $\to$ $\cdot$A $\to$ B) $\to$ $\cdot$A $\to$ B

self-distribution: (on the major)   (A $\to$ $\cdot$B $\to$ C) $\to$ $\cdot$A $\to$ B $\to$
                               $\cdot$A $\to$ C

           (on the minor)   A $\to$ B $\to$ $\cdot$(A $\to$ $\cdot$B $\to$ C) $\to$
                               $\cdot$A $\to$ C

replacement of the middle: D $\to$ B $\to$ $\cdot$(A $\to$ $\cdot$B $\to$ C) $\to$
                              (A $\to$ $\cdot$D $\to$ C)

replacement of the third: C $\to$ D $\to$ $\cdot$(A $\to$ $\cdot$B $\to$ C) $\to$ $\cdot$A $\to$
                             $\cdot$D $\to$ B $\to$ $\cdot$D $\to$ C

prefixing in the consequent: (A $\to$ $\cdot$B $\to$ C) $\to$ $\cdot$A $\to$ $\cdot$D $\to$ B $\to$
                               $\cdot$D $\to$ C

suffixing in the consequent: (A $\to$ $\cdot$B $\to$ C) $\to$ $\cdot$A $\to$ $\cdot$C $\to$ D $\to$
                               $\cdot$B $\to$ D

restricted permutation: (A $\to$ $\cdot$B $\to$ C $\to$ D) $\to$ $\cdot$B $\to$ C $\to$ $\cdot$A $\to$ D

restricted conditioned modus ponens: B $\to$ C $\to$ $\cdot$(A $\to$ $\cdot$B $\to$ C $\to$ D) $\to$
                               $\cdot$A $\to$ D

restricted assertion: A $\to$ B $\to$ $\cdot$A $\to$ B $\to$ C $\to$ C

specialized assertion: A $\to$ A $\to$ B $\to$ B

The foregoing seems to us to be a strong and natural list of valid entailments, all of which are *necessarily* true, and in each of which the antecedent is *relevant* to the consequent. We shall consider the matter of relevance subsequently, but as regards necessity, we observe here that, as might be expected, a theory of *logical necessity* is forthcoming in E_I. We define "it is necessary that A" as follows:

$$NA = df\ A \rightarrow A \rightarrow A.$$

Of course we do not mean to suggest that in saying that A is necessary we *mean* that A follows from $A \rightarrow A$; we mean rather that if one *were* to mean this by "A is necessary," or "NA," then it would turn out that N had all the right properties.

The motivation for the present definition of NA lies in the belief that A is necessary if and only if A follows from a logical truth. The choice of $A \rightarrow A$ as *the* logical truth from which a necessary A must follow is justified by the fact that if A follows from any true entailment $B \rightarrow C$, then it follows from $A \rightarrow A$, a fact expressed in the following theorem.

1	$B \rightarrow C_{\{1\}}$	hyp
2	$B \rightarrow C \rightarrow A_{\{2\}}$	hyp
3	$A \rightarrow A_{\{3\}}$	hyp
4	$B \rightarrow C_{\{1\}}$	1 reit
5	$B \rightarrow C \rightarrow A_{\{2\}}$	2 reit
6	$A_{\{1,2\}}$	$4\ 5 \rightarrow E$
7	$A_{\{1,2,3\}}$	$3\ 6 \rightarrow E$
8	$A \rightarrow A \rightarrow A_{\{1,2\}}$	$3\text{-}7 \rightarrow I$
9	$B \rightarrow C \rightarrow A \rightarrow NA_{\{1\}}$	$2\text{-}8 \rightarrow I$
10	$B \rightarrow C \rightarrow \cdot B \rightarrow C \rightarrow A \rightarrow NA$	$1\text{-}9 \rightarrow I$

We find support for this proposal in the fact that in such systems as M (Feys 1937; von Wright 1951), S4, and S5, NA (either taken as primitive, or defined as not-possible-not A) is strictly equivalent to (hence intersubstitutable with) $A \rightarrow A \rightarrow A$. (This observation for S4 and S5 was made by Lemmon et al. 1956.)

We give as examples some further proofs of theorems involving necessity.

1	$A \rightarrow A \rightarrow A_{\{1\}}$	hyp
2	$A_{\{2\}}$	hyp
3	$A_{\{2\}}$	2 rep
4	$A \rightarrow A$	2–3 $\rightarrow$ I
5	$A_{\{1\}}$	1 4 $\rightarrow$ E
6	$\mathcal{N}A \rightarrow A$	1–5 $\rightarrow$ I

1	$A \rightarrow A \rightarrow B_{\{1\}}$	hyp
2	$B \rightarrow B_{\{2\}}$	hyp
3	$A_{\{3\}}$	hyp
4	$A_{\{3\}}$	3 rep
5	$A \rightarrow A$	3–4 $\rightarrow$ I
6	$A \rightarrow A \rightarrow B_{\{1\}}$	1 reit
7	$B_{\{1\}}$	5 6 $\rightarrow$ E
8	$B_{\{1,2\}}$	2 7 $\rightarrow$ E
9	$B \rightarrow B \rightarrow B_{\{1\}}$	2–8 $\rightarrow$ I
10	$A \rightarrow A \rightarrow B \rightarrow \mathcal{N}B$	1–9 $\rightarrow$ I

The first says that necessity implies truth (a special case of the *specialized law of assertion*), and the second that if B follows from the *law of identity*, then B is necessarily true (which accords with previous informal observations). We add some other easily provable theorems.

$$A \rightarrow B \rightarrow \cdot \mathcal{N}A \rightarrow \mathcal{N}B$$
$$A \rightarrow B \rightarrow \mathcal{N}(A \rightarrow B)$$
$$A \rightarrow B \rightarrow C \rightarrow \cdot A \rightarrow B \rightarrow \mathcal{N}C$$
$$\mathcal{N}B \rightarrow \cdot (A \rightarrow \cdot B \rightarrow C) \rightarrow \cdot A \rightarrow C$$
$$\mathcal{N}A \rightarrow \mathcal{N}\mathcal{N}A$$

The first expresses distributivity of necessity over entailment. The second (a special case of *restricted assertion*) says that entailments, if true at all, are necessarily true. The third that if C follows from an entailment, then the necessity of C also follows from that entailment (which we may also express by saying that if C follows from an entailment, then if the entailment is true, then C is necessary). The next says that where B is necessary, we may infer $A \rightarrow C$ from $A \rightarrow \cdot B \rightarrow C$. And the last says that necessity implies necessary necessity (so to speak): a corollary of $A \rightarrow B \rightarrow \mathcal{N}(A \rightarrow B)$ together with the fact that necessity is defined in terms of entailment.

   5. Fallacies. The developments of the preceding section (and indeed of two millennia of history) seem to us to provide a set of indisputable truths about entailment. And of course each is provable not only in E_I, but also in each of the systems H_I, $S4_I$, and R_I. But the latter all contain in addition paradoxical assertions which we now discuss under two headings: fallacies of modality and fallacies of relevance.

   5.1. Fallacies of modality. Discussion of this topic necessitates introducing some ugly terminology. We do so forthwith, and apologize just this one time.

   It has been customary in the philosophical literature on logic to consider some propositions as positive, and some as negative. Without going into the difficulties raised by e.g., Eaton 1931, concerning "negative properties" such as "baldness," "orphanhood," and the like, it is clear that one sensible thing *might* be meant by describing a proposition as negative: we say that A is *negative* just in case there is some proposition B such that A is equivalent to the denial of B. Trivially, of course, all propositions are negative by this criterion (unless one hews to the intuitionistic theory of negation). We might define with equal triviality a "conjunctive" proposition A as a proposition equivalent to a conjunction B & C (whence again every proposition becomes conjunctive, in view of $A \leftrightarrow A \& A$). But a more sane way of looking at the matter would require that B and C be distinct from (i.e., not equivalent to) A. Similarly for "disjunctive proposition."

   Unfortunately there seems to be nothing parallel to say, in ordinary logical-philosophical language, about a proposition A such that A is equivalent with $\mathcal{N}B$, for some B. As a result, we are driven to the desperate expedient of coining "necessitive," on the analogy of "negative," "conjunctive," and the like, to refer to such propositions.

   Using this terminology, we may distinguish between *necessary* propositions and *necessitive* propositions. $A \rightarrow A$ is both necessary (i.e., we have $\mathcal{N}(A \rightarrow A)$) and necessitive (we also have $(A \rightarrow A) \leftrightarrow \mathcal{N}(A \rightarrow A)$). However, $A \vee \overline{A}$, though necessary, is not necessitive; there is no proposition B such that $(A \vee \overline{A}) \leftrightarrow \mathcal{N}B$. We shall try to give appropriate arguments for rejecting e.g., $(A \lor \overline{A}) \leftrightarrow \mathcal{N}(A \lor \overline{A})$ later; meanwhile we consider fallacies of modality as they arise in pure implicational calculuses.

Modal fallacies depend upon misdescribing the logical relations between necessitive and non-necessitive propositions. We can, however, put the matter in a different way for the pure systems now under discussion. In the first place, observe that entailments are one and all necessitives, since as was seen in 4, $(A \rightarrow B) \leftrightarrow \mathcal{N}(A \rightarrow B)$; and conversely, necessitives are one and all entailments in virtue of the definition $\mathcal{N}A \leftrightarrow (A \rightarrow A \rightarrow A)$. Secondly, and as a corollary, non-necessitives are in this setting just exactly propositional variables. It follows that, in the tiny area covered by E_I (Bennett 1965), a modal fallacy is a mistake concerning the logical relations between propositional variables and entailments. Such mistakes can occur in two distinguishable ways.

In the first place a system may mistakenly permit us to *use* propositional variables to establish entailments, in defiance of the condition mentioned at the outset of 2 above. Such use arises through reiterating propositional variables into subordinate proofs designed to establish entailments, as for example in the following fragmentary proof:

$$
\begin{array}{lll}
 & \vdots & \\
 & \vdots & \\
i & A & (?) \\
 & \vdots & \\
 & \vdots & \\
j & A \rightarrow B & \text{hyp} \\
j+1 & A & i \text{ reit} \\
j+2 & B & j \; j+1 \rightarrow E \\
j+3 & (A \rightarrow B) \rightarrow B & j - j+2 \rightarrow I \\
\end{array}
$$

Where A is a propositional variable, step $j + 1$ involves a reiteration, and subsequent use, of a non-necessitive proposition in the proof of the necessitive proposition $j + 3$; restrictions on reiteration in E_I^* and

$S4_I$* prohibit this move, whereas H_I* and R_I* allow it. So the subordinate proof formulations make it plain that $S4_I$* and E_I* do not commit modal fallacies of this sort. Notice that the subordinate proof format is essential in describing this sort of fallacious inference, since the idea of reiterating non-necessitives is at the heart of it.

But closely related fallacies of modality arise if a system permits us to prove that a non-necessitive entails a necessitive proposition; i.e., if it permits proof of a formula $A \rightarrow D$, with A a propositional variable and D some entailment $B \rightarrow C$.

One might think that it is hard to distinguish between systems which (a) allow the *use* of a propositional variable in establishing an entailment, and systems which (b) allow us to prove that a propositional variable entails an entailment. This is indeed a difference without a distinction in systems in which one can prove $A \rightarrow D$ when and only when one can use A in establishing D. As would be expected, E_I* commits neither sort of fallacy, and R_I* commits both. But the distinction does have point, and for two reasons: (1) $S4_I$* commits (b) without (a), since in it we can prove $A \rightarrow \cdot B \rightarrow B$, with A a propositional variable, it being obvious, as we observed earlier, that A is not *used* in establishing $B \rightarrow B$, and (2) the condition (b), unlike (a), is applicable to axiomatic formulations, whether or not subproof formulations are available — for it amounts simply to the provability of formulas $A \rightarrow \cdot B \rightarrow C$, where A is a propositional variable.

That E_I is free of modal fallacies in the second sense is shown by the following:

THEOREM. $A \rightarrow \cdot B \rightarrow C$ is unprovable in E_I whenever A is a propositional variable (Ackermann 1956).

Proof. Consider the following matrix (adapted from Ackermann):

	0	1	2
0	2	2	2
1	0	2	0
*2	0	0	2

The theorems of E_I always take the value 2; but for any $A \rightarrow \cdot B \rightarrow C$, where A is a propositional variable, we can assign A the value 1, giving

$A \rightarrow \cdot B \rightarrow C$ the value 0 regardless of the values of B and C. Hence no such $A \rightarrow \cdot B \rightarrow C$ is provable.

The theorem serves to rule out such formulas as $A \rightarrow \cdot A \rightarrow A$ and $A \rightarrow \cdot B \rightarrow B$, which are standard "implicational paradoxes" embodying modal fallacies, and this fact clearly accords with (untutored) intuitions. Consider $A \rightarrow \cdot A \rightarrow A$. Though that snow is white and that that snow is white entails that snow is white are both true — the latter necessarily so — it seems implausible that that snow is white should entail that it entails itself. It does entail itself, of course, but the color of snow seems irrelevant to that fact of logic. We should think someone arguing rather badly if he tried to convince us that snow is white entails itself by showing us some snow.

Also ruled out as involving fallacies of modality are such formulas as the unrestricted "law" of assertion:

$$A \rightarrow \cdot A \rightarrow B \rightarrow B,$$

and the "law" of permutation

$$(A \rightarrow \cdot B \rightarrow C) \rightarrow \cdot B \rightarrow \cdot A \rightarrow C,$$

which would lead from $A \rightarrow B \rightarrow \cdot A \rightarrow B$ to the "law" of assertion.

$A \rightarrow \cdot B \rightarrow A$ also involves a modal fallacy, as we have argued before. Of the systems considered previously $A \rightarrow \cdot B \rightarrow A$ is provable only in H_I; but $S4_I$, though containing no fallacies of the first kind, does embrace mistakes like

$$A \rightarrow B \rightarrow \cdot C \rightarrow \cdot A \rightarrow B, \quad \text{and}$$
$$B \rightarrow \cdot A \rightarrow A.$$

And R_I is chock-full of modal fallacies, of which the worst is no doubt

$$A \rightarrow \cdot A \rightarrow A \rightarrow A, \quad (\text{i.e., } A \rightarrow \mathcal{N}A).$$

5.2. Fallacies of relevance. Many of the foregoing modal fallacies also embody fallacies of relevance, sanctioning the inference from A to B even though A and B may be totally disparate in meaning. The archetype of fallacies of relevance is $A \rightarrow \cdot B \rightarrow A$, which would enable us to infer that Bach wrote the Coffee Cantata from the premise that the Van Allen belt is doughnut-shaped — or indeed from any premise you like.

In arguing that E_I satisfies a principle of relevance, we venture, somewhat gingerly, on new ground. We offer two conditions, the first as necessary and sufficient, the second as necessary only.

(i) The subscripting technique as applied in R_I and E_I may be construed as a formal analysis of the intuitive idea that for A to be relevant to B it must be possible to *use* A in a deduction of B from A. It need not be *necessary* to use A in the deduction of B from A — and indeed this is a familiar situation in mathematics and logic. It not infrequently happens that the hypotheses of a theorem, though all relevant to a conclusion, are subsequently found to be unnecessarily strong. An example is provided by Gödel's original incompleteness theorem, which required the assumption of ω-consistency. Rosser subsequently showed that this condition was not required for the proof of incompleteness — but surely no one would hold that ω-consistency was *irrelevant* to Gödel's original proof. Similarly in the following example (due to Smiley 1959), effort is wasted, since the antecedent is used in the proof of the consequent, though it need not be.

1	$A \rightarrow B_{\{1\}}$	hyp
2	$B \rightarrow A_{\{2\}}$	hyp
3	$B_{\{3\}}$	hyp
4	$B \rightarrow A_{\{2\}}$	2 reit
5	$A_{\{2,3\}}$	$3\ 4 \rightarrow E$
6	$A \rightarrow B_{\{1\}}$	1 reit
7	$B_{\{1,2,3\}}$	$5\ 6 \rightarrow E$
8	$A_{\{1,2,3\}}$	$4\ 7 \rightarrow E$
9	$B \rightarrow A_{\{1,2\}}$	$3\text{–}8 \rightarrow I$
10	$B \rightarrow A \rightarrow \cdot B \rightarrow A_{\{1\}}$	$2\text{–}9 \rightarrow I$
11	$A \rightarrow B \rightarrow \cdot B \rightarrow A \rightarrow \cdot B \rightarrow A$	$1\text{–}10 \rightarrow I$

A similar proof yields

$$B \rightarrow A \rightarrow \cdot A \rightarrow B \rightarrow \cdot B \rightarrow A.$$

The point in both cases is that the antecedent and the antecedent of the consequent can be made to "cycle," producing one or the other as consequent of the consequent.

The law $A \rightarrow B \rightarrow \cdot B \rightarrow A \rightarrow \cdot B \rightarrow A$ requires special attention, because it appears to violate a plausible condition due to Smiley 1959;

he demands that every true entailment be a "substitution instance of a tautological implication whose components are neither contradictory nor tautological." Thus Smiley's criterion allows $A \to A \to \cdot A \to A$ (with the consequent necessary) on the grounds that it is a substitution instance of $B \to B$ (with consequent possibly contingent). But it would seem to exclude $A \to B \to \cdot B \to A \to \cdot B \to A$ on the ground that the latter is not a substitution instance of a tautology with a possibly contingent consequent.

From the point of view we have been urging, Smiley's criterion is misguided. The validity of an entailment has nothing to do with whether or not the components are true, false, necessary, or impossible; it has to do solely with whether or not there is a necessary connection between antecedent and consequent. Hence it is a mistake (we feel) to try to build a sieve which will strain out entailments from the set of material or strict "implications" present in some system of truth-functions, or of truth-functions with modality. It is debatable, in fact, whether Smiley's criterion is even applicable to $A \to B \to \cdot B \to A \to \cdot B \to A$ since this formula involves nested entailment, and Smiley is concerned with entailments as between truth-functions. We remark that if A and B are truth-functions, then the true entailments $A \to B$ are all substitution-instances of true entailments with both A and B contingent, as Smiley requires. In particular, where $A \supset B =$ df $\overline{A} \lor B$, $A \supset B \to \cdot B \supset A \supset \cdot B \supset A$ is not true entailment; details can be worked out easily from Anderson and Belnap 1962.

But where A or B involves entailment, this sort of approach fails; and in particular, though of course $A \to B$ should be a sufficient condition for a material "implication" from A to B, there seems no good reason to suppose that the result of substituting the horseshoe of material "implication" for the arrow throughout an arbitrary truth concerning entailments would be a truth-functional tautology. For example, we have reason to believe that $\overline{A \to A \to \cdot A \to A}$ might be a truth about entailment, but $\overline{A \supset A \supset \cdot A \supset A}$ is clearly no tautology. We seem to be unable to give criteria involving only extensional considerations for detecting the fundamentally intensional notion of entailment.

Though the entailment $A \to B \to \cdot B \to A \to \cdot B \to A$ may appear to violate Smiley's condition, we can quote Smiley himself in support of it and of its proof: ". . . inferences may be justified on more grounds than one, and the present theory requires not that there should be *no* cogent way of reaching the conclusion *without* using all the premises, but only that there should be *some* cogent way of reaching it *with* all the premises used.''

Actually, this condition won't do either, as is easily seen by examples. Proof of the uniqueness of the identity element in an Abelian group does not invoke the fact that the group operation is commutative; it nevertheless follows from the axioms for an Abelian group that the identity element is unique — or at any rate everyone says so. What *is* required is that there be some cogent way of reaching the conclusion with some of the (conjoined) premises used. But this point will have to await discussion of truth-functions in connection with entailment.

(ii) The second formal condition is prompted by the consideration that informal discussions of implication or entailment have frequently demanded "relevance" of A to B as a necessary condition for the truth of $A \rightarrow B$, where relevance is construed as involving some "meaning content" common to both A and B. This call for common "meaning content" comes from a variety of quarters. Nelson 1930, (p. 445) says that implication "is a necessary connection between meanings"; Duncan-Jones 1934 (p. 71) that A implies B only when B "arises out of the meaning of" A; Baylis 1931 (p. 397) that if A implies B then "the intensional meaning of B is identical with a part of the intensional meaning of A"; and Blanshard 1939 (Vol. 2, p. 390) that "what lies at the root of the common man's objection [to strict implication] is the stubborn feeling that implication has something to do with the *meaning* of propositions, and that any mode of connecting them which disregards this meaning and ties them together in despite of it is too artificial to satisfy the demand of thought."

A formal condition for "common meaning content" becomes almost obvious once we note that commonality of meaning in propositional logic is carried by commonality of propositional variables. So we propose as a *necessary*, but by no means sufficient, condition for the relevance of A to B in the pure calculus of entailment, that A and B must share a variable. If this property fails, then the variables in A and B may be assigned propositional values, in such a way that the resulting propositions have no meaning content in common, and are totally irrelevant to each other. E_I avoids such fallacies of relevance, as shown by the following:

THEOREM. If $A \rightarrow B$ is provable in E_I, then A and B share a variable.

Proof. Consider the following matrix (a finite adaptation of a matrix of Sugihara 1955):

$$
\begin{array}{c|ccc}
\rightarrow & 0 & 1 & 2 \\
\hline
0 & 2 & 2 & 2 \\
*1 & 0 & 1 & 2 \\
*2 & 0 & 0 & 2 \\
\end{array}
$$

The axioms of E take values 1 or 2 for all assignments of values to the variables, and the rule → E preserves this property. But if A and B share no variables, then we may assign the value 2 to all the variables of A (yielding A = 2), and 1 to all the variables of B (yielding B = 1), and 2 → 1 takes the undesignated value 0. Hence if A and B fail to share a variable, A → B is unprovable.

We remark that the first of the two conditions has to do with entailment in its guise as the converse of deducibility, and in this sense is a purely syntactical completeness theorem: A is *relevant* to B, when A → B, just if there exists a proof (satisfying certain conditions) of B *from* the hypothesis A. The second condition, however, concerns entailment conceived of as a relation of logical consequence, and is semantical in character, since it has to do with possible assignments of values to the propositional variables.

The matrix given in the second condition above also satisfies (A → ·B → C) → ·B → ·A → C; it follows that R_I is also free of fallacies of relevance in the sense of satisfying the necessary condition of sharing variables, as we would expect from the previous discussion. Among fallacies of relevance which are *not* modal fallacies we mention A → A → ·B → B. (A → *N*A, mentioned above, has the converse property; it is a fallacy of modality, but not of relevance.)

With this section we complete the main argument of this chapter. We have argued that valid inferences are necessarily valid, and that the antecedent in a valid inference must be relevant to the consequent. In view of the long history of logic as a topic for investigation, and the near unanimity on these two points among logicians, it is surprising, indeed startling, that these issues should require re-arguing. That they do need arguing is a consequence of the almost equally unanimous contradictorily opposed feeling on the part of contemporary logicians that material and strict "implication" are implication relations, and that therefore necessity and relevance are not required for true implications. But, if we may be permitted to apply a result of the ingenious Bishop of Halberstadt (Albert of Saxony, *ca.* 1316–1390; see Boehner 1952, pp. 99–100), if both of these views are correct, it follows that Man is a donkey.

Lewis . . . has explicitly argued that the paradoxes of strict "implication" "state a fact about deducibility" (Lewis and Langford 1932, p. 251) and has presented "independent proofs" of their validity. Since there is a clear opposition between our position and that of Lewis (and practically everyone else), we will examine one of these proofs in detail.

The argument concerns A & ∼ A → B, and has two steps, (i) "A entails B" or "A → B" means that B is deducible from A "by some mode of inference which is valid" (Lewis and Langford 1932, p. 248), and (ii) there is a "valid mode of inference" from A & ∼ A to B.

We may accept (i) without cavil. Arguments for (ii), that is, for the proposition that there is a valid mode of inference from a contradiction to any arbitrary proposition, were known to several logicians flourishing circa the year 1350, and are found in extant writings of the astute Bishop of Halberstadt, Albert of Saxony (see Boehner 1952, pp. 99–100). Lewis and Langford's presentation of the argument (p. 250) does not differ significantly from Albert's, although it is almost certain that the modern appearance of the argument represents a rediscovery rather than a continuity of tradition. The argument has also been accepted by a variety of other modern logicians — e.g., Popper 1940, pp. 407–10, and 1943 — and indeed, as Bennett points out (Bennett 1954, p. 451), "this acceptance has not been an entirely academic matter. William Kneale 1945–46 and Popper 1947 have both used the paradoxes as integral parts of their respective accounts of the nature of logic."

Though departing in insignificant detail from Lewis' own, the following is a convenient presentation of the argument. Grant that the following are "valid modes of inference":

1. from A & B to infer A,
2. from A & B to infer B,
3. from A to infer A ∨ B, and
4. from A ∨ B and ∼A to infer B.

The argument then proceeds in this way:

(a)	A & ∼A	premise
(b)	A	from (a) by 1
(c)	A ∨ B	from (b) by 3
(d)	∼A	from (a) by 2
(e)	B	conclusion: from (c) and (d) by 4.

Than which nothing could be simpler: if the four rules above are "valid modes of inference" and if "A → B" means that there is a valid mode of inference from A to B, then a contradiction such as A & ∼A surely does entail any arbitrary proposition, B, whence A & ∼A → B represents a fact about deducibility.

We agree with those who find the argument from (a) to (e) self-evidently preposterous, and from the point of view we advocate it is immediately obvious where the fallacious step occurs; namely, in passing from (c) and (d) to (e). The principle 4 (from A ∨ B and ∼A to infer B), which commits a fallacy of relevance, is not a tautological entailment. We therefore reject 4 as an entailment, and as a valid principle of inference.

We seem to have been pushed into one of the "peculiar positions" of which Prior speaks (1955, p. 195), for we are explicitly denying that the principle of the disjunctive syllogism — or detachment for material "implication" — is a "valid mode of inference." The validity of this form of inference is something Lewis never doubts (see, for example, Lewis and Langford 1932, pp. 242–43) and is something which has perhaps never been seriously questioned before (though the possibility of dispensing with the disjunctive syllogism is raised by Smiley 1959). Nevertheless, we do hold that the inference from ∼A and A ∨ B to B is an error: it is a simple inferential mistake. Such an inference commits nothing less than a fallacy of relevance. We shall first anticipate possible misinterpretations of this thesis and then proceed to an "independent proof" of the invalidity of ∼A(A ∨ B) → B.

In the first place, we do not deny that the inference from |−A and |−A ∨ B to |−B is valid, where "|−A" means "A is a theorem of the two-valued propositional calculus." However, from this it does not follow that B follows from ∼A and A ∨ B, nor does it follow that if |−A and |−A ∨ B then B follows from ∼A and A ∨ B. We even admit that if |−B then B is necessarily true, and still hold that the argument from ∼A and A ∨ B to B is invalid even when |−∼A and

$\vdash -A \vee B$ (and hence $\vdash -B$). Such a claim would be senseless on Lewis' doctrine, for to admit B is necessarily true is to admit that any argument for B is valid.

Secondly, we do not say that the inference from $\sim$A and A $\vee$ B to B is invalid for all choices of A and B; it will be valid at least when A entails B (in which case $\sim$A is not required) or when $\sim$A entails B (in which case A $\vee$ B is not required); more generally, it will be valid when A & $\sim$A entails B (in which case the disjoined premise B is not required).

Furthermore, in rejecting the principle of the disjunctive syllogism, we intend to restrict our rejection to the case in which the "or" is taken truth-functionally. In general and with respect to our ordinary reasonings this would not be the case; perhaps always when the principle is used in reasoning one has in mind an intensional meaning of "or," where there is relevance between the disjuncts. But for the intensional meaning of "or," it seems clear that the analogues of A $\rightarrow$ A $\vee$ B are invalid, since this would hold only if B was relevant to A; hence, there is a sense in which the real flaw in Lewis' argument is not a fallacy of relevance but rather a fallacy of ambiguity: the passage from (b) to (c) is valid only if the "$\vee$" is read truth-functionally, while the passage from (c) and (d) to (e) is valid only if the "$\vee$" is taken intensionally. We shall further consider the intensional "or" below.

Our final remark concerns what Lewis might have meant be "some valid form of inference." It is hardly likely that he meant that a form of inference is valid if and only if either the premises are false or the conclusion true ("material validity"); more plausibly, he might have meant that a form of inference is valid if and only if it is necessary that either the premises are false or the conclusion true ("strict validity"). If this is what Lewis meant, then we agree at once that the inference from A and $\sim$A $\vee$ B to B is valid in this sense. However, if this is all that Lewis meant by "some valid form of inference," then his long argument for A & $\sim$ A $\rightarrow$ B is a quite unnecessary detour, for in this sense we should have agreed at once that there is a valid form of inference from A & $\sim$A to B: it is surely true that necessarily either the premise is false or the conclusion is true inasmuch as the premise is necessarily false. In short, Lewis' "independent proof" of A & $\sim$ A $\rightarrow$ B is convincing if "valid inference" is defined in terms of strict implication; but in that case it is superfluous and circular. And his argument serves a useful purpose only if "valid inference" is

thought of in some other sense, in which case he has failed to prove —
or even to argue for — his premises. Finally, should he wish to escape
the horns of this dilemma by remarking that the various forms of inference used in the argument are valid in the sense of having always been
accepted and used without question, then we should rest our case on
the fallacy of ambiguity noted above.

Such a thesis so strongly stated will seem hopelessly naive to those
logicians whose logical intuitions have been numbed through hearing
and repeating the logicians' fairy tales of the past half century, and
hence stands in need of further support. It will be insisted that to deny
detachment for material and strict implication, as well as to deny the
principle of the disjunctive syllogism, surely goes too far: "from $\sim$A
and A $\vee$ B to infer B," for example, is surely valid. For one of the
premises states that at least one of A and B is true, and since the other
premise, $\sim$ A, says that A can't be the true one, the true one must be B
(see Popper 1943, p. 48). Our reply is to remark again that this argument commits a fallacy of ambiguity. There are indeed important
senses of "or," "at least one," etc., for which the argument from $\sim$ A
and A–or–B is perfectly valid, namely, senses in which there is a true
relevance between A and B, for example, the sense in which "A–or–B"
means precisely that $\sim$A entails B. However, in this sense of "or,"
the inference from A to A–or–B is fallacious, and therefore this sense of
"or" is not preserved in the truth-functional constant translated by the
same word. As Lewis himself argued in some early articles, there are
intensional meanings of "or," "not both," "at least one is true," etc.,
as well as of "if . . . then . . . ." Those who claim that only an intensional sense of these words will support inferences are right — Lewis'
only error was in supposing he captured this sense by tacking a modal
operator onto a fundamentally truth-functional formula. . . .

BIBLIOGRAPHY

ACKERMANN, Wilhelm, "Begründung einer strengen Implikation," *Journal of Symbolic Logic*, Vol. 21 (1956), pp. 113–128.

ANDERSON, Alan Ross, and BELNAP, Nuel D., Jr., "The Pure Calculus of Entailment," *Journal of Symbolic Logic*, Vol. 27 (1962), pp. 19–52.

BAYLIS, Charles A., "Implication and Subsumption," *Monist*, Vol. 41 (1931), pp. 392–399.

BELNAP, Nuel D., Jr., *A Formal Analysis of Entailment*, Technical report no. 7, Office of Naval Research Contract no. SAR/Nonr-609(16), New Haven, 1960.

BENNETT, Jonathan F., "Meaning and Implication," *Mind*, n.s., Vol. 63 (1954), pp. 451–463.

———, "Review," *Journal of Symbolic Logic*, Vol. 30 (1965), pp. 240–241.

BOEHNER, Philotheus, *Medieval Logic*, Manchester, 1952.

CHURCH, Alonzo, "The Weak Theory of Implication," *Kontrolliertes Denken* (Festgabe zum 60 Geburtstag von Prof. W. Britzelmayr), Munich, 1951.

———, *Introduction to Mathematical Logic*, Vol. 1, Princeton, 1956.

CURRY, Haskell B., "The Interpretation of Formalized Implication," *Theoria*, Vol. 25 (1959), pp. 1–26.

DUNCAN-JONES, Austin E., "Is Strict Implication the Same as Entailment?" *Analysis*, Vol. 2 (1935), pp. 70–78.

EATON, R. M., *General Logic*, New York, 1931.

FEYS, Robert, "Les Logiques Nouvelles des Modalités," *Revue Neoscolastique de Philosophie*, Vol. 40 (1937), pp. 517–553, and Vol. 41 (1938), pp. 217–252.

FITCH, Frederic B., *Symbolic Logic*, New York, 1952.

GENTZEN, Gerhard, "Untersuchungen über das Logische Schliessen," *Mathematische Zeitschrift*, Vol. 39 (1934), pp. 176–210.

HACKING, Ian, "What is Strict Implication?" *Journal of Symbolic Logic*, Vol. 28 (1963), pp. 51–71.

HEYTING, Arend, "Die formalen Regeln der intuitionistischen Logik," *Sitzungsberichte der Preussischen Akademie der Wissenschaften*, Physikalisch-mathematische Klasse (1930), pp. 42–56, 57–71, 158–169.

JAŚKOWSKI, Stanislaw, "Trois Contributions au Calcul des Propositions Bivalent," *Studia Societatis Scientarum Torunensis*, Sectio A, Vol. 1, No. 1 (1948), pp. 1–15.

KNEALE, William, "Truths of Logic," *Proceedings of the Aristotelian Society*, Vol. 46 (1945–46), pp. 207–234.

LEMMON, E. J., MEREDITH, C. A., MEREDITH, D., PRIOR, A. N., and THOMAS, I., *Calculi of Pure Strict Implication* (mimeographed), 1956.

LEWIS, C. I., and LANGFORD, C. H., *Symbolic Logic*, New York, 1932.

ŁUKASIEWICZ, Jan, "Elementy Logiki Matematycznej," mimeographed Warsaw 1929, printed Warsaw 1958.

SHAW-KWEI, Moh, "The Deduction Theorems and Two New Logical Systems," *Methodos*, Vol. 2 (1950), pp. 56–75.

MONTAGUE, Roger, and HENKIN, Leon, "On the Definition of 'Formal Deduction,'" *Journal of Symbolic Logic*, Vol. 21 (1956), pp. 129–136.

MOORE, G. E., "External and Internal Relations," *Proceedings of the Aristotelian Society*, n.s. Vol. 20 (1920), pp. 40–62.

NELSON, E. J., "Intensional Relations," *Mind*, n.s., Vol. 39 (1930), pp. 440–453.

POPPER, Karl R., "What is Dialectic?" *Mind*, n.s., Vol. 49 (1940), pp. 403–426.

———, "Are Contradictions Embracing?" *Mind*, n.s., Vol. 52 (1943), pp. 47–50.

———, "New Foundations for Logic," *Mind*, n.s., Vol. 56 (1947), pp. 193–255.

PRAWITZ, Dag, "Normal Deductions," *Journal of Symbolic Logic*, Vol. 29 (1964), p. 152.

———, *Natural Deduction*, Stockholm, 1965.

PRIOR, A. N., *Formal Logic*, Oxford, 1955.

QUINE, Willard Van Orman, *Methods of Logic*, New York, 1950.

SMILEY, T. J., "Entailment and Deducibility," *Proceedings of the Aristotelian Society*, Vol. 59 (1959), pp. 233–254.

STRAWSON, P. F., *Introduction to Logical Theory*, London, 1952.

SUGIHARA, Takeo, "Strict Implication Free from Implicational Paradoxes," *Memoirs of the Faculty of Liberal Arts, Fukui University*, Series I (1955), pp. 55–59.

VON WRIGHT, Georg H., *An Essay in Modal Logic*, Amsterdam, 1951.

LOGIC AND
EXISTENCE

In many of the preceding selections questions have arisen as to what sorts of things there are and what we mean when we say of something that it exists. Once the apparatus of logic is developed to the point of including the so-called "existential quantifier," usually symbolized "(∃x)," it becomes possible to see these questions in a new light. There is at least a presumption, given the name "existential quantifier," that the formal system which exhibits the logical behavior of this quantifier can help us to get clear about the concept of existence or being. In the selections which follow we shall indeed as often see the resources of modern logic being used to deal with philosophical problems which arise independent of logic and are often discussed without reference to it, as we shall see technical logic giving rise to philosophical problems of its own.

Although Meinong distinguishes "existence" from other kinds of "being," it is possible, despite the terminological variations, to regard his argument as manifesting in an extreme form the tendency, also observable in Selections 1 and 4 above, to say that there are many different kinds of existence and that many different things exist in these different ways. Indeed, the things for which different kinds of existence are required are often just the puzzling things, such as propositions or universals, whose existence was controversial in those selections. (That Meinong's views represent a kind of extreme of "permissiveness" and of what White calls "multivocalism" may be seen by comparing the discussion of Meinong by Russell, himself permissive enough, in the piece listed under Suggestions for Further Reading on The Logic of Categorical Propositions.) White attempts to bring some order out of what he regards as the chaos of these senses of "existence" or "being" and argues, as against the view expressed by Russell in Selection 4 and the rather different (from Meinong) sort of "multivocalism" espoused by Ryle (see Suggestions for Further Reading), that "the use of 'there are' which is symbolized by the existential quantifier of modern logic — '(∃x)' — is clear, and that with its help a large number of ordinary and scientific statements of existence may be formulated." He suggests, furthermore, that those apparent statements of existence which cannot be so formulated should for this very reason be regarded with suspicion.

Given that "ontological" statements can be formulated with the help of the existential quantifier, Quine proposes a criterion, summed up in the sentence, "to be assumed as an entity is, purely and simply, to be reckoned as the value of a variable," which is an attempt to make clear just when we have

113

committed ourselves to saying that something exists. (It is worth while attempting to see how this criterion compares with any criterion implicit in Selections 1, 4, or 10.) As presented here, Quine's criterion does not carry much immediate indication of what will survive its application and emerge as something to whose existence we are still committed, but it is at least clear that many of Meinong's "Objects" will be found in the same slum as the imaginary Wyman's "possibles" and that Quine's clearance project is directed against them both.

Alston considers the import of the kinds of translations both White and Quine propose in their attempt to say what we want to say without committing ourselves to the existence of any "dubious" entities. He argues that if, in fact, a statement involves an ontological commitment, any adequate translation, any different way of making the same statement, must as well, so that Quine's project cannot possibly succeed. One of the issues here is the identification of the items which entail ontological assertions or, indeed, the items which entail anything, precisely the issue raised in Selections 1–3. Alston's notion of a "statement" should be compared with Quine's and with various notions of "proposition" in earlier selections to see if, as Alston suggests, there is "a confusion of sentence and statement lurking in the criterion of 'ontological commitment.' " Alston concludes rather guardedly that "possibilities do not exist in the same way as chairs," which is some of the way back to where we started with Meinong, for all the vast differences in tone and style. Alston's final remark about the "unfortunate effect of philosophical preoccupation with artificial languages" looks ahead to the issues discussed especially in Selections 20 and 21 below.

If Quine and White emphasize the adequacy of the notion symbolized by "$(\exists x)$" to the concept of existence, there are considerations which have led some philosophers to assert not only that the notion thus symbolized is inadequate to some important senses of "exist" but even that it has practically nothing to do with "existence." If such a formula as "$(\exists x)\ (Fx \lor \sim Fx)$," which is a theorem in standard developments of quantificational logic, is interpreted as standing for a proposition beginning "There exists something such that . . .," it appears that our system involves us in saying that there is some logical truth which asserts or at least entails some fact about the world, namely, that it is not empty. But this would be in sharp conflict with the view seen in Selections 4–6, all of which agree to the extent that they *contrast* logical truths with "factual" truths.

Lejewski argues that this dilemma can be solved by recognizing that "existential quantifications have no existential import." He insists that it is necessary to *separate* the notion of existence from the idea of quantification as captured by the so-called "existential" quantifier, and he sketches a formal system which purports to do just that. Cohen argues that Lejewski's proposal raises as many problems as it solves and appears to assert that, when they are properly understood, the theorems which bother Lejewski really do represent logical truths. (Quine's view, which is that there is no difficulty at all, since the notion of logical truth which gives rise to it is excessively obscure, may be examined in the piece mentioned in Suggestions for Further Reading. This view depends, of course, on his views about logical truth, as expounded in the article mentioned in Suggestions for Further Reading on Logical Truth.)

Existence and Being

10 Alexius Meinong: KINDS OF BEING (1904)

I. THE PROBLEM

That knowing is impossible without something being known, and more generally, that judgments and ideas or presentations (*Vorstellungen*) are impossible without being judgments about and presentations of something, is revealed to be self-evident by a quite elementary examination of these experiences. I have been able to show, almost without special investigation, that this is also true in the realm of assumptions (*Annahmen*), even though psychological research has but recently turned in their direction.[1] The situation is more complicated in this respect, however, in the case of feelings. There is no doubt that language is somewhat misleading in referring to joy or grief, or to pity or envy, and the like, as being that which one feels. There are also complications in the area of desires, insofar as we think from time to

Reprinted with permission of The Macmillan Company from *Realism and the Background of Phenomenology*, edited by Roderick M. Chisholm. © The Free Press, a Corporation 1960. Translated by Isaac Levi, D. B. Terrell, and Roderick M. Chisholm. The essay from which this selection is drawn, "The Theory of Objects," first appeared in *Untersuchungen zur Gegenstandstheorie und Psychologie* (Leipzig, 1904), edited by Meinong. Other essays, by philosophers and psychologists associated with Meinong at the University of Graz, were included in the same volume. The essay also appears in Volume II of Meinong's collected works.

[1] *Über Annahmen* (Leipzig, 1902), pp. 256 f. [The references in the present selection to *Über Annahmen* are to the first edition, not to the second, revised edition of 1910.]

time that we should revert to the possibility of desires which are not desires for anything, despite the linguistic evidence, which is here once again entirely unambiguous. However, even one who would disagree with my view that feelings, like desires, are dependent psychological states insofar as they have ideas as their indispensable "psychological presuppositions,"[2] would unhesitatingly concede that we are happy about something, interested in something, and, at least in the majority of cases, do not wish or intend without wishing for or intending something. To put it briefly, no one fails to recognize that psychological events so very commonly have this distinctive "character of being directed to something" (*auf etwas Gerichtetsein*) as to suggest very strongly (at least) that we should take it to be a characteristic aspect of the psychological as opposed to the non-psychological.

The purpose of the following remarks is, nevertheless, not to explain why I hold this way of looking at the matter to be firmly established, despite the many difficulties confronting it. There are so many cases in which reference, indeed explicit directedness (*Gerichtetsein*), to that "something," or (as we say quite naturally) to an object, unquestionably forces itself upon our attention that, even if they alone were to be considered, the question would soon be answered for anyone who investigated these matters scientifically.

The partitioning of whatever deserves and needs theoretical consideration into different scientific realms, and the careful delimitation of these realms, may often be of little practical importance in advancing the research connected with it. What matters in the final analysis is the work that is accomplished, and not the banner under which it is done. However, obscurities as to the boundaries of the diverse areas of science can become significant in two contrasting ways: either the areas which are actually investigated encroach upon one another, or they are separated from each other, and consequently leave an intermediate area untouched. The significance of such obscurities, within the sphere of our theoretical interest, is exactly the opposite of their significance within the sphere of practical affairs. In the latter, the "neutral zone" is a guarantee (always desired but rarely capable of being realized) of amicable neighborly relations, while the overlapping of territorial claims presents the typical case of conflict of interests. But in the realm of theoretical activity, where such conflicts, at least, have

---

[2] See my *Psychologisch-ethischen Untersuchungen zur Werttheorie* (Graz, 1894), pp. 34 f. Also Höfler, *Psychologie*, p. 389.

no justification, it is a gain, objectively considered, if the frontier districts coincide, for as a result they are investigated from different sides. A separation, on the other hand, is always a disadvantage, the seriousness of which depends on the size and significance of the intermediate territory.

The intent of the problem raised here is to call attention to just such an area of knowledge, which is sometimes overlooked, sometimes not sufficiently appreciated in its distinctive character. The question concerns the proper place for the scientific investigation of the Object (*Gegenstand*) taken as such and in general — we wish to know whether, among the sciences that are accredited by scientific tradition, there is one within which we could attempt a theoretical consideration of the Object as such, or from which we could at least demand this.

II. THE PREJUDICE IN FAVOR OF THE ACTUAL

It was no accident that the foregoing account took cognition as its starting point in order to arrive at the Object. To be sure, cognition is not unique in "having" an Object. It has it in such a distinctive manner, however, that whenever we are speaking of Objects, we are influenced to think first of all of the Object of cognition. For, to be precise, the psychological event we call cognition does not constitute the cognitive situation in and of itself: knowledge is, so to speak, a double fact (*Doppeltatsache*) in which what is known confronts the act of knowing as something relatively independent. The act of knowing is not merely directed toward what is known, in the way in which a false judgment may be directed toward its Object. In knowing, on the contrary, it is as though what is known were seized or grasped by the psychological act, or however else one might attempt to describe, in an unavoidably pictorial way, something which is indescribable. If one concentrates exclusively on the Object of knowledge, the problem about the science of Objects which was raised above is initially placed in a rather unfavorable light. A science of the Objects of cognition: does this mean anything more than the demand that what is already known as the Object of cognition be now made the Object of a science, and thus the Object of cognition for a second time? In other words, are we not asking for a science which either is made up of the sum-total of the sciences taken together, or one which would have to accomplish all over again what the recognized sciences jointly accomplish anyway?

We should guard ourselves against concluding from these considerations that the idea of a universal science, in addition to the special sciences, is absurd. This understanding of the nature of the world in its entirety and of its ultimate foundations, which the best minds have always considered to be the final and most estimable goal of their pursuit of knowledge, can only be the subject of a comprehensive science *in addition to* the special sciences. Indeed, the discipline which goes under the name of metaphysics has been thought to be exactly such a science. No matter how many disappointments have been associated with this name, and are associated with it, the responsibility for them lies with our intellectual capacities, and not with the idea of such a science. May one go so far, therefore, as to take metaphysics to be the science whose legitimate function is to deal with Objects as such — or Objects in their totality?

If we remember how metaphysics has always been conceived as including in its subject matter the farthest and the nearest, the greatest and the smallest alike, we may be surprised to be told that metaphysics cannot take on such a task. It may sound strange to hear that metaphysics is not universal enough for a science of Objects, and hence cannot take on the task just formulated. For the intentions of metaphysics have been universal (a fact which has so often been disastrous to its success). Without doubt, metaphysics has to do with everything that exists. However, the totality of what exists, including what has existed and will exist, is infinitely small in comparison with the totality of the Objects of knowledge. This fact easily goes unnoticed, probably because the lively interest in reality which is part of our nature tends to favor that exaggeration which finds the non-real a mere nothing — or, more precisely, which finds the non-real to be something for which science has no application at all or at least no application of any worth.

How little truth there is in such a view is most easily shown by ideal Objects[3] which do indeed subsist (*bestehen*), but which do not by any means exist (*existieren*), and consequently cannot in any sense be real (*wirklich*). Similarity and difference are examples of objects of this type: perhaps, under certain circumstances, they subsist between realities; but they are not a part of reality themselves. That ideas, as well as

[3] Concerning the sense in which I intend to employ the expression "ideal," which unfortunately is ambiguous in ordinary language, see my essay, "Über Gegenstände höherer Ordnung, etc.," *Zeitschrift für Psychologie*, XXI, 198. [This essay appears in Volume II of Meinong's collected works.]

assumptions and judgments, are nevertheless concerned with such Objects (and often have reason to be very intimately concerned with them) is, of course, beyond question. Similarly, number does not exist in addition to what is numbered, supposing the latter does exist; this we clearly know from the fact that we can also count what does not exist. Again, a connection does not exist in addition to what is connected, supposing the latter does exist: That their existence is not indispensable is proven by the connection between the equilaterality and equiangularity of a triangle. Moreover, where existing objects are concerned, such as atmospheric and thermometric or barometric conditions, the connectedness does not unite these realities themselves so much as it does their being or even their non-being. In knowing such a connection, we are already dealing with that special type of Object (*mit jenem eigentumlichen Gegenstandartigen*), which, as I hope I have shown,[4] is related to judgment and assumptions (*Urteilen und Annahmen*) in the way in which the Object, in a strict sense (*der eigentliche Gegenstand*), is related to presentations (*Vorstellungen*). I have recommended the name "Objective" (*Objektiv*) for this type of Object, and I have shown that the Objective itself can assume the functions of an Object in the strict sense. In particular, it can become the Object (*Gegenstand*) of a new judgment, or of some other intellectual operation, which is related to it as to an ordinary object (*Objekt*). If I say, "It is true that the antipodes exist," truth is ascribed not to the antipodes, but to the Objective, "that the antipodes exist." But this existence of the antipodes is a fact (*Tatsache*) which, as everyone sees immediately, can very well have a subsistent status, but cannot be still another existent entity in its own turn, as it were.* This holds, likewise, for all other objectives, so that every cognitive act which has an Objective as its Object represents thereby a case of knowing something which does not exist.

What has been stated here only in terms of isolated examples is supported by the testimony of a very highly developed science — indeed the most highly developed one: mathematics. We would surely not want to speak of mathematics as alien to reality, as though it had nothing to do with what exists. Indeed, we cannot fail to recognize that mathematics is assured of an extensive sphere of application in practical life no less than in the theoretical treatment of reality. However, pure

---

* [*dass sie zwar sehr wohl bestehen, aber nicht ihrerseits sozusagen noch einmal existieren kann.*]

[4] *Über Annahmen*, chap. vii.

nathematical knowledge is never concerned with anything which must, in the nature of the case, be actual. The form of being (*Sein*) with which mathematics as such is occupied is never existence (*Existenz*). In this respect, mathematics never transcends subsistence (*Bestand*): a straight line has no more existence than a right angle; a regular polygon, no more than a circle. It can be regarded only as a peculiarity of the mathematical use of language that this usage makes quite explicit existence-claims.[5] Even though the mathematician may use the term "existence," he cannot but concede that what we would otherwise call "possibility" is, in the final analysis, all that he requires of the objects of his theoretical consideration; it is very noteworthy, however, that a positive turn is being given to this ordinarily merely negative concept.

Together with the prejudice in favor of our knowledge of reality, alluded to previously, the basic independence of mathematics from existence enables us to understand a fact which would be fairly surprising if these points were not considered. Attempts to systematize the sciences as parts of a whole usually find themselves in an embarrassing position in connection with mathematics, and they must be extricated, with varying degrees of success, by more or less artificial expedients. This is in striking contrast to the recognition — one might straightaway say popularity — which mathematics has acquired for itself even in lay circles by its achievements. But the organization of all knowledge into the science of nature and the science of mind (*Natur- und Geisteswissenschaft*), appearing to be an exhaustive disjunction, really takes into account only the sort of knowledge which has to do with reality (*Wirklichkeit*). Consequently, when we look at the matter more closely, we should not be at all surprised to find that this organization does not do full justice to mathematics.

III. SOSEIN AND NICHTSEIN

There is thus not the slightest doubt that what is supposed to be the Object of knowledge need not exist at all. But our account up to now may seem to leave room for the conjecture that wherever existence is absent, it not only *can* be but *must* be replaced by subsistence. But even this restriction is inadmissable, as may be seen by contrasting

---

[5] Cf. K. Zindler: "Beiträge zur Theorie der mathematischen Erkenntnis," *Sitzungsberichte der kais. Akademis der Wissenschaften in Wien, phil. hist. Kl.*, CXVIII (1889), p. 33 and 53f.

the characteristic functions of judging and assuming, a distinction I
have attempted to maintain by contrasting the "thetic and synthetic
function" of thought.[6] In the former case, the act of thought grasps a
Sein, in the latter a "*Sosein.*" In each case, naturally, it is an Objective
that is grasped; it is reasonable to speak of a *Seinsobjektiv* and of a
Soseinsobjektiv, respectively.* Now it would accord very well with the
aforementioned prejudice in favor of existence to hold that we may
speak of a *Sosein* only if a *Sein* is presupposed. There would, indeed, be
little sense in calling a house large or small, a region fertile or unfertile,
before one knew that the house or the land does exist, has existed, or will
exist. However, the very science from which we were able to obtain the
largest number of instances counter to this prejudice shows clearly that
any such principle is untenable. As we know, the figures with which
geometry is concerned do not exist. Nevertheless, their properties, and
hence their *Sosein*, can be established. Doubtless, in the area of what can
be known merely a posteriori, a claim as to *Sosein* will be completely
unjustifiable if it is not based on knowledge of a *Sein*; it is equally certain
that a *Sosein* which does not rest on a *Sein* may often enough be utterly
lacking in natural interest. None of this alters the fact that the *Sosein*
of an Object is not affected by its *Nichtsein*. The fact is sufficiently important to be explicitly formulated as the principle of the independence
of *Sosein* from *Sein*.[7] The area of applicability of this principle is best
illustrated by consideration of the following circumstance: the principle
applies, not only to Objects which do not exist in fact, but also to
Objects which could not exist because they are impossible. Not only
is the much heralded gold mountain made of gold, but the round
square is as surely round as it is square. To be sure, insights of actual
importance regarding such Objects have been noted only in exceptional
cases. Nevertheless, even from them some light might be shed on
domains which are especially important for us to know.

* [Approximate translations of the German terms in the text are the following.
The *Sein* of an object is its existing, or its being real; its *Nichtsein* is its not existing, or its being unreal; its *Sosein* is its having characteristics. A *Seinsobjektiv* is an
objective consisting of something existing, or of something being real; analogously
for *Soseinsobjektiv* and *Nichtseinobjektiv*.]

[6] *Über Annahmen*, pp. 142ff.

[7] This principle was first enunciated by E. Mally in his treatise which was
honored by the Wartinger prize in 1903, and which appears in completely revised
form as No. III of these papers; see chap. 1, §3, of Mally's paper. [Meinong here
refers to the volume in which his own essay originally appeared. Mally's paper is
entitled "Untersuchungen zur Gegenstandstheorie des Messens."]

But such things may be alien to our natural way of thinking; it is even more instructive to recall this trivial fact, which does not yet go beyond the realm of the *Seinsobjektiv*: Any particular thing that isn't real (*Nichtseiendes*) must at least be capable of serving as the Object for those judgments which grasp its *Nichtsein*. It does not matter whether this *Nichtsein* is necessary or merely factual; nor does it matter in the first case whether the necessity stems from the essence of the Object or whether it stems from aspects which are external to the Object in question. In order to know that there is no round square, I must make a judgment about the round square. If physics, physiology, and psychology agree in asserting the so-called ideal character of sense-qualities, they implicitly assert something about color as well as about sound, namely, that the one exists no more than the other. Those who like paradoxical modes of expression could very well say: "There are objects of which it is true that there are no such objects." The fact, familiar the world over, which is meant by this statement throws such a bright light on the relation of objects to reality, or their relation to being, generally, that a somewhat closer examination of the matter, which is of fundamental importance in its own right, is entirely in place in our present study.

IV. THE AUSSERSEIN OF THE PURE OBJECT

A recourse to certain psychological experiences suggests itself as a natural way of resolving the paradox which seems to lie before us. I have attempted to present the most essential points pertaining to this problem in another work.[8] But, according to my account here, if we were now to maintain the aforementioned subjectivity of sense-qualities, we could speak of the object of a presentation of blue only in the sense of something which is a capacity of that presentation, from which reality withholds, as it were, the opportunity for its realization. Considered from the standpoint of the presentation, this still seems to me to touch on something of essential significance. However, I cannot conceal from myself at present the fact that it is no more necessary to an Object that it be presented in order not to exist than it is in order for it to exist. Further, even if there were a reference to it, the most that could result from its being presented would be a sort of existence — "existence by way of idea (*in der Vorstellung*)" — and so, more precisely,

[8] *Über Annahmen*, pp. 98ff.

"pseudo-existence."[9] To express it more exactly: If I say, "Blue does not exist," I am thinking just of blue, and not at all of a presentation and the capacities it may have. It is as if the blue must have being in the first place, before we can raise the question of its being (*Sein*) or non-being (*Nichtsein*). But in order not to fall into new paradoxes or actual absurdities, perhaps the following turn of expression may be appropriate: Blue, or any other Object whatsoever, is somehow given prior to our determination of its being or non-being, in a way that does not carry any prejudice to its non-being. We could also describe the situation from its psychological side in this way: if I should be able to judge that a certain Object is not, then I appear to have had to grasp the Object in some way beforehand, in order to say anything about its non-being, or more precisely, in order to affirm or to deny the ascription of non-being to the Object.

This fact, despite its commonplace character, is seen to be of a very peculiar type. We could hope to do justice to it with somewhat greater theoretical rigor by means of the following considerations. As I have stated elsewhere,[10] that a certain thing, A, is not — more briefly, the *Nichtsein* of A — is just as much an Objective as is the *Sein* of A. And the degree of certainty with which I am justified in saying that A "is not" is the degree of certainty that the Objective, "*Nichtsein* of A," itself has a *Sein* (or, more precisely, as mentioned above, that it has subsistence [*Bestand*]). Now an Objective, whether it is a *Seinsobjektiv* or *Nichtseinsobjektiv*, stands in relation to its Object (*Objekt*), albeit *cum grano salis*, as the whole to its parts. But if the whole has being, so must its parts. This seems to mean, when it is extended to the case of the Objective: if the Objective has being (*ist*), so, in some sense or other, must the object which belongs to it, even when the Objective is an objective of non-being (*Nichtseinsobjektiv*). Furthermore, since the Objective strictly prevents us from assuming that A has being (being, as we have seen, can sometimes be understood as existence, sometimes as subsistence), it appears that the requirement that the Object have being (which was inferred from the being of the *Nichtseinsobjektiv*) makes sense only insofar as the being in question is neither existence nor subsistence — only insofar as a third order of being, if one may speak this way, is adjoined to existence and subsistence. This sort of being must belong, therefore, to every Object as such. A *Nichtsein* of the same type

---

[9] See "Über Gegenstände höherer Ordnung," *loc. cit.*, pp. 186 f.
[10] *Über Annahmen*, chap. vii.

cannot be set in opposition to it, for a *Nichtsein* even in this new sense would have to immediately produce difficulties analogous to those which arise from *Nichtsein* in its ordinary sense, and which the new concept was to have eliminated. The term *"Quasisein"* seemed to me for a while to be a completely suitable expression for this rather oddly constituted type of being.

This designation, however, like others that were approved earlier (for instance, *"Pseudoexistenz"* and *"Quasitranszendenz,"*[11]) runs the risk of causing confusion. More important, meanwhile, are the following pertinent considerations. Can being which is in principle un-opposed by non-being be called being at all? However much we are permitted in this connection to judge that there is a being which is neither existence nor subsistence, nowhere else do we find grounds for such a postulate. Must we not take thought to avoid it in our case also wherever it is possible? The consideration which seems to force us to such a postulate is, to be sure, an experience which is easily observed. As we have seen, A must be "given" to me in some way or other if I am to grasp its non-being. This produces, however, as I have already shown elsewhere,[12] an assumption (*Annahme*) possessing affirmative quality: in order to deny A, I must first assume the being of A. What I refer to, so far as the being of A is concerned, is thus something which is to a certain extent only a claimant to being (*ein gewissermassen vor-gegebenes Sein des A*). But it is of the essence of assumption that it direct itself upon a being which itself does not need to be.

Without a doubt, it would be comforting to be able to say that the strange kind of being which belongs to that which does not have being (*Sein des Nichtseienden*) is just as absurd as it sounds. Such a view could recommend itself to us were it not for the fact that the Objective, which has being, always seems to require in turn an Object which has being. For the present, this requirement is based solely on the analogy to the part-whole relation: an Objective is thereby treated as a complex of some kind and the Object belonging to it as a kind of component. In many respects this may be in accordance with our insight into the nature of an Objective, which is as yet still exceedingly defective. However, no one will deny that this analogy is only an initial expedient in our embarrassment and that there would be no grounds for follow-ing this analogy rigorously even for part of the way. Thus, instead of

[11] *Über Annahmen*, p. 95.
[12] *Loc. cit.*, pp. 105 ff.

deriving the being of an Object from the being of an Objective, even on the basis of a questionable analogy where the Objective is an Objective of non-being, it would be better to conclude from the facts with which we are concerned that this analogy does not apply to the Objective of non-being — i.e., that the being of the Objective is not by any means universally dependent upon the being of its Object.

This is a position which speaks for itself without any further ado. If the opposition of being and non-being is primarily a matter of the Objective and not of the Object, then it is, after all, clearly understandable that neither being nor non-being can belong essentially to the Object in itself. This is not to say, of course, that an Object can neither be nor not be. Nor is it to say that the question, whether or not the Object has being, is purely accidental to the nature of every Object. An absurd Object such as a round square carries in itself the guarantee of its own non-being in every sense; an ideal Object, such as diversity, carries in itself the guarantee of its own non-existence. Anyone who seeks to associate himself with models which have become famous could formulate what has been shown above by saying that the Object as such (without considering the occasional peculiarities or the accompanying Objective-clause which is always present) stands "beyond being and non-being." This may also be expressed in the following less engaging and also less pretentious way, which is in my opinion, however, a more appropriate one: The Object is by nature indifferent to being (*ausserseiend*), although at least one of its two Objectives of being, the Object's being or non-being, subsists.

What one could thus call with propriety the principle of the indifference of pure Objects to being (*den Satz vom Aussersein des reinen Gegenstandes*) finally eliminates the appearance of a paradox which was the immediate occasion for the assertion of this principle. As soon as it is recognized that, apart from special cases, both being and non-being are equally external to an Object, it is then understandable that nothing more, so to speak, is involved in comprehending the non-being of the Object than there is in comprehending its being. The above-mentioned principle of the independence of *Sosein* from *Sein* now presents a welcome supplement to this view. It tells us that that which is not in any way external to the Object, but constitutes its proper essence, subsists in its *Sosein* — the *Sosein* attaching to the Object whether the object has being or not. We are finally in a position to see with sufficient clarity what confronted us above as the prejudice in favor of the existence, or at least the being, of all possible Objects of knowledge. Being is not the presupposition under which knowledge finds, as it were, its point of attack; it is itself such a point of attack. Non-being is equally as good a point of attack. Furthermore, in the *Sosein* of each Object, knowledge already finds a field of activity to which it may have access without first answering the question concerning being or non-being, or without answering this question affirmatively.

11 Morton White: THE USE OF 'EXISTS' (1956)

I. THREE VIEWS ON THE USE OF 'EXISTS'

Up to now we have concentrated on arguments for the existence of universals and physical objects, arguments that emerge in the writings of the earlier figures in the history of the analytic movement. We have distilled two that parallel each other — one that allegedly proves the existence of at least one meaning by accepting as a premise some true statement containing the word 'understand' or the phrase 'know a priori,' another that allegedly proves the existence of at least one physical object by accepting as a premise some statement like 'Here is a human hand.' In this chapter we shall look into the notion of existence involved in these "proofs." It may be helpful to begin by quoting two memorable passages in which Russell explains his view that a universal like the relation *north of* does not exist in the same sense in which the physical objects Edinburgh and London exist.

If we ask "Where and when does this relation exist?" the answer must be "Nowhere and nowhen." There is no place or time where we can find the relation "north of." It does not exist in Edinburgh any more than in London, for it relates the two and is neutral as between them. Nor can we say that it exists at any particular time. Now everything that can be apprehended by the senses or by introspection exists at some particular time. Hence the relation "north of" is radically different from such things. It is neither in space nor in time, neither material nor mental; yet it is something.[1]

We shall find it convenient only to speak of things *existing* when they are in time, that is to say, when we can point to some time *at* which they exist (not excluding the possibility of their existing at all times). Thus thoughts and feelings, minds and physical objects *exist*. But universals do not exist in this sense; we shall say that they *subsist* or *have being*, where "being" is opposed to "existence" as being timeless. The world of universals, therefore, may also be described as the world of being. The world of being is unchangeable, rigid, exact, delightful to the mathematician, the logician, the builder of metaphysical systems, and all who love perfection more than life. The world of existence is fleeting, vague, without sharp boundaries, without any clear plan or arrangement, but it contains all thoughts and feelings, all the data of sense, and all physical objects, everything that can do either good or harm, everything that makes any difference to the value of life and the world. According to our temperaments, we shall prefer the contemplation of the one or of the other. The one we do not prefer will probably seem to us a pale shadow of the one we prefer, and hardly worthy to be regarded as in any sense real. But the truth is that both have the same claim on our impartial attention, both are real, and both are important to the metaphysician. Indeed no sooner have we distinguished the two worlds than it becomes necessary to consider their relations.[2]

Russell's view in these passages lies between two positions that have been taken in the history of speculation about the word 'exists.' At one extreme there is a view that certainly may be attributed to John Stuart Mill, according to which the word 'exists' is univocal; I shall call this view 'univocalism.' At the other extreme is the view that the word 'exists' has more than two uses; indeed that it has as many distinct uses as there are categories; I shall call this 'multivocalism.' Russell seems willing to stop at two uses of 'exist' and so the most felicitous name for his view appears to be 'duovocalism.'

While for Russell in the *Problems of Philosophy* the grand break comes at the line between universals and nonuniversals, Gilbert Ryle, one of the most vocal and most recent exponents of multivocalism, appears willing to say that both within the class of Russell's universals and Russell's nonuniversals there are breaks that entail a shift in the meaning of 'exists.' Thus he says, for example: "It may be true that there exists a cathedral in Oxford, a three-engined bomber, and a

---

[1] *Problems of Philosophy*, p. 98 [p. 41, this volume].
[2] *Ibid.*, pp 99–100 [p. 42f., this volume].

number between 9 and 25. But the naïve passage to the conclusion that
there are three existents, a building, a brand of aircraft and a number
soon leads to trouble. The senses of 'exists' in which the three subjects
are said to exist are different and their logical behaviors are different."[3]
Here numbers and brands, both of them species of universals on
Russell's view and hence said by him to exist in the same sense, are
said to exist in *different* senses by Ryle. And elsewhere Ryle says:

> It is perfectly proper to say, in one logical tone of voice, that there exist
> minds and to say, in another logical tone of voice, that there exist bodies. But
> these expressions do not indicate two different species of existence, for 'existence'
> is not a generic word like 'coloured' or 'sexed.' They indicate two different
> senses of 'exist,' somewhat as 'rising' has different senses in 'the tide is rising,'
> 'hopes are rising,' and 'the average age of death is rising.' A man would be
> thought to be making a poor joke who said that three things are now rising,
> namely the tide, hopes, and the average age of death. It would be just as good
> or bad a joke to say that there exist prime numbers and Wednesdays and public
> opinions and navies; or that there exist both minds and bodies.[4]

Here *minds* and *bodies* are said to exist in different senses, again contrary
to the quoted passage from Russell in the *Problems of Philosophy*.

In a neglected part of his *System of Logic*,[5] Mill not only defends
univocalism but also expresses a number of worries over it that have
reappeared in more recent literature on this question. Mill is faced
with (what he regards as) a terminological problem arising from the
fact that he wants to divide the class of namable things into three categories: *feelings*, *substances*, and *attributes* ('feelings' is synonymous with
'states of mind' for Mill). His trouble lies in not being able to find a
concrete term corresponding to the abstract term 'existence' which
will be broad enough to embrace these three categories as subclasses of
the grandest category of all. One difficulty is that obvious candidates
among common nouns, like 'object' and 'thing,' are usually understood
as denoting only substances. Mill, therefore, wants a word like 'entity'
(although he thinks it is also sullied), which will permit him to say
that *whiteness*, for example, is an entity without implying that it is a
substance. He is troubled by precisely the thing that troubles Carnap

[3] *Philosophical Arguments* (Oxford: Clarendon Press, 1945), pp. 15–16.
[4] *The Concept of Mind* (London: Hutchinson's University Library, 1949), p. 23.
[5] Bk. 1, ch. 3, "Of the Things denoted by Names," expecially sec. 2, "Ambiguity
of the most general names."

at one point in his *Meaning and Necessity*.[6] Both want to avoid what Carnap calls "hypostatization or substantialization or reification." Now what is this sin? Carnap, like Mill, thinks that it consists in saying that all entities are things or substances. It is *not* hypostatization from Carnap's point of view to say that attributes are *beings* or *entities*, but Mill carries his terminological anxiety even to the point of fear about using the predicate 'is a being' as the most general of all, because, he remarks, "if we were to say, extension, colour, wisdom, virtue, are beings, we should perhaps be suspected of thinking with some of the ancients, that the cardinal virtues are animals; . . . We should be supposed, in short, to believe that Attributes are Substances." And Russell, by making the word 'exists' an elliptical shorthand for 'exists in space and time,' treats it, not as Mill uses the word 'exists' in the following passage, but rather as Mill uses the phrase 'is a thing'; "When we have occasion for a name which shall be capable of denoting whatever exists . . . there is hardly a word applicable to the purpose which is not also, and even more familiarly, taken in a sense in which it denotes only substances. But substances are not all that exists; attributes, if such things are to be spoken of, must be said to exist; feelings certainly exist. Yet when we speak of an *object*, or of a *thing*, we are almost always supposed to mean a substance. There seems a kind of contradiction in using such an expression as that one *thing* is merely an attribute of another thing."[7]

II. DUOVOCALISM: THE DOCTRINE THAT 'EXISTS' HAS TWO USES

Russell's duovocalism in the *Problems* deserves special attention because, as might already be evident, it is compatible with the kind of univocalism advocated by Mill. The fact that Russell himself says of being north of that "It is neither in space nor in time, neither material nor mental; *yet it is something* [my italics]" suggests that even Russell thinks there is a generic notion of which his *exists* and *subsists* are species, so to speak. It suggests that Russell might be obliged to accept a univocalistic view, were it understood that a univocalist merely maintains that, in the sentences 'The relation *north of* is something,' 'Edinburgh is something,' 'Russell's mind is something,' the phrase 'is something' is used univocally. In adding that "we shall find

[6] See *Meaning and Necessity*, pp. 22–23.
[7] Mill, *System of Logic*, p. 30. And yet "such *things* are to be spoken of" by Mill.

it convenient only to speak of things existing when they are in time,''
Russell says nothing of great philosophical importance from the point
of view of the univocalist. From that point of view, once we have gotten
to see that the relation *north of* is something just as Edinburgh is, we
may, if we wish, now say that the relation *north of* is so different from
Edinburgh that we would do well to say that one *sub*sists while the
other *ex*ists, even though they are both something in the same sense of
'are both something.' This would be a good deal like the sort of instruc-
tion that a parent might be forced to give to a child who had just come
to realize what men and women have in common. After the child had
discovered that men and women are both men from the point of view
of their biological class, the parent might tell him that because males
and females are so very different it is customary to use two different
words — 'men' and 'women' — for them. To dispel confusion, however, he would have to remind the child that it is, unfortunately, also
customary to call *all* animals of the class *man* 'men' and therefore to use
the word 'men' in a general and a special sense. Is this very different
from what goes on when one decides to apply the word 'exists' only to
things in space and time, even though one commonly applies it more
generally? I don't think so; both situations are similar insofar as we
are led to use 'exists,' after the fashion of 'man,' in a general and a
special way. But why should the fact that one thing exists in space and
time, while another does not, make it convenient for Russell to say
that only the first exists and that only the second subsists? Reasons
that are no more indicative of a profound philosophical point than those
which impel us to call only males 'men' and only females 'women' in
certain contexts; or those which impel us to call males handsome and
females beautiful even though we think that there is some univocal
predicate that can be applied to both of them; or those that impel us to
use 'church' sometimes as meaning *place of worship* and sometimes as
meaning *Christian place of worship*. The discussion reminds one of the
sports writer who could invent similar distinctions (of little philosophical interest) in the case of the obviously logical word 'class,' which is in
this respect very much like 'exists':

We all know that lots of wolves together make a pack, lots of lions a pride, and
then there is a gaggle of geese, a shoal of fish and a bevy of (what else?) beauties.
Add these impertinent ones by Smith: "A yammer of radio announcers . . . a
gangle of basketball players . . . a grouse of ball players . . . a Braille of um-
pires . . . a doze of race stewards . . . a dawdle of baseball magnates . . . a

venality of managers . . . a quiescence of fighters . . . a dissonance of com-
missioners . . . a scheme of jockeys . . . a prevarication of golfers . . . a vagrance
of amateur tennis players . . . an indigence of writers (sports) . . . a congealing
of editors."[8]

In concluding our discussion of Russell's view, we may repeat that
the crucial statement in the passage quoted from him is the following:
"It [the relation *north of*] is neither in space nor in time, neither material nor mental; yet it is something." From this statement one infers
that being something is a genus of which being in space and time and
being something not in space and time are species. We can therefore
say that there is a correspondingly general expression, namely 'There
is at least one,' which we can put before the phrase 'physical object'
and before the word 'universal.' In both of the resulting sentences,
'There is at least one physical object' and 'There is at least one universal,' the phrase 'there is at least one' is used in the same sense, and this
is reflected in the fact that we can use logical notation and symbolize
these two sentences as follows: '$(\exists x)$ (x is a physical object)' and '$(\exists x)$
(x is a universal).' Now, if Russell was prepared in the *Problems of
Philosophy* to symbolize the two sentences as indicated, then he should
have granted that the symbol '$(\exists x)$,' read in English as 'there is an x
such that,' is used in the same way in both cases. The alternative view,
according to which it means one thing in one context and another in
the other, is as doubtful and pointless as the view that the copula 'is a,'
as it appears in both contexts before the predicates 'universal' and
'physical object,' is used in two different senses.

III. FORESTALLING A POSSIBLE MISUNDERSTANDING

A few remarks should be added in order to forestall a misunderstanding. If we hold that physical objects exist in space and time, we
can certainly form an expression like 'exists in space and time' which
will not replace the unqualified expression 'exists.' And if Russell
could make some sense of the phrase 'out of space and time,' he might
form a third expression like 'exists out of space and time.' This is not
denied. We would then have three terms: 'exists,' 'exists in space and
time,' and 'exists out of space and time,' no one of which could be replaced by any other in the trio. I suggest, in fact, that using the term

---

[8] "Books of the Times," *New York Times*, July 10, 1954.

'exists' quite generally is tantamount to using Russell's 'is something,' using the second tantamount to using 'exists' narrowly, and the third term could replace Russell's 'subsists.' I also suggest that the parallel in the case of 'man' is this: The biologist's use of 'man' as a generic term (which I will write in capitals from now on when it is used generically) is analogous to my completely general word 'exists' and Russell's 'is something'; the ordinary use of 'man' as meaning *male* is analogous to the use of 'exists in space and time' and Russell's special use of 'exists'; and finally the use of 'woman' is analogous to the use of 'exists out of space and time' and Russell's 'subsists.' For purposes of easy reference I will write these down in three adjoining columns, using Russell's phrase 'space and time' rather than what might best be read 'space-time' in the light of contemporary physics.

List I	List II (Russell's)	List III
(1) exists	(1′) is something	(1″) MAN
(2) exists in space and time	(2′) exists	(2″) man
(3) exists out of space and time	(3′) subsists	(3″) woman

Now I suggest that the word 'exists' in List I is a term that Mill might have been contented with, instead of looking for common nouns like 'object,' 'thing,' 'entity,' though I sympathize with his motives for avoiding them. (Maybe 'existent' is the common noun he sought.) In each column above, no term is replaceable by any other, but in each column the notion expressed by the first term is generic in the sense that it appears as a component of, or of some expansion of, the second and third. I also suggest that List II is less illuminating than List I for someone who thinks that whatever exists or subsists (in the List II sense) *is something.* For similar reasons, List III is less illuminating than List IV below.

List IV

1‴: MAN
2‴: male MAN
3‴: female MAN

IV. AN ALTERNATIVE APPROACH TO SOME USES OF 'EXISTS'

After all of this, however, it should be observed that we are not forced to say that the word 'exists' or the phrases 'there are,' 'there exists,' and others like them, are *always* used in ordinary life in a way that is profitably or clearly rendered from a philosophical point of view by straightforward translation into modern logical symbolism. The latter is likely to clarify only one of the many ways in which these words and phrases are used in ordinary language. It is quite satisfactory for straightforward paraphrase of 'There is at least one red thing,' 'There is at least one horse,' or 'There is at least one chair in that room.' Such illustrations seem to raise no profound philosophical puzzles when they are rendered with the help of logical symbolism as indicated. But the matter is somewhat different when we come to sentences like 'There is a difference in age between John and Tom' or 'There is a possibility that James will come.' Here, of course, we can, *if we wish*, translate these sentences respectively into '(∃x) (x is an age-difference and x is between John and Tom),' and '(∃x) (x is identical with the possibility that James will come).' But if we do choose to translate them in this way, we will not clarify them. On the contrary, we will be saddled with the conclusion that there are in the universe different sorts of entities like red objects, prime numbers, age-differences, and possibilities. Such a conclusion is unwelcome to some philosophers, either because they think they understand it and think it false, or because they think it nonsensical. Thinking that such a conclusion is unwelcome — for whatever reason — they are inclined to say — and rightly — that if you want to translate the original sentences of ordinary language into statements which are clear and acceptable, it won't do to take the obvious way out, so to speak: it won't do to use the more or less obvious pattern of translation illustrated by translating 'There is at least one red thing' in the manner indicated above.

A similar feeling may be voiced, as Russell does, by saying that 'there is' in 'There is a possibility that James will come' is not used in the same sense as 'there is' in 'There is a red thing,' but this is a very dangerous way of speaking, given the philosophical motives in question. For in spite of protestations to the contrary, it gives the impression that it is quite all right to translate 'There is a possibility that James will come' into '(∃x) (x is identical with the possibility that James will come),' provided only that you recognize that the phrase '(∃x)' means something different from what it means in '(∃x) (x is red).' One might just as well introduce a new existential quantifier. And yet if the philosopher who operates in this way is asked just how this difference of meaning between these two quantifiers is registered, he cannot answer clearly.

How, then, can we clarify these puzzling sentences and yet avoid the unwelcome conclusion that there are possibilities and age-differences in our universe, without adopting something like Russell's device of saying that possibilities and age-differences exist in one sense and human beings in another? Before answering, let us consider our examples.

In the case of 'There is a difference in age between John and Tom,' we might begin by saying that we understand the relational predicate 'is as old as' and that we test statements of the form 'x is as old as y' without having to see that x has some queer thing called an age, that y has one, and that these ages are identical. In that event, the belief of the ordinary man that there is a difference in age between John and Tom would be rendered in language that is not misleading by saying instead, simply, 'It is not the case that John is as old as Tom.' We might offer an analogous translation of 'There is a possibility that James will come' in which we replace it by some statement about the statement 'James will come,' for example by the statement that this statement is not certainly false. But having clarified the original puzzling statement in this way, it is misleading to sum up our attitude toward the situation by saying that 'there is' is used in one sense in the case of 'There is a man' and in another in the case of 'There is a difference in age between John and Tom.' For what we have done is to show that we *need not assert the existence* of age-differences or the existence of possibilities in communicating what we want to communicate. Now I do not deny that some philosophers are eager to translate these puzzling statements into a notation which parallels that of '($\exists x$) (x is a man),' because they really believe that possibilities and age-differences exist along with men. Such philosophers are not being addressed at this point. Here I appeal to those philosophers who, in my opinion, want to say the right thing, but who say it in a way that is not calculated to avoid confusion. Their point of view must be distinguished from that of Russell in the *Problems of Philosophy* in spite of the fact that he too speaks of the different senses of 'exists.' Russell did *not* treat the statement 'There are universals' in a manner analogous to that in which we have just treated 'There is a difference in age between John and Tom' and 'There is a possibility that James will come.' In effect, Russell adopted the translation of 'There are universals' into '($\exists x$) (x is a universal)' (though he doesn't say so in so many words), and he also adopted a similar translation of 'There are physical objects.' He made no effort to elucidate the former in any way analogous to that in which we have tried to elucidate our examples. On the contrary, he wanted *to prove* that universals exist, but then, recognizing their queerness, was driven to saying that they exist in another sense. The result is a deliberate effort to distinguish two expressions of the form 'there exist,' having all of their so-called logical properties in common and yet differing in sense. But, as we have seen, even that effort was undercut by Russell's tendency to use the phrase 'is something' univocally.

V. THE MULTIVOCALISM OF RYLE

Having distinguished two kinds of philosophers who *say* that there are different senses of the word 'exists,' I now wish to turn to the views of Gilbert Ryle on this difficult subject because he too talks of 'exists' as having different senses. I should like to say in advance that while certain substantive philosophical views expressed in Ryle's *Concept of Mind* resemble the clarifications offered in the earlier handling of 'There is a difference in age between John and Tom' and 'There is a possibility that James will come,' Ryle's own formulation of his philosophical procedure sometimes suggests that his own multivocalism is merely a generalization of Russell's duovocalism.

The passages which give strongest support to this second interpretation of Ryle are those I have already quoted from his *Philosophical Arguments* and his *Concept of Mind*. There we have an explicit statement that 'exist' has different senses, indeed many more senses than Russell assigned to it. In these passages one gets the impression that Ryle thinks that there are many different "categories" and that we assert the non-emptiness of those categories in as many different senses of 'exist' as there are categories. Moreover, Ryle seems to avoid anything like Russell's general notion of *being something* and seems, therefore, to have conducted a more consistent and thoroughgoing attack on univocalism. When we say 'There exist minds' and when we say 'There exist bodies,' according to Ryle, we use two different senses of 'exist,' "somewhat as 'rising' has different senses in 'the tide is rising,' 'hopes are rising,' and 'the average age of death is rising,' " and he adds that uttering the conjunctive statement 'There exist bodies and there exist minds' is about as funny as saying 'Three things are now rising, namely the tide, hopes, and the average age of death.'

The following discussion of Ryle's views is divided into two parts.

I wish to show in this section that some things he says suggest that he merely espouses a generalization of Russell's duovocalism — and these things I will criticize adversely. Then I will try to show in the next section how Ryle's general view might be defended by treating the statement 'There are minds' in a manner analogous to that in which we treated 'There is a difference in age between John and Tom' and similar examples. Indeed, I think that this may be the main direction of Ryle's work.

In considering Ryle's view it is useful to begin with a distinction drawn by Quine between two kinds of existential statements.[9] On the one hand there are *singular* existence statements of the form 'There is such a thing as so-and-so,' and on the other *general* existence statements of the form 'There are so-and-so's.' The idea of a singular existential statement is illustrated by

> (a) There is such a thing as Edinburgh

and by

> (b) There is such a thing as being north of.

The general existential statement is illustrated by

> (c) There are cities in Scotland

and by

> (d) There are relations.

Now statement (a) is not profound but it is clear and true. I shouldn't imagine that anyone would protest or be alarmed at hearing someone utter it. But (b) is just the sort of thing that a philosopher (like Russell) was moved to *argue* for; moreover it is an example of the sort of thing that philosophers say and defend while trainmen don't. And yet a trainman might easily say in answer to the question 'Is there such a place as Edinburgh?' that there is, and only a bit of straightforward questioning on the part of a philosopher might lead that trainman to say that if there is such a *place* as Edinburgh, then there is such a *thing* as Edinburgh. There is a parallel difference between (c) and (d). In other words, (c) is to (d) as (a) is to (b) in this respect. Statements (a) and (c) are ordinary or semi-ordinary, while (b) and (d) are philosophical jargon.

While (b) 'There is such a thing as being north of' is, like (d) 'There are relations,' more "philosophical" than examples (a) and (c),

---

[9] "Designation and Existence," *Journal of Philosophy*, vol. 36 (1939); reprinted in Feigl and Sellars, *Readings in Philosophical Analysis*. See pp. 44–45 of the latter.

(d) is the more "philosophical" of the pair (b) and (d). This may be more evident if we compare the parallel examples of 'There is such a thing as manhood' and 'There are attributes.' The second of this last pair is much more likely to cause puzzlement than is the first. I leave aside the reasons for this, since, as a matter of fact, I suspect that most ordinary people who do accept 'There is such a thing as manhood' accept it because they think it means neither more nor less than 'There are men.' But it doesn't for platonists, since the very reasons that lead them to assert the existence of whiteness and *north of* should lead them to assert the existence of unicornhood even though there are no unicorns. The point is that they say manhood exists, it will be recalled, merely because they understand the term 'man,' so that the mere fact that they understand the term 'unicorn' *should* lead them to assert the existence of unicornhood.

If we make this distinction between singular existence statements and general existence statements, it is possible to discuss the issues at stake between Mill's univocalism and an extension of Russell's duovocalism by concentrating on either kind of statement. For (a) 'There is such a thing as Edinburgh' and (b) 'There is such a thing as *north of*' (the two singular existence statements) and (c) 'There are cities in Scotland' and (d) 'There are relations' (the two general existence statements) can be translated into logical jargon as the following respectively:

(a') ($\exists x$) (x is identical with Edinburgh.)
(b') ($\exists x$) (x is identical with being north of.)
(c') ($\exists x$) (x is a city in Scotland.)
(d') ($\exists x$) (x is a relation.)

Now, as I see it, one issue between univocalism and multivocalism (or duovocalism) can be stated in either of the following two ways:

(1) Is the symbol '($\exists x$)' as it occurs in (a') used as it is used in (b')?
(2) Is the symbol '($\exists x$)' as it occurs in (c') used as it is used in (d')?

In answer, I should say that *all* occurrences of it are used in the same way. Nevertheless, I recognize that someone who immediately translated 'There is such a thing as *manhood*' by '($\exists x$) (x is a man)' or who, in the same spirit, translated (b) 'There is such a thing as being north of,' not by (b') above, but by (b'') '($\exists x$) ($\exists y$) (x is north of y),' would be *tempted* to say that the phrase 'there is such a thing as' in (b) is used in a different sense from the same phrase in (a). Why? Simply because *the pattern* of translation advocated would be different. Statement (a)'s translation into (a′) follows the pattern of taking the singular name of a concrete object and prefacing '($\exists x$) (x is identical with)' to it. But clearly the philosopher who translated (b) by putting in its place not (b′) but (b″) would follow an entirely different pattern. It is this difference of *pattern* of translation, then, that causes some philosophers to say that the original phrase 'there is such a thing as' means something different in context (b) from what it means in (a). I should say at once that there are no insuperable objections to speaking in this way, provided we understand each other. Nevertheless, we must be perfectly clear about the difference between a strict duovocalism like Russell's, in which 'There is such a thing as being north of' is *not* rendered by 'Some things are north of others,' and one in which it is. Were we prepared to take certain risks, we might say that Russell "really" says that 'there are' is used in different senses, while the hypothetical philosopher last considered does not. I suspect that Ryle is more like this hypothetical philosopher than he is like Russell, no matter how much like Russell Ryle may sound. For the moment, however, I shall concentrate on those statements by Ryle which are dangerously like Russell's.

There is another point that might be made by reference to the distinction between singular and general statements of existence. It arises from something that Ryle says in a passage previously quoted. He says that we must assert the existence of minds and bodies in "different logical tones of voice" because the conjunction of 'There are minds and there are bodies' sounds absurd and punnish, like 'She came home in a flood of tears and a sedan chair' and 'Three things are now rising, namely the tide, hopes, and the average age of death.' This suggests that what Ryle might be worried about are conjunctions not of *singular* but rather of *general* existence statements, which contain "category-words" like 'minds,' 'bodies,' 'universals,' etc., as their predicates. (When I say that a general existence statement contains something as its predicate, I mean merely that it is like 'There are cities in Scotland' in containing the expression 'cities in Scotland' as its predicate.)

Now it may very well be that Ryle's dismay over 'There are minds and there are bodies' is stimulated not by the fact that it is a conjunction of *existential* statements but by the fact that it is a conjunction of two *general* existential statements. This would be confirmed if hearing Russell conjoin two singular existential statements like 'There is such a thing as Edinburgh' ['Edinburgh is something'] and 'There is such a thing as being north of' ['Being north of is something'] did not cause us to suppose he was telling jokes, as, of course, it doesn't. So even if 'There are physical objects and there are meanings' were to leave us in stitches, still, if 'There is such a thing as Edinburgh and there is such a thing as being north of' didn't, we might conclude that the source of mirth was not in the double occurrence of 'there are' but rather in the expressions 'physical object' and 'meaning.' However, once the conjunction 'There are minds and there are bodies' is thought to be funny because of combining a reference to such differently described things, then, of course, we can point out that even *within one category* there will be pairs of species which are such that the conjunctive asserton of the fact that they both contain members would raise a titter. For example, if one were to say after reading Lewis Carroll, "Yes, there are cabbages and there are kings and there are bits of sealing wax," one might be thought to be mildly funny, but that would not justify our thinking that 'there are' was being used in three different senses. The point is that sometimes the humor (or attempt at it) comes from punning on a word like 'rising' or 'in' and sometimes from the discrepancy of the subject matter involved, as in the case of 'exists.'

So far I have argued that if minds and bodies *are* very different sorts of things and if physical objects and meanings are, it would not follow that the strangeness or comic quality of a conjunction of general existential statements containing these categorical predicates would prove that 'there exists' was being used in different senses in one sentence. On the contrary, the very phrase 'different sorts of things' suggests that they are species of the genus *thing*, just as cabbages and kings are. And, moreover, when Ryle speaks of "categories" he gives the impression that there are different pigeonholes in the desk that makes up everything. Why, then, *must* someone who says, 'There is something in category *A*' use 'there is' in a sense different from that in which he uses it when he says, 'There is something in category *B*'?

One principle which Ryle seems to use when he says that 'there are' has two meanings in the context 'There are minds and there are bodies' appears to be this: No expression that can be combined with one categorial predicate like 'body' to form a true statement is synonymous with the same expression combined in the same way with another categorial predicate like 'mind.' Thus Ryle says that 'I bought a left-hand glove and I bought a right-hand glove and I bought a pair of gloves' illustrates this situation because gloves and pairs are in different categories. According to Ryle's view, the last occurrence of 'I bought' must differ in sense from the first two because pairs are bought in a sense different from that in which single gloves are bought. And similarly, I suppose, with 'There are right-hand gloves and there are left-hand gloves and there are pairs of gloves.' Similarly with 'There are bodies and there are minds' and with 'There are bodies and there are universals.' But, of course, Ryle must say that the situation is different with 'There are kings and there are cabbages and there are bits of sealing wax.' This last involves no multivocality of 'there are,' so that the question naturally arises: What distinguishes the last case from the others?

And furthermore, which is the fundamental notion? Is it the nonsynonymy of the different occurrences of 'there are' or is it the categorial difference of 'mind' and 'body'? Are the predicates 'body' and 'mind' seen to be different categorial predicates on the basis of our seeing the multivocality of 'there is a' as prefixed to both of them, or do we come to see that 'there is a' is multivocal as prefixed to each of them because we know that they each represent a distinct category? I confess that I can *see* neither directly. I know that cabbages are not kings and, conversely, I know that universals are not physical objects; but I don't see that the first is a noncategorial mutual exclusion while the second is a case of two categories excluding each other. For this reason I can't use this as a basis for concluding that while 'There are cabbages and there are kings' involves no pun, 'There are minds and there are bodies' does.

Now I don't deny that there are some things that one can say truly about universals that one can't say truly about physical objects, for I think the statement 'Johnson kicked a physical object' is true, while 'Johnson kicked a meaning' is not. But if a man were to say 'Johnson kicked a physical object and Johnson kicked a meaning,' and for some strange reason insisted on regarding the conjunction as true, he might add that 'Johnson kicked' meant something different the second time it occurred in the conjunction from what it meant the first time, because, as he might say, "Of course, we don't kick meanings in the sense in which we kick physical objects." I think that the contrast between a cartesian who uses the devices of modern logic and Ryle (in one of his moods) may now be stated fairly clearly. The simple-minded logistic cartesian who is also a logistic platonist would say that minds, physical objects, and universals, all exist in the same sense — even though they are very different sorts of things. Mill is a case in point. He would therefore leave himself open to the attack of another philoso- pher, who might then flatly deny or query the meaningfulness of the statement that universals exist as well as the statement that minds exist. But Ryle, who is certainly not a cartesian but who sometimes seems bent on so construing 'There are minds' in such a way as to allow it to be true, thinks he is forced to say that 'there are' is here used in a sense which is different from that in which it is used in 'There are bodies.' And sometimes, as I have said, this leads to language which is danger- ously like Russell's in the *Problems of Philosophy*.

In concluding this discussion of one interpretation of Ryle's multivocalism — his tendency to speak without qualification about 'exists' as having different senses — I should like to reiterate my own positive view on this point. Once a philosopher decides to assert the existence of minds or meanings without providing further clarification or translation of his assertion, or worse, once he goes so far as to adopt anything like the quantifier of modern logic in formulating his existen- tial statements, he will find it difficult to speak of the different senses of 'exist' without confusing the issue. Indeed he may even find himself defeating his own ends. For consider the following statement: 'There are exactly two places at which the phrase 'there are' occurs in the sentence 'There are minds and there are bodies,' *and* there are exactly two meanings of 'there are' expressed in that sentence.' This is one (admittedly dangerous) way of expressing Ryle's fundamental thesis. But does he suppose that in saying this we are making a pun on 'There are exactly two' because in one case we count physical ink marks (Category A) and in the other meanings (Category B)? I should think not, because the very thesis to the effect that 'there are' is ambiguous implies that two distinct ink marks have two distinct meanings in the *same* sense of 'two.' Here, by Ryle's own standards, the two occurrences of the phrase 'two distinct' have two distinct meanings in turn, thereby making it impossible for him to say that the number of occurrences of 'there are' is two in the same sense as the number of meanings of 'there are' is two.

And finally, it should be repeated that a duovocalist like Russell in the *Problems* is bent on *proving* the existence of universals to ordinary men who believe in the existence of physical objects but not in univer- sals. Is it not strange, then, that Russell should say to the ordinary man that he is proving the existence of universals in another sense of 'exists'? Think how unpersuasive it would be to argue as follows: "You think that only articles of clothing are capes, but you are wrong. Some bodies of land are too, only in a different sense of 'cape.'" If a philosopher is going to be clever and prove that there are more things than an ordinary man thinks there are, he should not change the meaning of 'there are' in the middle of the argument. Something similar is clearly relevant in theology.

VI. HOW RYLE MIGHT DISPENSE WITH MULTIVOCALISM

Very often in the *Concept of Mind* Ryle suggests that the puzzling sentence 'There are bodies and there are minds' might be profitably replaced by what I shall write as 'There are bodies and there are bodies that behave mentally.' I am not so much interested now in the truth or philosophical usefulness of Ryle's thesis when formulated in this (oversimplified) way as in its implication for his approach to the notion of existence. And therefore I will not pause to discuss the difficult expression 'behave mentally,' which is telescopic in the extreme. What I wish to point out is that this translation or replacement of a puzzling statement by another one which is presumed to be less puzzling should not lead us to say that 'there are' in 'There are minds' has a different sense from the same expression in 'There are bodies.' For the effect of this translation resembles the effect of our suggested translations of 'There is a difference in age between John and Tom,' 'There is a possibility that James will come,' and 'There is such a thing as manhood' (where the last is translated, symbolically, into '$(\exists x)$ (x is a man)'). And what is the general effect of these translations of existential statements of ordinary language? From our present point of view they all *free us from the need to assert the existence* of things like age-differences, possibilities, and attributes, insofar as they allow us to say what some of us want to say, without ever having to admit *their* existence in the way that we cheerfully admit the existence of men. Moreover, we are saved from having to say that the phrase 'exists' applies to some "entities" in one sense and to others in another "sense." And because it seems to me that Ryle's philosophy of mind needs no such appeal to different senses, I see no reason for his concluding that 'there exist' when it precedes 'minds' means something different from what it means when it precedes 'bodies' — unless that is merely understood as a way of saying that, while it's all right to translate 'There are bodies' into '($\exists x$) (x is a body)' and to stop there, it's not only not all right to do something analogous with 'There are minds,' but you've got to translate it according to some other pattern.

Here we are reminded of the non-platonic rendering of 'There is such a thing as manhood' discussed earlier. A non-platonist might refuse to render it '($\exists x$) (x is identical with manhood)' and to stop there, though he might be quite willing in the case of 'There is such a thing as Edinburgh' to render it as '($\exists x$) (x is identical with Edinburgh)' and stop. He paraphrases the puzzling statement (whether correctly from a broader philosophical point of view doesn't interest us now) by using a different pattern of translation: he renders it as '($\exists x$) (x is a man).' And this is something like what the Ryle-like translator of 'There are minds' does when he paraphrases it as 'There are bodies that behave mentally' and ultimately as '($\exists x$) (x is a body and x behaves mentally).'

In passing we might observe certain differences within the class of clarifying translations just considered. In some cases, as in the translations of 'There are minds' and 'There is such a thing as *manhood*,' we do not free ourselves from asserting existence altogether, for in the translation we continue to assert the existence of bodies of a certain kind and of men. But when we move from 'There is a difference in age between John and Tom' to 'It is not the case that John is as old as Tom,' we move to a nonexistential statement altogether. This difference merely underscores the fact that philosophical clarification of statements which seem to commit us to the existence of things that don't exist, or which seem to imply existential statements we don't understand, can be accomplished by different patterns of translation. The temptation is to suppose that the original contexts *use* the word 'exists' differently if the pattern of translation is different, but I think this way of speaking should be resisted. The whole thing may be described in a clearer and less puzzling way.

VII. CONCLUSION

It should not be concluded from this chapter that 'exists' or 'there are' *must* always be used in exactly the same way. That would be absurd. One conclusion is that the use of 'there are' which is symbolized by the existential quantifier of modern logic — '($\exists x$)' — is clear, and that with its help a large number of ordinary and scientific statements of existence may be formulated. But there are some existential statements in ordinary language which, when translated according to the simple pattern whereby we go from 'There are men' to '($\exists x$) (x is a man),' merely have their puzzling nature exposed. If they are so translated, therefore, it can only be to dramatize their peculiarity and to show that something further must be done. This can sometimes take the form of further translation which clarifies and removes puzzlement by removing the need to postulate obscure entities or nonentities.

Some very serious philosophical problems involving existence have not been mentioned in this chapter. They arise from a consideration of existential statements in ordinary language or science which cannot be paraphrased in a way that quiets our anxieties. The existential statements of arithmetic fall into this group. They explicitly assert the existence of numbers, they are naturally rendered by the use of the existential quantifier, and yet they are not easily translated into statements which do not assert the existence of puzzling things, or which assert the existence of nonpuzzling things. Here, it might be said, we must surely distinguish a new sense of 'exists,' for one thing because we cannot contextually eliminate the existential quantifier, and for another because arithmetic is a priori true. We cannot deny that this raises a profound philosophical problem, but we must question the argument in favor of distinguishing a new sense of 'exists'. It amounts to saying that arithmetical statements like 'There are prime numbers between 5 and 50' are a priori true and therefore that the phrase 'there are' is used differently in arithmetical statements from the way in which it is used when we say 'There are mountains in Alaska,' which is not a priori. Whatever merit there may be in the claim — and I admit none — this argument for it is fallacious. Frege provides its refutation implicitly when he says that the phrase 'is identical with' is used in the same way in the context 'The evening star is identical with the evening star' and in the context 'The evening star is identical with the morning star,' even though the first is a priori true and the second not.[10] Furthermore, he does not conclude that a conjunction of his two statements is like 'She came home in a flood of tears and a sedan chair.' His example is instructive because the phrase 'there is,' like 'is identical with,' is a logical constant and can therefore appear in a statement of any epistemological status. Think how absurd it would be to conclude that the logical constant 'or' is used differently in the law of excluded middle from the way in which it is used in 'She fell or she was pushed,'' just because one is ''a priori'' and the other not. 'There are' is in the same boat as 'or.'

[10] "On Sense and Nominatum" in Feigl and Sellars.

Ontological
Commitment

12 Willard Van Orman Quine: ON WHAT THERE IS (1948)

A curious thing about the ontological problem is its simplicity. It can be put in three Anglo-Saxon monosyllables: 'What is there?' It can be answered, moreover, in a word — 'Everything' — and everyone will accept this answer as true. However, this is merely to say that there is what there is. There remains room for disagreement over cases; and so the issue has stayed alive down the centuries.

Suppose now that two philosophers, McX and I, differ over ontology. Suppose McX maintains there is something which I maintain there is not. McX can, quite consistently with his own point of view, describe our difference of opinion by saying that I refuse to recognize certain entities. I should protest, of course, that he is wrong in his formulation of our disagreement, for I maintain that there are no entities, of the kind which he alleges, for me to recognize; but my finding him wrong in his formulation of our disagreement is unimportant, for I am committed to considering him wrong in his ontology anyway.

When *I* try to formulate our difference of opinion, on the other hand, I seem to be in a predicament. I cannot admit that there are some things which McX countenances and I do not, for in admitting that there are such things I should be contradicting my own rejection of them.

It would appear, if this reasoning were sound, that in any onto-logical dispute the proponent of the negative side suffers the disadvantage of not being able to admit that this opponent disagrees with him.

This is the old Platonic riddle of nonbeing. Nonbeing must in some sense be, otherwise what is it that there is not? This tangled doctrine might be nicknamed *Plato's beard*; historically it has proved tough, frequently dulling the edge of Occam's razor.

It is some such line of thought that leads philosophers like McX to impute being where they might otherwise be quite content to recognize that there is nothing. Thus, take Pegasus. If Pegasus *were* not, McX argues, we should not be talking about anything when we use the word; therefore it would be nonsense to say even that Pegasus is not. Thinking to show thus that the denial of Pegasus cannot be coherently maintained, he concludes that Pegasus is.

McX cannot, indeed, quite persuade himself that any region of space-time, near or remote, contains a flying horse of flesh and blood. Pressed for further details on Pegasus, then, he says that Pegasus is an idea in men's minds. Here, however, a confusion begins to be apparent. We may for the sake of argument concede that there is an entity, and even a unique entity (though this is rather implausible), which is the mental Pegasus-idea; but this mental entity is not what people are talking about when they deny Pegasus.

McX never confuses the Parthenon with the Parthenon-idea. The Parthenon is physical; the Parthenon-idea is mental (according anyway to McX's version of ideas, and I have no better to offer). The Parthenon is visible; the Parthenon-idea is invisible. We cannot easily imagine two things more unlike, and less liable to confusion, than the Parthenon and the Parthenon-idea. But when we shift from the Parthenon to Pegasus, the confusion sets in — for no other reason than that McX would sooner be deceived by the crudest and most flagrant counterfeit than grant the nonbeing of Pegasus.

The notion that Pegasus must be, because it would otherwise be nonsense to say even that Pegasus is not, has been seen to lead McX into an elementary confusion. Subtler minds, taking the same precept as their starting point, come out with theories of Pegasus which are less patently misguided than McX's, and correspondingly more difficult to eradicate. One of these subtler minds is named, let us say, Wyman. Pegasus, Wyman maintains, has his being as an unactualized possible. When we say of Pegasus that there is no such thing, we are saying, more precisely, that Pegasus does not have the special attribute of actuality. Saying that Pegasus is not actual is on a par, logically, with saying that the Parthenon is not red; in either case we are saying something about an entity whose being is unquestioned.

Wyman, by the way, is one of those philosophers who have united in ruining the good old word 'exist.' Despite his espousal of unactualized possibles, he limits the word 'existence' to actuality — thus preserving an illusion of ontological agreement between himself and us who repudiate the rest of his bloated universe. We have all been prone to say, in our common-sense usage of 'exist,' that Pegasus does not exist, meaning simply that there is no such entity at all. If Pegasus existed he would indeed be in space and time, but only because the word 'Pegasus' has spatio-temporal connotations, and not because 'exists' has spatio-temporal connotations. If spatio-temporal reference is lacking when we affirm the existence of the cube root of 27, this is simply because a cube root is not a spatio-temporal kind of thing, and not because we are being ambiguous in our use of 'exist.'[1] However, Wyman, in an ill-conceived effort to appear agreeable, genially grants us the nonexistence of Pegasus and then, contrary to what *we* meant by nonexistence of Pegasus, insists that Pegasus *is*. Existence is one thing, he says, and subsistence is another. The only way I know of coping with this obfuscation of issues is to *give* Wyman the word 'exist.' I'll try not to use it again; I still have 'is.' So much for lexicography; let's get back to Wyman's ontology.

Wyman's overpopulated universe is in many ways unlovely. It offends the aesthetic sense of us who have a taste for desert landscapes, but this is not the worst of it. Wyman's slum of possibles is a breeding ground for disorderly elements. Take, for instance, the possible fat man in that doorway; and, again, the possible bald man in that doorway. Are they the same possible man, or two possible men? How do we decide? How many possible men are there in that doorway? Are there more possible thin ones than fat ones? How many of them are alike?

---

[1] The impulse to distinguish terminologically between existence as applied to objects actualized somewhere in space-time and existence (or subsistence or being) as applied to other entities arises in part, perhaps, from an idea that the observation of nature is relevant only to questions of existence of the first kind. But this idea is readily refuted by counter-instances such as 'the ratio of the number of centaurs to the number of unicorns.' If there were such a ratio, it would be an abstract entity, viz. a number. Yet it is only by studying nature that we conclude that the number of centaurs and the number of unicorns are both 0 and hence that there is no such ratio.

Or would their being alike make them one? Are no *two* possible things alike? Is this the same as saying that it is impossible for two things to be alike? Or, finally, is the concept of identity simply inapplicable to unactualized possibles? But what sense can be found in talking of entities which cannot meaningfully be said to be identical with themselves and distinct from one another? These elements are well-nigh incorrigible. By a Fregean therapy of individual concepts, some effort might be made at rehabilitation; but I feel we'd do better simply to clear Wyman's slum and be done with it.

Possibility, along with the other modalities of necessity and impossibility and contingency, raises problems upon which I do not mean to imply that we should turn our backs. But we can at least limit modalities to whole statements. We may impose the adverb 'possibly' upon a statement as a whole, and we may well worry about the semantical analysis of such usage; but little real advance in such analysis is to be hoped for in expanding our universe to include so-called *possible entities*. I suspect that the main motive for this expansion is simply the old notion that Pegasus, for example, must be because otherwise it would be nonsense to say even that he is not.

Still, all the rank luxuriance of Wyman's universe of possibles would seem to come to naught when we make a slight change in the example and speak not of Pegasus but of the round square cupola on Berkeley College. If, unless Pegasus were, it would be nonsense to say that he is not, then by the same token, unless the round square cupola on Berkeley College were, it would be nonsense to say that it is not. But, unlike Pegasus, the round square cupola on Berkeley College cannot be admitted even as an unactualized *possible*. Can we drive Wyman now to admitting also a realm of unactualizable impossibles? If so, a good many embarrassing questions could be asked about them. We might hope even to trap Wyman in contradictions, by getting him to admit that certain of these entities are at once round and square. But the wily Wyman chooses the other horn of the dilemma and concedes that it is nonsense to say that the round square cupola on Berkeley College is not. He says that the phrase 'round square cupola' is meaningless.

Wyman was not the first to embrace this alternative. The doctrine of the meaninglessness of contradictions runs away back. The tradition survives, moreover, in writers who seem to share none of Wyman's motivations. Still, I wonder whether the first temptation to such a doctrine may not have been substantially the motivation which we have observed in Wyman. Certainly the doctrine has no intrinsic appeal; and it has led its devotees to such quixotic extremes as that of challenging the method of proof by *reductio ad absurdum* — a challenge in which I sense a *reductio ad absurdum* of the doctrine itself.

Moreover, the doctrine of meaninglessness of contradictions has the severe methodological drawback that it makes it impossible, in principle, ever to devise an effective test of what is meaningful and what is not. It would be forever impossible for us to devise systematic ways of deciding whether a string of signs made sense — even to us individually, let alone other people — or not. For it follows from a discovery in mathematical logic, due to Church, that there can be no generally applicable test of contradictoriness.

I have spoken disparagingly of Plato's beard, and hinted that it is tangled. I have dwelt at length on the inconveniences of putting up with it. It is time to think about taking steps.

Russell, in his theory of so-called singular descriptions, showed clearly how we might meaningfully use seeming names without supposing that there be the entities allegedly named. The names to which Russell's theory directly applies are complex descriptive names such as 'the author of *Waverley*,' 'the present King of France,' 'the round square cupola on Berkeley College.' Russell analyzes such phrases systematically as fragments of the whole sentences in which they occur. The sentence 'The author of *Waverley* was a poet,' for example, is explained as a whole as meaning 'Someone (better: something) wrote *Waverley* and was a poet, and nothing else wrote *Waverley*.' (The point of this added clause is to affirm the uniqueness which is implicit in the word 'the,' in '*the* author of *Waverley*.') The sentence 'The round square cupola on Berkeley College is pink' is explained as 'Something is round and square and is a cupola on Berkeley College and is pink, and nothing else is round and square and a cupola on Berkeley College.'

The virtue of this analysis is that the seeming name, a descriptive phrase, is paraphrased *in context* as a so-called incomplete symbol. No unified expression is offered as an analysis of the descriptive phrase, but the statement as a whole which was the context of that phrase still gets its full quota of meaning — whether true or false.

The unanalyzed statement 'The author of *Waverley* was a poet' contains a part, 'the author of *Waverley*,' which is wrongly supposed by McX and Wyman to demand objective reference in order to be meaningful at all. But in Russell's translation, 'Something wrote *Waverley* and was a poet and nothing else wrote *Waverley*,' the burden of objective reference which had been put upon the descriptive phrase is now taken over by words of the kind that logicians call bound variables, variables of quantification, namely, words like 'something,' 'nothing,' 'everything.' These words, far from purporting to be names specifically of the author of *Waverley*, do not purport to be names at all; they refer to entities generally, with a kind of studied ambiguity peculiar to themselves. These quantificational words or bound variables are, of course a basic part of language, and their meaningfulness, at least in context, is not to be challenged. But their meaningfulness in no way presupposes there being either the author of *Waverley* or the round square cupola on Berkeley College or any other specifically preassigned objects.

Where descriptions are concerned, there is no longer any difficulty in affirming or denying being. 'There *is* the author of *Waverley*' is explained by Russell as meaning 'Someone (or, more strictly, something) wrote *Waverley* and nothing else wrote *Waverley*.' 'The author of *Waverley* is not' is explained, correspondingly, as the alternation 'Either each thing failed to write *Waverley* or two or more things wrote *Waverley*.' This alternation is false, but meaningful; and it contains no expression purporting to name the author of *Waverley*. The statement 'The round square cupola on Berkeley College is not' is analyzed in simiiar fashion. So the old notion that statements of nonbeing defeat themselves goes by the board. When a statement of being or nonbeing is analyzed by Russell's theory of descriptions, it ceases to contain any expression which even purports to name the alleged entity whose being is in question, so that the meaningfulness of the statement no longer can be thought to presuppose that there be such an entity.

Now what of 'Pegasus'? This being a word rather than a descriptive phrase, Russell's argument does not immediately apply to it. However, it can easily be made to apply. We have only to rephrase 'Pegasus' as a description, in any way that seems adequately to single out our idea; say, 'the winged horse that was captured by Bellerophon.' Substituting such a phrase for 'Pegasus,' we can then proceed to analyze the statement 'Pegasus is,' or 'Pegasus is not,' precisely on the analogy of Russell's analysis of 'The author of *Waverley* is' and 'The author of *Waverley* is not.'

In order thus to subsume a one-word name or alleged name such as 'Pegasus' under Russell's theory of description, we must, of course, be able first to translate the word into a description. But this is no real restriction. If the notion of Pegasus had been so obscure or so basic a one that no pat translation into a descriptive phrase had offered itself along familiar lines, we could still have availed ourselves of the following artificial and trivial-seeming device: we could have appealed to the *ex hypothesi* unanalyzable, irreducible attribute of *being Pegasus*, adopting, for its expression, the verb 'is-Pegasus,' or 'pegasizes.' The noun 'Pegasus' itself could then be treated as derivative, and identified after all with a description: 'the thing that is-Pegasus,' 'the thing that pegasizes.'

If the importing of such a predicate as 'pegasizes' seems to commit us to recognizing that there is a corresponding attribute, pegasizing, in Plato's heaven or in the minds of men, well and good. Neither we nor Wyman nor McX have been contending, thus far, about the being or nonbeing of universals, but rather about that of Pegasus. If in terms of pegasizing we can interpret the noun 'Pegasus' as a description subject to Russell's theory of descriptions, then we have disposed of the old notion that Pegasus cannot be said not to be without presupposing that in some sense Pegasus is.

Our argument is now quite general. McX and Wyman supposed that we could not meaningfully affirm a statement of the form 'So-and-so is not,' with a simple or descriptive singular noun in place of 'so-and-so,' unless so-and-so is. This supposition is now seen to be quite generally groundless, since the singular noun in question can always be expanded into a singular description, trivially or otherwise, and then analyzed out *à la* Russell.

We commit ourselves to an ontology containing numbers when we say there are prime numbers larger than a million; we commit ourselves to an ontology containing centaurs when we say there are centaurs; and we commit ourselves to an ontology containing Pegasus when we say Pegasus is. But we do not commit ourselves to an ontology containing Pegasus or the author of *Waverley* or the round square cupola on Berkeley College when we say that Pegasus or the author of *Waverley* or the cupola in question is *not*. We need no longer labor under the delusion that the meaningfulness of a statement containing a singular term presupposes an entity named by the term. A singular term need not name to be significant.

An inkling of this might have dawned on Wyman and McX even

without benefit of Russell if they had only noticed — as so few of us do — that there is a gulf between *meaning* and *naming* even in the case of a singular term which is genuinely a name of an object. The following example from Frege will serve. The phrase 'Evening Star' names a certain large physical object of spherical form, which is hurtling through space some scores of millions of miles from here. The phrase 'Morning Star' names the same thing, as was probably first established by some observant Babylonian. But the two phrases cannot be regarded as having the same meaning; otherwise that Babylonian could have dispensed with his observations and contented himself with reflecting on the meanings of his words. The meanings, then, being different from one another, must be other than the named object, which is one and the same in both cases.

Confusion of meaning with naming not only made McX think he could not meaningfully repudiate Pegasus; a continuing confusion of meaning with naming no doubt helped engender his absurd notion that Pegasus is an idea, a mental entity. The structure of his confusion is as follows. He confused the alleged *named object* Pegasus with the *meaning* of the word 'Pegasus,' therefore concluding that Pegasus must be in order that the word have meaning. But what sorts of things are meanings? This is a moot point; however, one might quite plausibly explain meanings as ideas in the mind, supposing we can make clear sense in turn of the idea of ideas in the mind. Therefore Pegasus, initially confused with a meaning, ends up as an idea in the mind. It is the more remarkable that Wyman, subject to the same initial motivation as McX, should have avoided this particular blunder and wound up with unactualized possibles instead.

Now let us turn to the ontological problem of universals: the question whether there are such entities as attributes, relations, classes, numbers, functions. McX, characteristically enough, thinks there are. Speaking of attributes, he says: "There are red houses, red roses, red sunsets; this much is prephilosophical common sense in which we must all agree. These houses, roses, and sunsets, then, have something in common; and this which they have in common is all I mean by the attribute of redness." For McX, thus, there being attributes is even more obvious and trivial than the obvious and trivial fact of there being red houses, roses, and sunsets. This, I think, is characteristic of metaphysics, or at least of that part of metaphysics called ontology: one who regards a statement on this subject as true at all must regard it as trivially true. One's ontology is basic to the conceptual scheme by which he interprets all experiences, even the most commonplace ones. Judged within some particular conceptual scheme — and how else is judgment possible? — an ontological statement goes without saying, standing in need of no separate justification at all. Ontological statements follow immediately from all manner of casual statements of commonplace fact, just as — from the point of view, anyway, of McX's conceptual scheme — 'There is an attribute' follows from 'There are red houses, red roses, red sunsets.'

Judged in another conceptual scheme, an ontological statement which is axiomatic to McX's mind may, with equal immediacy and triviality, be adjudged false. One may admit that there are red houses, roses, and sunsets, but deny, except as a popular and misleading manner of speaking, that they have anything in common. The words 'houses,' 'roses,' and 'sunsets' are true of sundry individual entities which are houses and roses and sunsets, and the word 'red' or 'red object' is true of each of sundry individual entities which are red houses, red roses, red sunsets; but there is not, in addition, any entity whatever, individual or otherwise, which is named by the word 'redness,' nor, for that matter, by the word 'household,' 'rosehood,' 'sunsethood.' That the houses and roses and sunsets are all of them red may be taken as ultimate and irreducible, and it may be held that McX is no better off, in point of real explanatory power, for all the occult entities which he posits under such names as 'redness.'

One means by which McX might naturally have tried to impose his ontology of universals on us was already removed before we turned to the problem of universals. McX cannot argue that predicates such as 'red' or 'is-red,' which we all concur in using, must be regarded as names each of a single universal entity in order that they be meaningful at all. For we have seen that being a name of something is a much more special feature than being meaningful. He cannot even charge us — at least not by *that* argument — with having posited an attribute of pegasizing by our adoption of the predicate 'pegasizes.'

However, McX hits upon a different strategem. "Let us grant," he says, "this distinction between meaning and naming of which you make so much. Let us even grant that 'is red,' 'pegasizes,' etc., are not names of attributes. Still, you admit they have meanings. But these *meanings*, whether they are *named* or not, are still universals, and I venture to say that some of them might even be the very things that I call attributes, or something to much the same purpose in the end.''

For McX, this is an unusually penetrating speech; and the only way I know to counter it is by refusing to admit meanings. However, I feel no reluctance toward refusing to admit meanings, for I do not thereby deny that words and statements are meaningful. McX and I may agree to the letter in our classification of linguistic forms into the meaningful and the meaningless, even though McX construes meaningfulness as the *having* (in some sense of 'having') of some abstract entity which he calls a meaning, whereas I do not. I remain free to maintain that the fact that a given linguistic utterance is meaningful (or *significant*, as I prefer to say so as not to invite hypostasis of meanings as entities) is an ultimate and irreducible matter of fact; or, I may undertake to analyze it in terms directly of what people do in the presence of the linguistic utterance in question and other utterances similar to it.

The useful ways in which people ordinarily talk or seem to talk about meanings boil down to two: the *having* of meanings, which is significance, and *sameness* of meaning, or synonymy. What is called *giving* the meaning of an utterance is simply the uttering of a synonym, couched, ordinarily, in clearer language than the original. If we are allergic to meanings as such, we can speak directly of utterances as significant or insignificant, and as synonymous or heteronymous one with another. The problem of explaining these adjectives 'significant' and 'synonymous' with some degree of clarity and rigor — preferably, as I see it, in terms of behavior — is as difficult as it is important. But the explanatory value of special and irreducible intermediary entities called meanings is surely illusory.

Up to now I have argued that we can use singular terms significantly in sentences without presupposing that there are the entities which those terms purport to name. I have argued further that we can use general terms, for example, predicates, without conceding them to be names of abstract entities. I have argued further that we can view utterances as significant, and as synonymous or heteronymous with one another, without countenancing a realm of entities called meanings. At this point McX begins to wonder whether there is any limit at all to our ontological immunity. Does *nothing* we may say commit us to the assumption of universals or other entities which we may find unwelcome?

I have already suggested a negative answer to this question, in speaking of bound variables, or variables of quantification, in connection with Russell's theory of descriptions. We can very easily involve ourselves in ontological commitments by saying, for example, that *there is something* (bound variable) which red houses and sunsets have in common; or that *there is something* which is a prime number larger than a million. But this is, essentially, the *only* way we can involve ourselves in ontological commitments: by our use of bound variables. The use of alleged names is no criterion, for we can repudiate their namehood at the drop of a hat unless the assumption of a corresponding entity can be spotted in the things we affirm in terms of bound variables. Names are, in fact, altogether immaterial to the ontological issue, for I have shown, in connection with 'Pegasus' and 'pegasize,' that names can be converted to descriptions, and Russell has shown that descriptions can be eliminated. Whatever we say with the help of names can be said in a language which shuns names altogether. To be assumed as an entity is, purely and simply, to be reckoned as the value of a variable. In terms of the categories of traditional grammar, this amounts roughly to saying that to be is to be in the range of reference of a pronoun. Pronouns are the basic media of reference; nouns might better have been named propronouns. The variables of quantification, 'something,' 'nothing,' 'everything,' range over our whole ontology, whatever it may be; and we are convicted of a particular ontological presupposition if, and only if, the alleged presuppositum has to be reckoned among the entities over which our variables range in order to render one of our affirmations true.

We may say, for example, that some dogs are white and not thereby commit ourselves to recognizing either doghood or whiteness as entities. 'Some dogs are white' says that some things that are dogs are white; and, in order that this statement be true, the things over which the bound variable 'something' ranges must include some white dogs, but need not include doghood or whiteness. On the other hand, when we say that some zoölogical species are cross-fertile we are committing ourselves to recognizing as entities the several species themselves, abstract though they are. We remain so committed at least until we devise some way of so paraphrasing the statement as to show that the seeming reference to species on the part of our bound variable was an avoidable manner of speaking . . . .

13   William P. Alston: ONTOLOGICAL COMMITMENTS (1958)

During the past half-century many philosophers have occupied themselves with translating one linguistic expression into another, or with providing general schema for such translations. And some of them, sensitive to charges of engaging in parlor games during working hours, have tried, in various ways, to exhibit the serious value of such activities. I want to consider one very popular sort of philosophic translation — the sort which goes from sentences of the form 'There are P's' (or from other sentences which obviously imply sentences of this form, such as 'The P is R') to sentences of some other form. And I want to consider one very common explanation of the point of such translations — viz., that they enable us to avoid "ontological commitments" to P's. It will be my contention that this explanation is basically confused, and that it only succeeds in raising a dust which obstructs our view of the real point of such translations.

Let's begin by considering an example from Morton White's recent book, *Toward Reunion in Philosophy*.[1] He is speaking of the sentences 'There is a difference in age between John and Tom' and 'There is a possibility that James will come.'

"How, then, can we clarify these puzzling sentences and yet avoid the unwelcome conclusion that there are possibilities and age-differences in our universe . . .

"In the case of 'There is a difference in age between John and Tom,' we might begin by saying that we understand the relational predicate 'is as old as' and that we test statements of the form 'x is as old as y' without having to see that x has some queer thing called an age, that y has one, and that these ages are identical. In that event, the belief of the ordinary man that there is a difference in age between John and Tom would be rendered in language that is not misleading by saying instead, simply, 'It is not the case that John is as old as Tom.' We might offer an analogous translation of 'There is a possibility that James will come' in which we replace it by some statement about the state-

Reprinted with the kind permission of the author and the editors from *Philosophical Studies*, 9, no. 1–2 (1958), 8–17.

[1] Cambridge, Mass.: Harvard University Press, 1956. [See above, p. 135.]

ment 'James will come,' for example by the statement that this statement is not certainly false. . . . what we have done is to show that we
need not assert the existence of age-differences or the existence of possibilities in communicating what we want to communicate." (pp. 68–69.)

Here are several philosophically interesting translations of this
sort (which I shall call 'existential reduction'):

1. There is a possibility that James will come.
2. The statement that James will come is not certainly false.
3. There is a meaning which can be given to his remarks.
4. His remarks can be understood in a certain way.
5. There are many virtues which he lacks.
6. He might conceivably be much more virtuous than he is.
7. There are facts which render your position untenable.
8. Your position is untenable in the light of the evidence.

Now it is puzzling to me that anyone should claim that these translations
"show that we need not assert the existence of" possibilities, meanings,
virtues, and facts "in communicating what we want to communicate."
For if the translation of (1) into (2), for example, is adequate, then
they are normally used to make the same assertion. In uttering (2)
we would be making the same assertion as we would make if we uttered
(1), i.e., the assertion that there is a possibility that James will come.
And so we would be asserting that there is a possibility (committing ourselves to the existence of a possibility) just as much by using (2) as by
using (1). If, on the other hand, the translation is not adequate, it
has not been shown that we can, by uttering (2), communicate what
we wanted to communicate when we uttered (1). Hence the point of
the translation cannot be put in terms of some assertion or commitment
from which it saves us.

This dilemma has more than a passing resemblance to the "paradox of analysis," which was extensively discussed a short while ago.
(If x is adequately analyzable as y, then 'x' and 'y' must be synonymous. But if so, how can we convey any information by saying 'x is y.')
Some philosophers attempted (unsuccessfully in my opinion) to resolve
the paradox of analysis by pointing out differences between the meanings of 'x' and 'y' which were sufficient to make the analysis informative, but not so great as to render it invalid. Similar gambits might be
tried here, although the omens are no more favorable than before.

A. It may be said that (1) differs from (2) only in carrying an imputation of 'ultimate reality' to possibilities, in implying that possibilities are among the 'ultimate furniture of the universe.' Thus in replacing (1) with (2) we continue to say everything we have any need or right to say, sloughing off only the groundless, and gratuitous, attribution of ultimate reality.

Before we can accept this account we must understand what is meant by 'ultimate reality' and this is not altogether easy. What can be meant by 'taking possibilities to be ultimately real,' other than simply asserting, seriously and with full awareness of what we are doing, that, for example, there is a possibility that James will come? And this can be done by the use of (2) as well as (1).[2] But suppose that some meaning can be given to the phrase 'ultimate reality,' such that (2) does not carry with it an implication of the ultimate reality of possibilities. It is still worthy of note that no one has given adequate reason for the supposition that (1), as ordinarily used, carries any such implication either. What evidence is there that the ordinary man in uttering (1), or the scientist in uttering a sentence like 'There are fourteen electrons in this atom,' is asserting the ultimate reality of possibilities or electrons in any sense which goes beyond the serious and deliberate use of these sentences to make assertions? Of course a philosopher who utters such sentences as 'Possibilities are ultimately real,' 'Possibilities are objective entities,' etc., is asserting the *ultimate* reality of possibilities if anyone ever is. But does that justify us in saying that he is making the same assertion when he utters (1)? Well, perhaps the fact that he uses these queer sentences is an indication that his use of (1) carries a metaphysical implication. But if it does then precisely for that reason he will not admit that by using (2) he can just as well say what he wanted to say when he used (1). This is our problem all over again. Wherever (1), unlike (2), does carry a metaphysical force, the translation is not adequate. Thus the analysis would only have the virtue of showing us that we could say what we want to say without making an ontological commitment to possibilities, except where we want to make an ontological commitment to possibilities. In this case it would be less than a parlor game.

B. Alternatively, admitting that talk of 'ultimate reality' is un-

[2] One sometimes suspects that it is some peculiar solemnity attaching to 'There is' (and especially to 'x') which leads philosophers to give sentences like (1) a metaphysical import not imputed to sentences like (2).

clear, or even unintelligible, one might locate the value of the analysis in the dissolution of this unclarity, i.e., in the fact that (2) says everything that is clearly said by (1) but without these confused suggestions of ultimate reality. But does (1) as ordinarily used carry such suggestions? Even if it does and even if this account is substantially correct, it offers no aid and comfort to the ontological interpretation. The ontological interpretation presupposes that there is an activity called 'admitting the (ultimate) existence of possibilities' which we might or might not perform, and the performance or nonperformance of which hinges on whether we employ (1) or (2) to say what we want to say (or on whether we use (1) with or without the realization that it can be translated by (2)). But to say that phrases like 'ultimate existence' are unintelligible is to say that we can't understand what such an activity would be, or what it would be like to perform it, and so are unable to specify what admission it is from which the translation saves us. In other words, on the present account, what the translation enables us to avoid is not certain commitments or assertions, but certain confusions. This clue will be taken up later. But first — back to the ontologist.

These moves have not proved fruitful. But there is indeed one thing, not yet explicitly mentioned, which the translation of (1) into (2) does enable us to avoid, and that is the *sentence*, (1). More generally the schema of which this translation is an instance enables us to say what we want to say without having to use any sentences of this form, i.e., any sentence beginning with 'There is (are),' followed by 'a possibility . . .' 'the possibility . . .' ('possibilities . . .' 'some possibilities . . .'), etc. And the hard-pressed ontologist may make a stand here by roundly declaring that the ability to avoid sentences of this form is what he *means* by avoiding an ontological commitment. That is, he will define 'ontological commitment to possibilities' as the inability to say what we want to say without using such sentences.

To be at all plausible this definition will have to be patched up. As it stands, we could avoid an ontological commitment to possibilities simply by introducing a new word as synonymous with 'there is,' or with 'possibility.' This makes the game too easy. The rules can be tightened by requiring that the restatement consist only of existing expressions with their established meanings. But that won't be enough. No one could consider the translation of (1) into 'The possibility exists that James will come' to constitute an evasion of an ontological commitment. The trouble is that there are a number of expressions in common use ('. . . exists,' 'some . . .') which do essentially the same job as 'there is'; let us speak of these expressions as having an explicitly existential force.[3] The sort of translation we are trying to specify is a translation from a sentence which contains one of these expressions, along with the crucial predicate terms, into a sentence which does not. Taking account of this let us restate the definition of ontological commitment as follows:

I. One is ontologically committed to P's if and only if he is unable to say what he wants to say without using a sentence of the form 'There is (are) a P . . . (the P . . ., P's . . ., etc.)' or some other sentence which deviates from this form only by replacing 'there is' by some other expression with explicit existential force or by replacing 'P' by a synonym (together with such grammatical changes as are required by these replacements, as in the change from 'There are some lions in this country' to 'Lions exist in this country').[4]

By a not so fortuitous circumstance this criterion is substantially equivalent to Quine's famous criterion for ontological commitment.

II. We are convicted of a particular ontological presupposition if, and only if, the alleged presuppositum has to be reckoned among the entities over which our variables range in order to render one of our affirmations true. (*From a Logical Point of View*, p. 13.)[5]

An entity is assumed by a theory if and only if it must be counted among the values of the variables in order that the statements affirmed in the theory be true. (*Ibid.*, p. 103.)

The equivalence can be seen as follows. The variables of a theory must range over P's in order to make the affirmations of that theory true if and only if one of those affirmations is either 'There are P's' or some

[3] The boundaries of this group are not precise. For example, there would be controversy over whether 'some . . .' belongs here.

[4] This criterion could be further made precise by making more explicit the scope of the 'etc.' Not any phrase containing 'possibility' can be combined with a 'there is' to produce a sentence which would normally be used to assert the existence of possibilities. Consider, for example, 'There is a man who is holding some good possibilities open for you.' More generally, what is required is that 'P' falls within the scope of the existential expression. This of course needs further clarification.

[5] Cambridge, Mass.: Harvard University Press, 1953. [See above, p. 156.]

statement which implies 'There are P's,' such as 'There are R's and all R's are P's.' Of course Quine's criterion applies explicitly only to "theories" which are in quantificational form. But he himself points out that the criterion is applicable to theories otherwise expressed provided they can be translated into this form. And I see no reason why any English sentence beginning with 'there is' cannot be translated into one beginning '∃x.' In fact II can be viewed as a narrower version of I, since '∃x' is one of the expressions which does essentially the same job as 'there is.' Hence although the following remarks will be explicitly directed, for the most part, to I, they will, I believe, apply equally to II.

Do we, then, adequately bring out the merits of existential reduction by saying that it enables us to avoid "ontological commitments," in the sense specified by these criteria? These criteria do point up the way in which such translations enable us to cut down the number of sentences of an explicitly existential form which we use (or to reduce the range of our variables). And in certain contexts this may be a virtue. There may be desires, widespread among logicians, which are satisfied by such reductions. And for certain purposes of theory construction or formalization it might be desirable to have as narrow a range of variable substitutions as possible. But it is at best misleading, and at worst flatly incorrect, to record this achievement by saying that we have avoided making an ontological commitment to P's, or avoided asserting the existence of P's. For the achievement consists, to return to our chief example, in finding some other sentence which can be used to make the same statement which one had been making in uttering (1). And, in any ordinary sense of these terms, whether a man admits (asserts) the existence of possibilities depends on what statement he makes, not on what sentence he uses to make that statement. One admits that possibilities exist whenever he assertorially utters (1), *or any other sentence which means the same* (would ordinarily be used to make the same statement). It is a question of *what* he says, not of *how* he says it. Hence he cannot repudiate his admission by simply changing his words.[6]

A man who was afraid of policemen would be reassured if he were convinced that there are no policemen. But he would not be reassured if he were convinced that one could express all one's beliefs in a language which took not policemen, but rather policemanship, as values

[6] Can there be a confusion of sentence and statement lurking in this criterion of 'ontological commitment'?

of variables (that one could avoid locutions like 'There is a policeman around the corner' in favor of 'Policemanship is exemplified around the corner'). Nor could we convince a scientist that the assumption of the existence of electrons can be dispensed with, simply by providing a way of translating every sentence of the form '($\exists$x) (x is an electron . . .)' into another sentence which has the same meaning but which does not require variables to range over electrons, though he would be convinced if we could provide a theory which did the same jobs as his electronic theory but contained no individual sentences which were synonymous with his sentences asserting the existence of electrons. That is, in any context where questions of existence arise the problem is whether or not we shall assert *that* so-and-so exists, not whether we shall choose some particular way of making this assertion. This means that assertion of existence, commitment to existence, etc., does not consist in the inflexible preference for one verbal formulation over any other, however gratifying such preferences may be to logicians, and that the use of the phrase 'ontological commitment' here is unjustifiable and misleading.

Of course Quine could say that the notational question is what he is interested in and that, ordinary usage be damned, this is what he is using 'ontological commitment' to mean. But the whole point of his using 'ontological commitment' for this purpose rather than some other phrase (and the associated use of cognate expressions like 'believe in the existence of,' 'countenance abstract entities,' etc.) is to associate, or identify, the terminological problem with existential problems as they are ordinarily conceived, and so transfer to the former the interest and importance which attaches to the latter. Otherwise why present the values of variables formula as a criterion for 'ontological commitment' instead of just as something which is interesting in its own right? The fact that Quine intends his criterion to be more than just notational in import is further brought out by (1) his insistence that ontological questions (as he formulates them) are not different in kind from scientific questions; (2) his use of considerations other than notational convenience (queerness, unobservability) in deciding what values of variables it might be desirable to avoid.

Thus in the last analysis the ontological interpretation can offer no rationale of existential reduction other than the notational convenience attaching to the avoidance of certain verbal forms. But surely this sort of analysis has more significance than that. To get at its significance

I shall relapse for a moment into ontological terminology and ask the hitherto neglected question 'Why should anyone wish to avoid an ontological commitment to, for example, possibilities?' More generally, why do the ontological analysts bend their efforts toward escaping from ontological commitments to "abstract entities" (attributes, classes, possibilities, meanings, facts, etc.) rather than to "concrete entities" (physical objects, events, persons, etc.). The reasons most commonly cited are these (Ockham's razor is not relevant here, since the question is not why we should ever try to avoid ontological commitments, but why we should aim at paring off abstract rather than concrete entities):

1. Possibilities, etc., are queer.
2. Possibilities, etc., are obscure in their nature.
3. Possibilities, etc., are unobservable (there is no empirical reason for supposing that there are any such things).

Obviously these reasons are not expressed very clearly. To say that a possibility is queer or obscure is no argument against its existence; on the contrary it is a conclusive argument for its existence. Possession of any characteristic entails, or presupposes, existence. And the unobservability of possibilities is not a matter of fact like the unobservability of mangoes on my desk or of unicorns. It is rather that we can't understand what it would be like to empirically observe a possibility.

These complaints are captious. But they do show that the objections to abstract entities would be more precisely expressed by talking not about possibilities, but about what people say about possibilities. It is because people sometimes say (and ask) such queer and obscure things about possibilities, and talk about them in empirically untestable ways, that our ontological analysts are so loath to "make an ontological commitment to possibilities," i.e., are so loath to use a sentence like (1). More specifically, the tendency to shy away from sentences like (1) is due to the fact that people who attach a great deal of importance to such sentences (and resist replacing them with sentences of other forms) are liable to:

1. Ask such puzzling questions as 'Are possibilities eternal?' 'Can a proposition be immediately intuited?' 'What are the parts of a fact?' 'Are there negative facts as well as positive ones?'
2. Propound 'theories' which are unintelligible, or at least such that we cannot find any relevant arguments for or against them. For example, 'Possibilities contain in their essence a reference

to actuality' 'Every true statement corresponds with a fact' 'Attributes have an existence independent of their exemplifications' 'Meanings are known by intuition.'

3. Take the existence (or *ultimate* existence) of such entities as problematic, subject to proof or disproof, even after ordinary sentences like (1) have been accepted, without giving an intelligible account of the difference between asserting ultimate existence in this problematic sense and simply assenting to the ordinary sentence.

But if (1) and (2) are synonymous, why should (1) and not (2) suffer this abuse, and how can the replacement of (1) with (2) alleviate the situation? It is at this point that the real virtue of this sort of translation can be seen. Consider the following parallels:

There is a possibility that James will come	There is a fruit that James will eat
There is a meaning which can be given to his words	There is a chair which can be given to his aunt
There are many virtues which he lacks	There are many articles of clothing which he lacks

In each case the strong verbal similarity provides a temptation to assimilate the two sorts of existents, i.e., to suppose that we can talk of one in the same way as the other. Since chairs have spatial locations, we are apt to ask about the (ontological) locus of meanings. (See Whitehead on God as the locus of "eternal objects.") Physical objects like chairs and fruits consist of parts which can be specified, unless they are atomic; and so we are led into asking whether facts or propositions are atomic, and if not what their parts are like.[7] Since this is a story which has been often, and ably, told in the recent literature, I shall not elaborate it further. The moral to be drawn here is that the only "ontological commitment" to possibilities which there is any reason to consider undesirable is the tendency to talk about possibilities in inappropriate ways ("category mistakes").

[7] There are many reasons why the grammatical similarity, which is symmetrical, leads to confusions on the left-hand rather than the right-hand side. The most important ones are these two: (1) We have, in our language a rich repertoire of locutions for talking about chairs, fruits, etc., whereas there are comparatively few ways of talking properly about possibilities, meanings, etc. Thus the pull is into the vacuum on the left. (2) Our tendency to picture everything we talk about entails a tendency to construe the unpicturable abstracta on the model of the picturable concreta.

It is the seductive grammatical family likenesses of sentences like (1) which render them objectionable, not any assertion of the existence of possibilities they carry with them, in any intelligible sense of that term. And the point of translating (1) into (2) lies in the fact that once anyone sees that what he says when he uses (1) can be just as well said by using (2), the power of the grammatical lure will be broken. To see that one can say that there is a possibility that James will come, by using either of two sentences of quite different grammatical forms, is to see that possibilities do not *have* to be talked about in the way which would be suggested by either of these forms, and hence that one does not *have* to ask about possibilities the same sort of questions one asks about chairs. To put it in a rather dangerous way, he sees that possibilities do not exist in the same way as chairs. Of course the translation doesn't prove that the same questions cannot be asked about possibilities and about chairs. It is rather that the realization that the translation holds relieves us of the compulsion to ask these questions about possibilities in spite of the impossibility of really making sense of them.

Thus we can make explicit the virtues of existential reduction, taking account of the (unconfused) motives which have led people to perform it, without having to say what we have seen to be untenable — viz., that it enables us to avoid admitting the existence of something.

This way of looking at the matter should also free us from the supposition, which the ontological account might suggest, that when we utter (1) we are inevitably saying something false, at least if we haven't seen that it can be translated into (2), whereas we wouldn't be subject to any such danger in using (2), even if we didn't realize that it is translatable into (1). This gives rise to the idea that there is something inherently objectionable about (1), a sort of ontological taint. But when we see that the point of the translation is the neutralizing of tendencies to confusions, we see that the problem is essentially a strategic one. One is not necessarily misled by (1), with or without a translation, nor is one necessarily safe from confusion by using (2). The translation is a device for removing confusions wherever they arise. They usually arise in connection with (1), in which case we show that (2) can be used to say the same thing; but the reverse procedure might conceivably be useful. Just as no sentence is necessarily misleading, so none is guaranteed, by its form, to be used without confusion. The supposition to the contrary is one of the unfortunate effects of philosophic preoccupation with artificial languages.

Quantification and Existence

14 Czeslaw Lejewski: LOGIC AND EXISTENCE (1955)[1]

I have given my essay this title because it roughly indicates the boundaries of the topic to be discussed and at the same time hints at the method that will be adopted in my analysis. The problem of existence will interest me only to the extent to which it enters the province of logical enquiry and I shall try to disentangle it a little by departing from the generally accepted interpretation of the quantifiers and by bringing in other concepts related to that of existence.

When we have to commit ourselves to asserting or rejecting propositions like

$$\text{electrons exist} \qquad (1)$$
$$\text{minds exist} \qquad (2)$$
$$\text{Pegasus exists,} \qquad (3)$$

our hesitation can be traced to twofold causes. In the first place we may not be willing to give our judgment because we are not quite certain what we mean by 'electrons' or 'minds,' or we may not understand the word 'Pegasus.' In the second place we may be confused as

Reprinted with the kind permission of the author and the editor from *British Journal for the Philosophy of Science*, Vol. V (1955), pp. 104–119.

[1] The first draft of this paper was presented to a post-graduate seminar at the London School of Economics on 12th November 1953, and was also read and criticised by Professors J. Łukasiewicz, K. R. Popper, W.V. Quine, and J. H. Woodger, from whose generous comments I have benefited much.

regards the meaning of the term 'exist(s).' It is the latter cause of our embarrassment that calls for closer attention. Let the physicist, the psychologist, and the mythologist deal with the meaning of the words 'electrons,' 'minds,' and 'Pegasus' respectively. The logician's task, as I understand it, will be to establish the meaning of the constant term 'exist(s)' as it occurs in the function 'x exist(s)' where 'x' is a variable for which any noun-expression can be substituted.

I hope that it will be a permissible simplification to say that in recent times the discussion over the logical side of the problem of existence centres around what Professor Quine has written on the subject.[2] In presenting the views of this author I shall have to use a little more quotation than is customary as the whole matter is of exceptional subtlety.

On page 150 of Quine's *Mathematical Logic* we read:

> To say that *something* does not *exist*, or that there *is* something which *is not*, is clearly a contradiction in terms; hence '$(x)(x$ exists$)$' must be true.

Let us translate this argument into a symbolic language so that its logical structure may become more perceptible. I think that the following translation stands a fair chance of being acceptable to Quine:

$$((\exists x)(x \text{ does not exist}) \equiv (\exists x) \ (x \text{ exists}. \sim (x \text{ exists})) \tag{4}$$

If instead of 'x does not exist' in the antecedent of (4) we write '$\sim(x$ exists$)$' then from (4) and from the circumstance that the consequent of (4), being a contradiction, is false, we get immediately

$$\sim (\exists x) \sim (x \text{ exists}), \tag{5}$$

which in accordance with the law relating the existential quantifier to its universal counterpart is equivalent to

$$(x)(x \text{ exists}). \tag{6}$$

[2] Quine's most important contributions in this connection are the following: "A Logical Approach to the Ontological Problem," *Journal of Unified Science*, Chicago, 1940, 9. This paper was read at the Fifth International Congress for the Unity of Science, Cambridge (Mass.), 1939; "Designation and Existence," *The Journal of Philosophy*, New York, 1939, 36, also in *Readings in Philosophical Analysis*, edited by H. Feigl and W. Sellars, New York, 1949; "Notes on Existence and Necessity," *The Journal of Philosophy*, New York, 1943, 40; "On What There Is," *The Review of Metaphysics*, New Haven, 1948, 2, also reprinted in *Proceedings of the Aristotelian Society, Supplementary Volume XXV*, London, 1951. [See above, pp. 146ff.]

This list would have to be supplemented with the titles of several, more technical papers, published by Quine in *The Journal of Symbolic Logic*, and also with some passages from his *Mathematical Logic*, Cambridge (Mass.), 1947 (second printing), and *Methods of Logic*, London, 1952.

This result seems to confirm our interpretation of the passage, which is in complete harmony with the opening paragraph of "On What There Is" as this paragraph runs as follows:

A curious thing about the ontological problem is its simplicity. It can be put into three Anglo-Saxon monosyllables: 'What is there?' It can be answered moreover in a word — 'Everything' — and everyone will accept this answer as true.'[3]

But let us revert to page 150 of *Mathematical Logic*. The passage which we began to analyse just now continues thus:

Moreover we should certainly expect leave to put any primitive name of our language for the 'x' of any matrix '. . . x . . . ,' and to infer the resulting singular statement from '(x)(. . . x . . .)'; it is difficult to contemplate any alternative logical rule for reasoning with names.

This logical rule, which in *Methods of Logic* is referred to by Quine as the rule of universal instantiation, owes its validity to a certain logical law which with the aid of symbols can be expressed in the following way:

$$(x)(Fx) \supset Fy. \tag{7}$$

Now difficulties begin to appear and Quine sets them out as follows:

But this rule of inference leads from the truth '(x)(x exists)' not only to the true conclusion 'Europe exists' but also to the controversial conclusion 'God exists' and the false conclusion 'Pegasus exists' if we accept 'Europe,' 'God,' and 'Pegasus' as primitive names in our language.[4]

From the whole passage quoted from page 150 of *Mathematical Logic* we seem to be entitled to conclude that for Quine (6), i.e. '(x)(x exists),' is a truth while (3), i.e. 'Pegasus exists,' is a falsehood. Regarding the rule which allows us to infer '*Fy*' from '(x)(Fx),' Quine cautiously remarks that "it is difficult to contemplate any alternative logical rule for reasoning with names." He is more outspoken in his "Notes on Existence and Necessity," to which we now turn.

In that paper Quine discusses inferences which would be exemplified by the one whereby from

$$\text{Pegasus does not exist} \tag{8}$$

we infer

$$(\exists x) \ (x \text{ does not exist}) \tag{9}$$

---

[3] See W. V. Quine, "On What There Is," *The Review of Metaphysics*, New Haven, 1948, 2, 21. [See above, p. 146.]

[4] See W. V. Quine, *Mathematical Logic*, Cambridge (Mass.), 1947, 150.

in virtue of the rule which allows us to infer '$(\exists x)(Fx)$' from 'Fy.'[5] In "Notes on Existence and Necessity" and in *Methods of Logic* this rule is described as the rule of existential generalisation, and we may add at once that it derives its validity from the following logical law:

$$Fy \supset (\exists x)(Fx). \tag{10}$$

According to Quine (8) would be true but (9) would be false. Regarding the rule he observes the following:

> The idea behind such inference is that whatever is true of the object designated by a given substantive is true of something; and clearly the inference loses its justification when the substantive in question does not happen to designate.[6]

I think that we have come to a point where a brief summary of Quine's argument may not appear to be superfluous. We have two inferences:

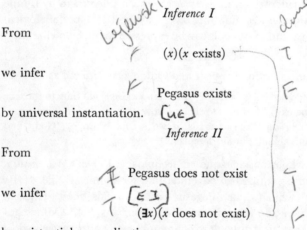

Inference I

From

$$(x)(x \text{ exists})$$

we infer

Pegasus exists

by universal instantiation.

Inference II

From

we infer

Pegasus does not exist

$(\exists x)(x \text{ does not exist})$

by existential generalisation.

According to Quine both these inferences are objectionable to our intuitions. In his opinion they lead from truths, '$(x)(x$ exists$)$' and 'Pegasus does not exist,' to falsehoods, 'Pegasus exists' and '$(\exists x)$ $(x$ does not exist$).$' In other words the logical laws (7) and (10), which we thought to be behind the rule of universal instantiation and the rule of

[5] See W. V. Quine, "Notes on Existence and Necessity," *The Journal of Philosophy*, New York, 1943, 40. The inference has been rephrased so that it may conform with the example taken from *Mathematical Logic*. The original propositions are 'There is no such thing as Pegasus' and '$\exists x$ (there is no such thing as x),' respectively. See op. cit. 116.

[6] See W. V. Quine, op. cit. 116.

existential generalisation, do not hold for every interpretation of 'F' and every substitution for the free variable. If we interpret 'F' as 'exists' and substitute 'Pegasus' for 'y,' (7) turns out to be false. Similarly, (10) turns out to be false for the same substitution if we interpret 'F' as 'does not exist.' But no difficulty arises if the noun-expressions substituted for 'y' in (7) and (10) are non-empty:

$$(x)(x \text{ exists}) \supset \text{Socrates exists} \tag{11}$$
$$\text{Socrates does not exist} \supset (\exists x)(x \text{ does not exist}) \tag{12}$$

are true propositions.

A remedy that might suggest itself to an unscrupulous mind would be to ban the use of empty noun-expressions and consider them as meaningless. Quine is right in not following this course. One may disagree as to the truth-value of the proposition 'Pegasus exists' but one would have to have attained an exceptionally high degree of sophistication to contend that the expression was meaningless. Quine does not think that empty noun-expressions are meaningless just because they do not designate anything. He allows for the use of such words as 'Pegasus,' 'Cerberus,' 'centaur,' etc. under certain restrictions and tries to distinguish between logical laws which prove to be true for any noun-expressions, empty or non-empty, and those which hold for non-empty noun-expressions only. It follows from his remarks that before we can safely use certain laws established by logic, we have to find out whether the noun-expressions we may like to employ, are empty or not. This, however, seems to be a purely empirical question. Furthermore, all the restrictions which according to Quine must be observed whenever we reason with empty noun-expressions, will have to be observed also in the case of noun-expressions of which we do not know whether they are empty or not.

This state of affairs does not seem to be very satisfactory. The idea that some of our rules of inference should depend on empirical information, which may or may not be forthcoming, is so foreign to the character of logical enquiry that a thorough re-examination of the two inferences may prove to be worth our while. Let us then try to find out on what grounds (6) is asserted as true while (9) is rejected as false, and let us find out also on what grounds the rules of universal instantiation and existential generalisation are regarded as inapplicable to reasoning with empty names. In seeking answers to the above questions we shall have to turn to the interpretation of the quantifiers.

Regarding Quine's interpretation of the quantifiers, which is the one accepted by the majority of modern logicians, we have a very useful passage in the *Methods of Logic*. It reads as follows:

If we think of the universe as limited to a finite set of objects a, b, ... , h, we can expand existential quantifications into alternations and universal quantifications into conjunctions; '$(\exists x)Fx$' and '$(x)Fx$' become respectively:

$$Fa \text{ v } Fb \text{ v } \ldots \text{ v } Fh, \qquad Fa \cdot Fb \ldots \ldots Fh^7$$

To have a still simpler though fictitious example let us think of the universe as limited to two objects **a** and **b**. Then the corresponding expansions would be:

$$Fa \text{ v } Fb \qquad \text{and} \qquad Fa \cdot Fb$$

Our language, which for reasons of simplicity needs not synonyms, may leave room for noun-expressions other than the singular names '**a**' and '**b**.' We may wish to have a noun-expression '**c**' which would designate neither of the two objects, in other words which would be empty, and also a noun-expression '**d**' which would designate either. Introducing noun-expressions is a linguistic matter. It does not affect our assumed universe, which continues to consist of **a** and **b** only. The new noun-expressions can now be put to use. For instance we can form the following true proposition; '**c** does not exist,' and on turning '**d**' into a predicate-expression '**D**' we can further assert that '$(x)(Dx)$' is true. To say that something exists means the same as to say that it belongs to the universe. Thus '**a** exists' and '**b** exists' are true propositions. From the expansion of the existential quantification we see that either of these two propositions implies '$(\exists x)(x \text{ exists})$.' But we have no ground to contend that '**c** does not exist' implies '$(\exists x)(x \text{ does not exist})$.' Again since '**a** does not exist or **b** does not exist' is false, we conclude from the expansion that '$(\exists x)(x \text{ does not exist})$' is also false. Hence '$(x)(x \text{ exists})$' is true. This is confirmed by the expansion of the universal quantification and in view of the circumstance that '**a** exists and **b** exists' is true. We also learn from this expansion that '$(x)(x \text{ exists})$' does not imply '**c** exists.' Within our fictitious universe the rule of universal instantiation and the rule of existential generalisation fail if applied to '**c**' or '**d**.' They are valid rules of inference if their application is restricted to reasoning with '**a**' and '**b**.'

But this is not the only possible interpretation of the quantifiers. With the aid of the same fictitious example I shall now present an inter-

[7] See W. V. Quine, *Methods of Logic*, London, 1952, 88.

BUT, CAN WE EXCLUDE C AND D FROM U & El ?

pretation which as far as I can judge, is in harmony with the one adopted for instance by Lesniewski of the Warsaw School.

Our universe consisting of **a** and **b** remains the same but the quantifiers read differently. Under the present interpretation '$(\exists x)(Fx)$' becomes:

$$Fa \lor Fb \lor Fc \lor Fd$$

Correspondingly, '$(x)(Fx)$' is to mean:

$$Fa \cdot Fb \cdot Fc \cdot Fd$$

Thus one can argue that '$(\exists x)(x \text{ does not exist})$' is true because '**c** does not exist,' which under the new interpretation is one of the components of the existential expansion, is true. Hence '$(x)(x \text{ exists})$' is false. This is confirmed by the corresponding universal expansion, which contains a false component, namely '**c** exists.' Under this interpretation the rule of universal instantiation and the rule of existential generalisation are valid without any restrictions. They can be safely applied in reasoning with any noun-expressions: singular non-empty like '**a**' and '**b**,' empty like '**c**,' or general non-empty like '**d**.' The noun-expression '**d**' need not be changed into the corresponding predicate-expression '**D**.'

" THERE IS" IMPLIES EXISTENCE

These two different interpretations of the quantifiers, which in what follows, will be referred to as the *restricted* interpretation and the *unrestricted* interpretation respectively, can now be generalised to apply to a universe with any number of objects. In the case of a finite universe we have finite expansions which are equivalent to their respective quantifications. If, however, we think of the universe as consisting of an infinite or unknown number of objects then we cannot have equivalences for the simple reason that we can never form complete expansions of our quantifications. Consequently we abandon equivalences in favour of implications. We say that an existential quantification is implied by any component of its infinite or unknown expansion and that a universal quantification implies any component of its infinite or unknown expansion. Now the expansions will vary depending on how we choose to interpret the quantifiers. Under the restricted interpretation every component of an expansion contains a noun-expression which designates only one of the objects belonging to the universe. *NON-EMPTY* Under the unrestricted interpretation every component of an expansion contains an expression of which we can only say that it is a meaningful *EMPTY* noun-expression. It may designate only one of the objects belonging to the universe, it may designate more than one, or it may designate nothing at all. IF SOMETHING IS DESIGNATED, MAY IT BE "NOTHING"?

The two interpretations of the quantifiers give rise to two different theories of quantification and we may well be expected to say a few words on the relation in which one theory stands to the other. In this respect the most important point is that whatever is said with the aid of the theory of restricted quantification, can be easily expressed in terms of the unrestricted quantification provided we are allowed to use the notion of existence. A few examples set out below in the form of two lists will suffice to illustrate the procedure:

I. Expressions to be understood in the light of the restricted interpretation:

LET F EXISTS BE or BE REGARDLESS

$$(x)(Fx) \supset Fy \tag{7}$$

$$Fy \supset (\exists x)(Fx) \tag{10}$$

$$(x)(Fx) \equiv \sim\left[(\exists x)(\sim Fx)\right] \tag{13}$$

II. Corresponding translations to be understood in the light of the unrestricted interpretation:

$$(x)(x \text{ exists} \supset Fx) \supset Fy \tag{7a}$$

$$Fy \supset (\exists x)(x \text{ exists} \cdot Fx) \tag{10a}$$

$$(x)(x \text{ exists} \supset Fx) \equiv \sim (\exists x)(x \text{ exists} \cdot \sim Fx) \tag{13a}$$

LET F BE

It is not difficult to check that under their respective interpretations the corresponding expressions in the two lists yield the same truth value for the same substitutions performed on the free variables regardless of how we choose to interpret the predicate letters. The general rule for translating expressions is simple: expressions of type '$(x)(Fx)$' and '$(\exists x)(Fx)$' become expressions of type '$(x)(x \text{ exists} \supset Fx)$' and '$(\exists x)(x \text{ exists} \cdot Fx)$' respectively; other expressions remain unchanged.

Thus, for instance, (6) and (9) translated for the purpose of the unrestricted interpretation become

$$(x)(x \text{ exists} \supset x \text{ exists}) \tag{14}$$

and

$$(\exists x)(x \text{ exists} \cdot x \text{ does not exist}) \tag{15}$$

respectively. These translations fully account for the assertion of (6) and the rejection of (9) under the restricted interpretation of the quantifiers. Similarly (7a) and (10a) make it clear why (7) and (10) do not turn out true for all interpretations of 'F' and for all substitutions for the free variable. For if we interpret 'F' as 'exists' and substitute say 'Pegasus' for 'y,' the antecedent of ($7a$) becomes a tautology but at the same time the consequent turns out to be false. And again, if we interpret 'F' as 'does not exist' and substitute 'Pegasus' for 'y' then the antecedent of ($10a$) comes out true but the consequent must be rejected as a contradiction. Thus for certain interpretations of 'F' (7) and (10) turn out to be false if we substitute an empty noun-expression for the free variable. Consequently the rules of universal instantiation and existential generalisation, which derive their validity from (7) and (10), can no longer be applied without restrictions.

The position is different if we choose to understand the quantifiers in the light of the unrestricted interpretation. (3), which is 'Pegasus exists,' and (8), which is 'Pegasus does not exist,' are meaningful propositions either of which contains a noun-expression, viz. 'Pegasus.' Thus (3) and (8) may be regarded as components of quantificational expansions. Now, (3) being false, the corresponding universal quantification, i.e. '$(x)(x$ exists),' which ought to imply any component of its expansion, must also be false. On the other hand, (8) being a true proposition the corresponding existential quantification, i.e. '$(\exists x)(x$ does not exist),' which is implied by any component of its expansion, must also be true. Thus under the unrestricted interpretation of the quantifiers the two inferences on p. 107 [p. 170 above] cannot be used as counterexamples to disprove the validity of the rules of universal instantiation and existential generalisation in application to reasoning with empty noun-expressions. In Inference I both the premise and the conclusion are false, while in Inference II both the premise and the conclusion are true. There is nothing wrong with the inferences provided we adopt the unrestricted interpretation of the quantifiers. Furthermore, under the unrestricted interpretation the logical laws (7) and (10) turn out to be universally true. For every proposition of type 'Fa' where 'a' stands for any noun-expression, empty or non-empty, is now regarded as a component of the quantificational expansions and consequently is implied by the corresponding proposition of type '$(x)(Fx)$' and implies, in turn, the corresponding proposition of type '$(\exists x)(Fx)$.' (7) and (10) being universally true, the rule of universal instantiation and the rule of existential generalisation are universally valid as the principles that are behind them are no longer principles by courtesy.[8]

[8] See W. V. Quine, "Notes on Existence and Necessity," *The Journal of Philosophy*, New York, 1943, 40, 118.

The unrestricted interpretation of the quantifiers seems to remove yet another difficulty from quantification theory. It has been argued by several authors that

$$(\exists x)(Fx \mathbf{\ v} \sim Fx) \tag{16}$$

and

$$(x)(Fx) \supset (\exists x)(Fx), \tag{17}$$

which are valid if the universe is not empty, fail for the empty universe as their truth depends on there being something.[9] When discussing these laws Quine tries to dismiss the case of the empty universe as relatively pointless and reminds us that in arguments worthy of quantification theory the universe is known or confidently believed to be non-empty.[10] This contention, however, does not quite remove our uneasiness particularly as (16) and (17), not unlike (7) and (10), are demonstrable in quantification theory.

On considering (16) and (17) we readily admit that these two formulae fail for the empty universe if we understand the quantifiers in accordance with the restricted interpretation. This becomes evident from

$$(\exists x)(x \text{ exists} \cdot (Fx \mathbf{\ v} \sim Fx)) \tag{16a}$$

and

$$(x)(x \text{ exists} \supset Fx) \supset (\exists x)(x \text{ exists} \cdot Fx), \tag{17a}$$

which are the corresponding translations of (16) and (17) to be understood in the light of the unrestricted interpretation. If there exists nothing then (16a) and the consequent of (17a) are obviously false while the antecedent of (17a) is obviously true. Under the unrestricted interpretation, however, (16) and (17) come out to be true irrespective of whether the universe is empty or non-empty. For (16) is implied by any component of type '$Fa \mathbf{\ v} \sim Fa$' where 'a' stands for a noun-expression. In particular it is implied by a component '$Fa \mathbf{\ v} \sim Fa$' in which 'a' stands for an empty noun-expression. Such a component is true for all choices of universe and so is (16). In the case of (17) we argue as follows: if we asume that the antecedent of (17) is true then a proposition of type 'Fa' where 'a' stands for an empty noun-expression must also be true in harmony with the unrestricted interpretation of the universal quantifier. Now any such proposition implies the proposition of type '$(\exists x)(Fx)$,' which again must be true. Thus in the establishing of the truth value of (16) and (17) the problem of whether the universe is empty or non-empty is altogether irrelevant on condition, of course, that we adopt the unrestricted interpretation of the quantifiers.

It ought to be evident from what has already been said that under the unrestricted interpretation existential quantifications have no existential import. In fact it would be misleading to read '$(\exists x)(Fx)$' as 'there exists an x such that Fx.' The non-committal 'for some x, Fx' seems to be more appropriate. Similarly the terms 'existential quantification' and 'existential quantifier' no longer apply and could be conveniently replaced by such expressions as 'particular quantification' and 'particular quantifier.' The rule of existential generalisation could perhaps be referred to as the rule of 'particular generalisation.'

Finally, the unrestricted interpretation in comparison with the restricted one appears to me to be a nearer approximation to ordinary usage. Somehow we do not believe that *everything exists* and we do not see a contradiction in saying that *something does not exist*. It is only from logicians who favour the restricted interpretation that we learn that things are the other way round. We may further add that the unrestricted interpretation of the quantifiers is in complete harmony with the formal quantification theory. I do not know of any formulae which are demonstrable in the formal quantification theory and which, under the unrestricted interpretation, are not applicable to reasoning with empty noun-expressions or do not hold for universes of some specific size.

When we consider (7), (10), (13), (16), and (17) as understood in the light of the restricted interpretation and compare them with their corresponding translations for the purpose of the unrestricted interpretation, i.e. with (7a), (10a), (13a), (16a), and (17a), we cannot fail to notice that the idea of the restricted quantification is not a simple one. The translations reveal that it can be analysed into two separate constituents: the idea of the unrestricted quantification on the one hand and the notion of existence on the other. In my opinion the most serious disadvantage of the theory of the restricted quantification is that by merging the idea of quantification with the notion of existence it has put logicians and philosophers on a wrong track in their endeavours to elucidate the problem of existence in logic. In what follows we shall adhere to the theory of unrestricted quantification and we shall attack the problem of existence in logic by determining the meaning of the constant term 'exist(s)' as used in the function 'x exist(s).'

From the logical point of view there are two satisfactory methods of determining the meaning of a constant term. The one consists in setting forth a set of axioms for the term in question. The other is adopted whenever we give a definition of the term in question with the aid of other terms whose meaning has already been determined axiomatically.[11] We may add at once that we shall employ the latter method.

The meaning of 'exist(s)' can best be determined on the basis of the logic of noun-expressions constructed as a deductive system by Lesniewski in Warsaw in 1920 and called by him 'Ontology.'[12] The original system of Lesniewski's Ontology is based on singular inclusion (a is b or in symbols $a \in b$) as the only primitive function. For various reasons, however, I prefer to continue my analysis of 'exist(s)' with reference to a system of Ontology based on ordinary inclusion, which I shall write in the following manner:

$$a \subset b \qquad\qquad (18)$$

I shall read it 'all a is b' or 'all a's are b's.' I prefer doing this because ordinary inclusion seems to be more intuitive to an English speaking reader than Lesniewski's singular inclusion. Thus for instance ordinary inclusion has recently been used by Woodger in his "Science without Properties"[13] for the purpose of constructing a language whose general tendency approximates the tendencies embodied in Ontology.

The functor of ordinary inclusion is a proposition forming functor for two arguments either of which is a noun-expression. If in (18) we substitute constant noun-expressions for the variables 'a' and 'b' then the result of the substitution will be true if and only if everything named, or designated, by the noun-expression substituted for 'a' is also named by the noun-expression substituted for 'b.' It may be of some historical interest to mention that the above semantic characterisation of inclu-

---

[11] See J. Łukasiewicz "The Principle of Individuation," *Proceedings of the Aristotelian Society*, Sup. Vol. 27, London, 1953, 77 sq.

[12] See S. Lesniewski, 'Über die Grundlagen der Ontologie,' *Comptes rendus des séances de la Société des Sciences et des Lettres de Varsovie*, Classe III, 1930, 23. For a brief account of Ontology see L. Ajdukiewicz, 'On the Notion of Existence,' *Studia Philosophica*, Posnaniae, 1951, 8 sq., or J. Łukasiewicz, 'The Principle of Individuation,' *Proceedings of the Aristotelian Society*, Supplementary Volume XXVII, London, 1953, 77 sq.

[13] See this *Journal*, 1951, 2.

sion can be traced back to Hobbes who used it in order to determine the meaning of the copula 'est' in propositions such as 'homo est animal.'[14]

From the semantic characterisation of inclusion[15] it is evident that the following propositions are true:

$$\text{man} \subset \text{animal}$$
$$\text{man} \subset \text{man}$$
$$\text{Socrates} \subset \text{man}$$
$$\text{Socrates} \subset \text{Socrates}$$
$$\text{Pegasus} \subset \text{animal}$$
$$\text{Pegasus} \subset \text{Socrates}$$
$$\text{Pegasus} \subset \text{Pegasus}$$

The last three propositions are true because nothing is designated by 'Pegasus.' Thus whatever is designated by 'Pegasus,' is designated by anything you like. The corresponding proposition can be formulated in symbols as follows:

$$(a)(\text{Pegasus} \subset a) \tag{19}$$

If instead of 'Pegasus' in (19) we write the constant noun-expression 'Λ,' which designates nothing, then we shall get the following ontological thesis:

$$(a)(\Lambda \subset a) \tag{20}$$

'Λ' can be defined in terms of inclusion but for the sake of simplicity I prefer to introduce it as an undefined term with the aid of (20).

In order to determine the meaning of 'exist(s)' we shall need three definitions, which I write below in the form of equivalences:

[14] Hobbes wrote: 'Ut qui dicit *homo est animal* intellegi ita vult ac si dixisset "si quem recte *hominem* dicimus eundem etiam *animal* recte dicimus".' See 'Leviathan,' *Opera Philosophica*, iii, 497 (Molesworth); see also 'De Corpore,' *Opera Philosophica* i, 27 (Molesworth).

[15] Strictly speaking the meaning of inclusion ought to have been determined axiomatically. I understand from Dr. B. Sobocinski that Lesniewski had an axiom for inclusion. It has never been published and I never saw it when I was studying with Lesniewski in Warsaw before the war. But I found some time ago that a system of Ontology can be built up on the basis of the following single axiom:

$$(a, b)((a \subset b) \equiv (c, d)(\sim(c \subset d) \cdot (c \subset a) \supset (\exists)e, f)(\sim(e \subset f) \cdot (e \subset c) \cdot (e \subset b) \cdot$$
$$(g, h, i)(\sim(h \subset i) \cdot (g \subset e) \cdot (h \subset e) \supset (g \subset h)))))\,.$$

FOR ALL A,B A⊂B ⟺ [FOR ALL C,D NOT C IS D AND C IS A] THEN [THERE IS

E,F SUCH THAT NOT E AND F AND E AND C AND E AND B AND
FOR ALL G,H,I NOT H AND I AND G AND E AND H AND E] THEN G AND H]

$$(a)(\mathrm{ex}(a) \ \equiv \ (\exists b)(\sim(a \subset b))) \tag{21}$$

$$(a)(\mathrm{sol}(a) \ \equiv \ (b, c, d)(\sim(c \subset d) \cdot (b \subset a) \cdot (c \subset a) \supset (b \subset c))) \tag{22}$$

$$(a)(\mathrm{ob}(a) \ \equiv \ \mathrm{ex}(a) \cdot \mathrm{sol}\ (a))^{16} \tag{23}$$

For the present we need not trouble ourselves with the question how to read the newly defined functors. We can proceed straight on to the consequences which can be deduced from (20) and the three definitions.

Thus from (21) we immediately get

$$\mathrm{ex}(\varLambda) \ \equiv \ (\exists a)(\sim(\varLambda \subset a)) \tag{24}$$

Since from (20) we know that

$$\sim (\exists a)(\sim (\varLambda \subset a)) \tag{25}$$

we use (25) and (24) to show that

$$\sim (\mathrm{ex}(\varLambda)) \tag{26}$$

From (26) we obtain, by particular generalization,

$$(\exists a)(\sim (\mathrm{ex}(a))) \tag{27}$$

which is equivalent to

$$\sim (a)(\mathrm{ex}(a)) \tag{28}$$

From (23) and (26) we conclude that

$$\sim (\mathrm{ob}(\varLambda)) \tag{29}$$

From (29) we get

$$(\exists a)(\sim (\mathrm{ob}(a))) \tag{30}$$

which is equivalent to

$$\sim (a)(\mathrm{ob}(a)) \tag{31}$$

We can now draw Pegasus into our deductions. From (19) we immediately obtain

$$\sim (\exists a)(\sim (\mathrm{Pegasus} \subset a)) \tag{32}$$

---

[16] In Lesniewski's original system of Ontology the three functors are defined as follows:

$$(a)(\mathrm{ex}(a) \ \equiv \ (\exists b)(b \ \epsilon \ a))$$

$$(a)(\mathrm{sol}(a) \ \equiv \ (b, c)((b \ \epsilon \ a) \cdot (c \ \epsilon \ a) \supset (b \ \epsilon \ c)))$$

$$(a)(\mathrm{ob}(a) \ \equiv \ (\exists b)(a \ \epsilon \ b))$$

See T. Kotarbinski, *Elementy teorji poznania, logiki formalnej i metodologji nauk* (Elements of Epistemology, Formal Logic, and Methodology), Lwów, 1929, 235 sq.; see also K. Ajdukiewicz, 'On the Notion of Existence,' *Studia Philosophica*, Posnaniae, 1951, 4, 8, and J. Łukasiewicz, "The Principle of Individuation," *Proceedings of the Aristotelian Society*, Supplementary Volume XXVII, London, 1953, 79 sq.

and use it together with (21) to show that

$$\sim (\text{ex}(\text{Pegasus})) \tag{33}$$

From (23) and (33) we derive

$$\sim (\text{ob}(\text{Pegasus})) \tag{34}$$

Now (27), (28), (30), (31), (33), and (34) show that the functors 'ex' and 'ob' are very close approximations of 'exist(s).' We remember that under the unrestricted interpretation of the quantifiers '$(x)(x$ exists)' is false and so is '$(a)(\text{ex}(a))$' and '$(a)(\text{ob}(a))$' as is evident from (28) and (31). Under the same interpretation '$(\exists x)$ (x does not exist)' comes out true and so does '$(\exists a)(\sim (\text{ex}(a)))$' and '$(\exists a)(\sim (\text{ob}(a)))$' as is evident from (27) and (30).

Further evidence is supplied by (33) and (34) from which it follows that 'ex(Pegasus)' and 'ob(Pegasus)' are false just as 'Pegasus exists' is admittedly false. It remains then to be explained what is the difference in the meaning of 'ex' and 'ob.' We can find the required explanation if we consider the meaning of (22), which is a definition of 'sol.' The right hand side of this definition turns out to be true in two cases: if there is no such a thing as a or if there is only one a. Thus 'sol(a)' can be read as 'there is at most one a.' Now if we agree to read 'ex(a)' as 'a exists' or as 'a's exist' then in accordance with (23) 'ob(a)' will have to be read as 'there exists exactly one a,' which is equivalent to 'a is an object' or to 'a is an individual.' Thus the distinction between 'ex' and 'ob' roughly corresponds to the one made by Quine in his "Designation and Existence," where he talks about *general* existence statements and *singular* existence statements.[17]

We have already remarked that under the restricted interpretation every component of quantificational expansions contains a noun-expression which designates only one of the objects belonging to the universe. It therefore follows that the function 'x exists' as used by us when we discussed the two interpretations of the quantifiers, means in fact the same as 'there exists exactly one x' which is the rendering of the symbolic 'ob(x).' The functor 'ex,' on the other hand, appears to be a very close approximation of the 'exist(s)' as used in ordinary language as it forms true propositions with noun-expressions which may designate more objects than one.

I wish to conclude with a brief summary of the results. The aim

[17] See W. V. Quine, "Designation and Existence," in *Readings in Philosophical Analysis*, edited by H. Feigl and W. Sellars, New York, 1949, 44 sq.

of the paper was to analyse rather than criticise. I started by examining
two inferences which appeared to disprove the validity of the rules of
universal instantiation and existential generalisation in application to
reasoning with empty noun-expressions. Then I distinguished two
different interpretations of the quantifiers and argued that under what
I called the unrestricted interpretation the two inferences were correct.
Further arguments in favour of the unrestricted interpretation of the
quantifiers were brought in, and in particular it was found that by
adopting the unrestricted interpretation it was possible to separate the
notion of existence from the idea of quantification. With the aid of
the functor of inclusion two functors were defined of which one expressed the notion of existence as underlying the theory of restricted
quantification while the other approximated the term 'exist(s)' as
used in ordinary language.

It may be useful to supplement this summary by indicating some
aspects of the problem of existence which have not been included in
the discussion. I analysed the theory of quantification so far as it was
applied in connection with variables for which noun-expressions could
be substituted and my enquiry into the meaning of 'exist(s)' was
limited to cases where this functor was used with noun-expressions
designating concrete objects or with noun-expressions that were empty.
It remains to explore, among other things, in what sense the quantifiers
can be used to bind predicate variables and what we mean when we
say that colours exist or that numbers exist. These are far more difficult
problems, which may call for a separate paper or rather for a number
of separate papers.

15 L. Jonathan Cohen: LOGIC AND THE EMPTY UNIVERSE (1962)

Von Wright considers that in the standard calculus of predicates the possibility of an empty universe is wrongly excluded and every
property is wrongly ascribed at least one positive or negative instance,
in the sense that some sentence attributing the property to a thing is

From *The Diversity of Meaning* by L. Jonathan Cohen. Herder and Herder,
New York, 1962. Reprinted with the permission of the publisher.

made either true or false. At its bluntest the feature to which he objects is found in the theorem '$(\exists x)(Fx \lor \sim Fx)$,' which he implies not to be a truth of logic at all because it 'disagrees with the possibility that the universe may be empty.'[1] He has therefore proposed a calculus of predicates in which neither the supposed analogue of this theorem nor any of its corollaries, such as '$(x)Fx \supset (\exists x)Fx$' is provable.

Whether or not such theorems have a rightful place in a logic of predicates, it is very doubtful whether von Wright's own system is as compatible with the possibility of an empty universe as he supposes. The universality of a property, in his system, is said not to imply its existence. But it is not at all clear why this implication should fail to hold, in view of von Wright's definitions for universality and existence. A property is called universal by him if all instances of it are positive, and is said to exist if at least one instance of it is positive. But a thing is said to be a positive instance of a property if and only if a proposition that attributes the property to the thing is true, and a negative instance if and only if it is false. Hence, so far as von Wright's explicit definitions go, no sense is given to the notion of a property that is both universal and non-existent. To entertain this notion we require to suppose that if a certain non-existent property had instances they would all be positive ones. But what can this mean for von Wright, unless it be that if certain strings of words expressed propositions, which they do not, the propositions would all be true? Further, why are these strings of words to be supposed incapable of expressing propositions, unless it be that their domain of discourse is supposed to be empty? But, if that is the reason, von Wright's system is not genuinely compatible with the possibility of an empty universe, because the system seems to presuppose that such a universe can never be the topic of propositional discussion.

Lejewski, on the other hand, believes that the standard calculus of predicates is not at fault, but only its standard interpretation.[2] The quantifiers, on his view, should not be assigned any existential significance. Suppose we take '$(\exists x)Fx$' to be equivalent to, or implied by, the expansion '$Fa \lor Fb \lor Fc \ldots$,' and '$(x)Fx$' to be equivalent to, or imply, the expansion '$Fa \cdot Fb \cdot Fc \ldots$' If we then take '$a$,' '$b$,' '$c$,' etc., to designate objects in the universe, we must assign an existential significance to our quantifiers. But Lejewski suggests that if we take 'a,' 'b,'

[1] 'On the Idea of Logical Truth' (1948) in *Logical Studies* (1957), pp. 22ff.
[2] 'Logic and Existence,' *British Journal for the Philosophy of Science*, v (1955), pp. 104ff. [See above, pp. 167ff.]

'*c*,' etc., merely as meaningful noun-expressions, which may or may not designate objects in the universe, our quantifiers need have no existential import and the controversial formulas will not imply, when interpreted, that something exists. On this interpretation, he believes, all theorems of the standard predicate calculus turn out to be patterns of logical truth that hold as well for reasoning with empty noun-expressions as with non-empty ones, and are as valid for the empty universe as for any other. For example, on the standard interpretation he thinks that '$(x)Fx \supset Fy$' and '$Fy \supset (\exists x)Fx$' are liable to lead to obvious paralogisms when 'Pegasus' is put for 'y,' and 'exists' or 'does not exist,' respectively, for 'F.' But on his own interpretation Lejewski claims that these formulas can be taken to express logical laws for the safe use of which one does not have to know whether the noun-expressions put for 'y' are empty or not.

Though Lejewski's reinterpretation of the predicate calculus is obviously uneconomical to the extent that it requires some other symbol than a quantifier to express the notion of existence, this lack of economy would be negligible if it were the sole price paid to avert a genuine paralogism. But it turns out that a much heavier price must also be paid.

The trouble is that if we try to interpret the standard predicate calculus along Lejewski's lines we run into paradoxes about predication in the empty universe. Take any empty noun-expression 'y.' On Lejewski's interpretation '$Fy \lor \sim Fy$' is a logical truth whatever meaning we assign to 'F,' and so is '$\sim(Fy \cdot \sim Fy)$.' Of the two statements 'Fy' and '$\sim Fy$' one must be true and the other false. But how are we to tell which is true and which is false, since neither is deducible within the system? If 'exists' is put for 'F' there is no difficulty: 'Fy' is false and '$\sim Fy$' is true, because *ex hypothesi* 'y' is empty. But suppose some other predicate-expression, like 'is winged,' 'is unwinged,' 'is hot,' 'is cold,' etc., is put for 'F.' There seems no conceivable reason for assigning one truth-value to 'Fy' and the other to '$\sim Fy$,' though perhaps, if it had not been for the theorems '$Fy \lor \sim Fy$' and '$\sim(Fy \cdot \sim Fy)$,' we might plausibly have said that both are equally true, because there can be no evidence against either, or that both are equally false because there can be no evidence in favour of either.

In other words, if the theorems '$(x)(Fx \lor \sim Fx)$' and '$(x) \sim (Fx \cdot \sim Fx)$' are to be valid for the empty universe we have to assume that of every predicate and its contradictory one but not the other holds for the empty universe. But whatever can there be in the empty universe that makes this so for any ordinary pair of mutually contradictory predicates as well as for 'exists' and 'does not exist'? What intelligible truth-conditions can there be for such predicates? We cannot even hope to divide all predicates into two groups, such that truth for the empty universe could be quite arbitrarily assigned to members of one group and falsehood to members of the other. For in order to do this we should need to know the truth-value of every statement of the form '$(x)(Fx \supset Gx)$,' in case we mistakenly decided to make 'F' hold for the empty universe and 'G' not. Nor could we just make all atomic statements, like 'Fy' and 'Gy,' false, and their denials correspondingly true, where 'y' is empty. This neat procedure is favoured by Quine where singular terms are retained in a standard interpretation of the predicate calculus,[3] since 'Fy' is certainly false when 'y' is empty and 'F' is read 'exists.' But the trouble for Lejewski with this assignment of truth-values would be that it would require all generalizations of the form '$(x)(\sim Fx \supset Gx)$' to be false, if we are not to be plunged in antinomy with regard to the truth-value of 'Ga.' If 'a' is empty, 'Ga' will be false, because atomic; but '$\sim Fa$' will be true and if '$(x)(\sim Fx \supset Gx)$' is also true, so must 'Ga' be. Can we always expect to be safe in denying, if our domain of discourse is the animal world, for instance, that anything not oviparous is mammalian, or if our domain is the physical universe, that anything not containing carbon is a mineral, or if our domain is even wider, that anything not physical is mental? It is not open to Lejewski, as it is to Quine, to circumvent these difficulties by refusing to apply the principle of universal instantiation in the case of empty noun-expressions, for it is an essential part of his purpose to ensure that all the basic principles of predicate logic are in fact applicable in such cases. Hence, on Lejewski's interpretation, we shall certainly avoid the alleged risk of paralogism in applying certain principles to the predicates 'exist' and 'does not exist' without knowing whether our noun-expressions are empty or not. But we shall do so at the cost of not being able to give the full truth-conditions for any predicate except 'exists' and 'does not exist' without knowing the truth-value of very many generalizations in which it occurs. Lejewski's interpretation simplifies the task of interpreting the quantifiers at the cost of making it well-nigh impossible to interpret fully most of the predicate letters. When this interpretation prevents the quantifiers from repre-

[3] *From a Logical Point of View*, p. 166.

senting the notion of existence, it does so at the cost of preventing the predicate letters from representing any other notion as fully.

Nor can Lejewski get out of the difficulty by being content to leave it unspecified how we are to say which predicates, apart from 'exists' and 'does not exist,' hold for the empty universe and which do not. For he cannot then claim to have devised a way of interpreting the standard predicate calculus that makes it as valid for the empty universe as for all others. The empty universe would constitute a special case for which a fully adequate interpretation can be given to very few of the calculus's predicate letters. He might just as well admit that as a theory of predicates his system does not apply to the empty universe because it allows nothing meaningful and consistent to be said about the contents of this universe except that they do not exist. Correspondingly he might just as well abandon his claim to accommodate empty noun-expressions. For, where 'y' is an empty but meaningful noun-expression, 'Fy' must now be almost always meaningless, since no rule for appraising its truth-value can be given unless 'F' is read 'exists' or 'does not exist.' Not that a proposal for interpreting the predicate calculus is obliged to give defining conditions of application for every predicate in every universe of discourse where the interpretation is to apply. But it must at least show in principle how this could safely be done without supposing factual omniscience. Admittedly, even when 'y' is empty, 'Fy' is still well-formed and the connectives in such theorems as '$Fy \lor \sim Fy$' and '$\sim(Fy \cdot \sim Fy)$' still have their meanings as logical constants. But when no truth-conditions can be given for 'Fy,' 'F' is not on all fours as a predicate with 'exists,' nor is the empty universe on all fours, in regard to the applicability of predicate logic, with non-empty universes.

Hence Lejewski's proposal for interpreting the standard predicate calculus fails to achieve its purpose, and the arguments against Lejewski's proposal would hold equally well against any other proposal to reinterpret the calculus's quantifiers so as to permit quantification over an empty domain. If we think that a logic of predicates should embrace the empty universe in its scope of application, we have no choice but to abandon the standard calculus altogether and to adopt some other basis for our logic, though von Wright's system, as already shown, will not serve the purpose. But there are good reasons to suppose it right for a logic of predicates to exclude, rather than include, the possibility of an empty domain of discourse.

Not that Quine's reasons[4] are adequate for this supposition. Quine points out that quantificational schemata which are valid for all choices of universe of a given size also turn out valid for all smaller universes that are not altogether empty. Thus nothing is gained if in formulating the laws of quantification theory we disregard universes of, say, one to ten objects in the hope of obtaining further laws that will be useful for seriously large universes. For there are no further laws, no laws not holding also for universes of sizes one to ten. It is only when we come to the empty universe that certain laws, holding for all larger universes, fail any longer to hold. Quine argues therefore that we should 'put aside the one relatively inutile case of the empty universe, so as not to cut ourselves off from laws applicable in all other cases.' But it is unsatisfactory to have to regard this as the only, or even the main argument, for disregarding the possibility of an empty universe. If there really are logical truths about the empty universe the economies obtained by omitting them from our systematization of logical truth are too dearly bought. If economy may be purchased here at the cost of comprehensiveness, then why not elsewhere also? The road seems open to those who would wish to disregard the logic of non-extensional discourse because all classical mathematics is extensional, and to advocates of other similar economies. Formal logic, so constructed, can no longer claim to be the impartial arbiter of all rational discourse. The problem of systematization is being shirked, not solved, once the ideal of comprehensiveness is sacrificed to considerations of economy. Certainly, in building a logical system we may need to determine the truth-value of certain statements about which ordinary usage is insufficiently explicit, as with vacuous conditionals and the so-called paradoxes of strict implication. But this enriches the system in the very act of simplifying it: to impoverish it for purposes of simplification is a much less profitable procedure.

Fortunately Quine's argument is not needed, because its supposition that there can be logical truths about the empty universe is mistaken. The notion of an empty domain of discourse is self-contradictory. What does it mean to say that such-or-such a term or universe is empty? This question seems prima facie answered if we say that a term is empty when it denotes nothing and a class is empty when it has no members. But such an answer would be insufficiently determinate. 'Pegasus' is commonly suggested as an example of a term that denotes nothing,

[4] *Ibid.*, pp. 161 f.

and the class of winged horses as an example of a class that has no members. But these suggestions provide adequate examples only on the assumption that terrestrial, rather than celestial, fauna are the objects of discussion. Certainly classes do not vary their membership in accordance with how they are being discussed, but a language-phrase may vary in the class it denotes in accordance with its context of occurrence. The null class, in particular, is not so often denoted as logicians sometimes seem to suppose. It is fairly safe to say that there are no winged horses — that the class of winged horses is empty — if and only if what is meant is that the class of terrestrial fauna, which are under discussion, and the class of winged horses have no common member, or that the product of these two classes is the null class. Perhaps the word 'Pegasus' itself justifies a presumption that terrestrial fauna are under discussion. But this presumption might be rebutted by the specific assertion that Pegasus is a celestial or supernatural creature. Someone might then want to claim that the term 'celestial fauna' is empty: 'There are no angels, seraphs or Olympian demi-gods,' he will say, 'so Pegasus does not exist after all.' But here again one would want to know exactly what was being claimed. Is it that no such fauna are visible? Then what is meant is that the class of visible objects, which are under discussion, does not intersect with the class of celestial fauna: the two classes have no common member. Or is it rather that celestial fauna are not worth while postulating in scientific theory? Then what is meant is that the class of celestial fauna does not intersect with the class of objects now under discussion, viz. objects that are worth while postulating in scientific theory. In short, all our ordinary, non-analytic assertions of existence and non-existence require the implicit or explicit assumption of a domain of discourse. The invariant element in the meaning of 'there exists' is the assertion of intersection with such a class: the variable element depends on what domain is implicitly or explicitly specified. If a term is said to be empty, this is normally because it denotes no member of the given domain: if a class is said to be empty, this is because it does not intersect with the given domain. What sense therefore could be attached to the notion of such a domain's being empty? Certainly we could at one time take physical objects for our domain of discourse and then later, as followers of Berkeley perhaps, deny that there are any physical objects. But on the later occasion our domain of discourse would have changed to what Berkeley called real things, and we should be claiming that the class of real — perceived or perceiving — things, which are under discussion, did not intersect with that of physical objects. A domain of discourse, as such, is something about which questions of emptiness or non-emptiness do not arise: if you ask whether a certain domain is empty or not, you imply that it is not, at least then, your domain of discourse.

It follows that the formula '$(\exists x)(Fx \lor \sim Fx)$' cannot be interpreted in general as 'The universe of discourse is not empty.' After all, '$(\exists x)Fx$' would not be taken to say that the universe of discourse is not empty, but rather that the class of things that are F is not empty. Similarly '$(\exists x)(Fx \lor \sim Fx)$' means that either the class of things that are F or the class of things that are not F is not empty. Hence it is no use objecting, like von Wright, that the ordinary predicate calculus on its standard interpretation excludes the possibility of an empty universe of discourse, for neither the inclusion nor the exclusion of this is conceivable. Moreover the law represented by '$(\exists x)(Fx \lor \sim Fx)$' is in fact, as it should be, a universal condition on the predicability of terms in statements. No term is truly or falsely predicable within a given domain unless either it or its contradictory picks out the members of a class that intersects with the domain. Again, '$(x)Fx \supset (\exists x)Fx$' seems most objectionable where 'F' is taken to represent the same term as that which denotes the universe of discourse. For then from the truism that anything denoted by this term is denoted by it we seem entitled to infer the apparently contingent fact that the term is not empty. But the non-emptiness of 'F' here stems from our own decision to take as values for quantified variables only those entities that are denoted by 'F': it no longer even appears as a contingent fact when we remember that decision.

Nor are formulas like '$Fy \supset (\exists x)Fx$' likely to lead to paralogism, even when 'F' is taken to mean 'does not exist.' For if 'y' functions here as an individual constant it cannot be an empty term but must denote some element in the universe of discourse. If you want to put 'Pegasus' for 'y' then you must choose celestial fauna or some other suitable class as your domain of discourse. Of course a proper name might be assigned in error. You might assign the name 'Pegasus' to the only winged horse on earth, not knowing that winged horses do not exist on earth. But how could this lead, as Lejewski suggests it does, to paralogism — to the deduction of a false conclusion from true premises? If you do not know that your term is empty, i.e. denotes no animal, you are not in a position to affirm the antecedent and detach the consequent from '$Fy \supset (\exists x)Fx$,' where 'y' is read 'Pegasus' and 'F' is read 'does not exist.' If you do know that your term 'Pegasus' is empty on earth you should either refuse to read 'y' or any other individual constant of your system as 'Pegasus,' or refuse to confine your universe of discourse — the range of values for your quantified variables — to terrestrial fauna. In other words, for the safe use of '$Fy \supset (\exists x)Fx$' as a principle of inference, where 'F' is read 'does not exist' and quantifiers have their standard interpretation, we do indeed have to know, as Lejewski claims, whether the expression put for 'y' is empty or not relative to the chosen domain of discourse. But in effect this is just a case of the general requirement that, for the safe use of any provable formula $A \supset B$ as a principle of valid inference to the truth of B, we must first know the truth of A.

LOGIC AND
LANGUAGE

Besides the contrast in the philosophy of logic, already amply illustrated in the foregoing selections, between those who are willing to "multiply entities" and those who resist, there is also a contrast between those who find the economy of basic means and the strict rules of operation, which are among the most striking features of logic, to be its main attractions and those who find them rather to be constricting and falsifying. (This latter impulse can already be seen in the concluding lines of Selection 13.) It should also be observed here that, although the multipliers of entities tend also to "multiply senses" (recall Selection 10), one can argue against the possibility of reducing all the many uses of key logical concepts to those expressible in standard logical systems without making any ontological commitments such as those made in Selections 1, 4, and 10. The present selections by Strawson, which are representative of criticism of formal logic by "ordinary language" philosophers, present arguments of this sort, where questions of the adequacy of the standard logical constants to the concepts they are supposed to represent and of the adequacy of translations in terms of them to the propositions they are supposed to represent, are raised quite apart from any ontological issues.

Strawson argues against claims identifying concepts such as "and," "or," and so on, with their alleged representations in truth-functional logic. His arguments against the identification of "if . . . then" with the truth-functional horseshoe are included here. (Recall the related issues in Selections 7-9.) His account of the "standard or primary use of 'if . . . then . . . ,'" on which the argument depends heavily, of course, should be scrutinized carefully, especially with regard to the question whether some of these features of the use of "if . . . then" are not matters which are irrelevant to questions about logical relations such as deducibility holding between propositions involving the concept "if . . . then." (In this connection, see also the last footnote to Selection 19, in which Strawson considers a similar point.) Here, as throughout this final group of selections, the question in Selections 1-3 about what sort of entities enter into logical relations is relevant as well. Faris's counter-argument to the effect that propositions of the form "If p, then q" and "$p \supset q$" are at least derivable from one another should be examined to see if what he calls "the only kind of connexion which can plausibly be held to be a necessary condition of the truth of *if p then q*" is in fact the only one. Given this much, he is able to show that, since this condition is also necessary for the truth of "$p \supset q$," "if . . .

193

then" and the horseshoe cannot be distinguished, as is often supposed, on any such grounds as the former's involving some "connection" between antecedent and consequent which the latter does not.

The selection from Brentano represents one of the earliest statements of a view which has become orthodox among modern logicians concerning logical relations among so-called "standard form categorical propositions." These relations were the subject of most logical investigation until perhaps a century ago, and the view represented in this selection, which can be arrived at by reflecting on the most natural way of rendering these propositions in the symbolism of quantificational logic, entails considerable modification of the traditional doctrines of the twenty-four valid syllogistic forms, the relations of "immediate inference," and the "square of opposition," which specifies relations of contradiction, contrariety, and sub-contrariety. Strawson defends the older logicians against the new, arguing that it is possible to interpret these propositions in such a way that the traditional laws all hold and the notions of "all" and "some" are, with some reservations, given "just the sense which they have in a vast group of statements of ordinary speech." The moral to be drawn from the disparities between the traditional system and that which emerges from representing the standard form categorical propositions in terms of quantificational logic is not that the traditional logic was at fault but that the formal machinery of quantificational logic is inadequate to the task of rendering these propositions.

Finally, Selections 20 and 21 give us statements by Strawson and Quine, perhaps the leading contemporary protagonists of their respective views, on the general question of the function and significance of formal logic. On the one hand, Strawson argues that the resources of formal logic are insufficient to deal with all the philosophically important distinctions in language and there is left over a less tidy but no less philosophically vital study of the "logical features of ordinary speech." Quine, on the other hand, defends the "regimentation" enforced by formal logic, in which we "minimize our stock of basic functions" and translate various sentences into the resulting "canonical notation." He goes on to argue that this "quest of a simplest, clearest overall pattern of canonical notation is not to be distinguished from a quest of ultimate categories, a limning of the most general traits of reality." No doubt the most basic question in the philosophy of logic concerns the nature of logic and its relation to philosophy in general; here we have a very strong claim indeed in behalf of the philosophical significance of logic, reminiscent of the assertion once made by Russell that "every philosophical problem, when it is subjected to the necessary analysis and purification, is found either to be not really philosophical at all, or else to be . . . logical."

Truth-Functions and Ordinary Language

16 P.F. Strawson: TRUTH-FUNCTIONAL CONSTANTS AND ORDINARY WORDS (1952)

What of the relations between the truth-functional constants and expressions of ordinary speech? The meaning, or interpretation, of those constants was given, in words, on p. 67, and this explanation was to be understood in the light of the subsequently developed procedures for determining truth-conditions and establishing logical rules. We have to ask, with regard to each of those constants, whether there is any expression of ordinary speech which has at least a standard use identifiable with the meaning of that constant. It is quite common to suggest, with certain reservations, the following identifications: '$\sim$' with 'not,' or 'it is not the case that'; '$\cdot$' with 'and'; '$\ldots \vee \ldots$' with 'either ... or ...'; '$\cdots \supset \cdots$' with 'if ... then ...'; '$\cdots \equiv \cdots$' with '... if and only if ....' Of these identifications the first two are the least misleading. We shall find that the remainder are not only misleading, but definitely wrong. We shall be entitled to say that such an identification is definitely wrong, wherever we find that the ordinary conjunction, in its standard or primary use, does not conform to a logical rule which holds for the truth-functional constant with which it is identified, and whenever we find, conversely, that the truth-functional constant does not conform to a logical rule which holds for the ordinary

Reprinted by permission of the publisher from *Introduction to Logical Theory* by P. F. Strawson. Methuen & Co. Ltd. (London, 1952.)

conjunction in its standard or primary use. But we shall also find that even the most mistaken of these identifications has a point: we shall find not only some degree of formal parallelism (which could be noted independently of interpretation) but some degree of interpenetration of meanings of the interpreted expressions of the system and of ordinary speech respectively. We could not, of course, find the latter without the former. . . .

The relations between 'if' and '⊃' have already, but only in part, been discussed. The sign '⊃' is called the Material Implication sign — a name I shall consider later. Its meaning is given by the rule that any statement of the form '$p \supset q$' is false in the case in which the first of its constituent statements is true and the second false, and is true in every other case considered in the system. That is to say, the falsity of the first constituent statement or the truth of the second are, equally, sufficient conditions of the truth of a statement of material implication; the combination of truth in the first with falsity in the second is the single, necessary and sufficient, condition of its falsity. The standard or primary[1] use of an 'if . . . then . . .' sentence, on the other hand, we saw to be in circumstances where, not knowing whether some statement which could be made by the use of a sentence corresponding in a certain way to the first clause of the hypothetical is true or not, or believing it to be false, we nevertheless consider that a step in reasoning from that statement to a statement related in a similar way to the second clause would be a sound or reasonable step; the second statement also being one of whose truth we are in doubt, or which we believe to be false. Even in such circumstances as these we may sometimes hesitate to apply the word 'true' to hypothetical statements (i.e., statements which could be made by the use of 'if . . . then . . .' in its standard significance), preferring to call them reasonable or well-founded; but if we apply the word 'true' to them at all, it will be in such circumstances as these. [Now one of the sufficient conditions of the truth of a statement of material implication may very well be fulfilled without the conditions for the truth (or reasonableness) of the corresponding hypothetical statement being fulfilled;] i.e., a statement of the form '$p \supset q$' does not entail the corresponding statement of the form 'if p, then q.' But if we

---

[1] The importance of this qualifying phrase can scarcely be overemphasized. There are uses of 'if . . . then . . .' which do not answer to the description given here, or to any other descriptions given in this chapter.

are prepared to accept the hypothetical statement, we must in consistency be prepared to deny the conjunction of the statement corresponding to the first clause of the sentence used to make the hypothetical statement with the negation of the statement corresponding to its second clause; i.e., a statement of the form 'if p, then q' does entail the corresponding statement of the form '$p \supset q$.'

The force of the word 'corresponding' in the above paragraph needs elucidation. Consider the three following very ordinary specimens of hypothetical sentences:

(1) If the Germans had invaded England in 1940, they would have won the war.
(2) If Jones were in charge, half the staff would have been dismissed.
(3) If it rains, the match will be cancelled.

The sentences which could be used to make statements *corresponding* in the required sense to the subordinate clauses can be ascertained by considering what it is that the speaker of each hypothetical sentence must (in general) be assumed either to be in doubt about or to believe to be not the case. Thus, for (1) to (3), the corresponding pairs of sentences are:

(1*a*) The Germans invaded England in 1940; they won the war.
(2*a*) Jones is in charge; half the staff has been dismissed.
(3*a*) It will rain; the match will be cancelled.

Sentences which could be used to make the statements of material implication *corresponding* to the hypothetical statements made by sentences (1) to (3) can now be framed from these pairs of sentences as follows:

(M1) The Germans invaded England in 1940 $\supset$ they won the war.
(M2) Jones is in charge $\supset$ half the staff has been dismissed.
(M3) It will rain $\supset$ the match will be cancelled.

The very fact that these verbal modifications are necessary, in order to obtain from the clauses of the hypothetical sentence the clauses of the corresponding material implication sentence is itself a symptom of the radical difference between hypothetical statements and truth-functional statements. Some detailed differences are also evident from these examples. The falsity of a statement made by the use of 'The Germans invaded England in 1940' or 'Jones is in charge' is a sufficient condition of the truth of the corresponding statements made by the use of (M1) and (M2); but not, of course, of the corresponding statements made by the use of (1) and (2). Otherwise, there would normally be no point in using sentences like (1) and (2) at all; for these sentences would normally[2] carry, in the tense or mood of the verb, an implication of the speaker's belief in the falsity of the statements corresponding to the clauses of the hypothetical. Its not raining is sufficient to verify a statement made by the use of (M3), but not a statement made by the use of (3). Its not raining is also sufficient to verify a statement made by the use of (M4) 'It will rain $\supset$ the match will *not* be cancelled.' The formulae '$p \supset q$' and '$p \supset \sim q$' are consistent with one another, and the joint assertion of corresponding statements of these forms is equivalent to the assertion of the corresponding statement of the form '$\sim p$.' But 'If it rains, the match will be cancelled' is inconsistent with 'If it rains, the match will not be cancelled,' and their joint assertion in the same context is self-contradictory.

Suppose we call the statement corresponding to the first clause of a sentence used to make a hypothetical statement the antecedent of the hypothetical statement; and the statement corresponding to the second clause, its consequent. It is sometimes fancied that whereas the futility of identifying conditional statements with material implications is obvious in those cases where the implication of the falsity of the antecedent is normally carried by the mood or tense of the verb (e.g., (1) or (2)), there is something to be said for at least a partial identification in cases where no such implication is involved, i.e., where the possibility of the truth of both antecedent and consequent is left open (e.g., (3)). In cases of the first kind ('unfulfilled' or 'subjunctive' conditionals) our attention is directed only to the last two lines of the truth-tables for '$p \supset q$,' where the antecedent has the truth-value, falsity; and the suggestion that '$\sim p$' entails 'if p, then q' is felt to be obviously wrong. But

---

[2] But not necessarily. One may use the pluperfect or the imperfect subjunctive when one is simply working out the consequences of an hypothesis which one may be prepared eventually to accept.

in cases of the second kind we may inspect also the first two lines, for the possibility of the antecedent's being fulfilled is left open; and the suggestion that '$p \cdot q$' entails 'if p, then q' is not felt to be obviously wrong. This is an illusion, though engendered by a reality. The fulfilment of both antecedent and consequent of a hypothetical statement does not show that the man who made the hypothetical statement was right; for the consequent might be fulfilled as a result of factors unconnected with, or in spite of, rather than because of, the fulfilment of the antecedent. We should be prepared to say that the man who made the hypothetical statement was right only if we were also prepared to say that the fulfilment of the antecedent was, at least in part, the explanation of the fulfilment of the consequent. The reality behind the illusion is complex: it is, partly, the fact that, in many cases, the fulfilment of both antecedent and consequent may provide confirmation for the view that the existence of states of affairs like those described by the antecedent is a good reason for expecting states of affairs like those described by the consequent; and it is, partly, the fact that a man who says, for example, 'If it rains, the match will be cancelled' makes a prediction (viz., that the match will be cancelled) under a proviso (viz., that it rains), and that the cancellation of the match because of the rain therefore leads us to say, not only that the reasonableness of the prediction was confirmed, but also that the prediction itself was confirmed.

Because a statement of the form '$p \supset q$' does not entail the corresponding statement of the form 'if p, then q' (in its standard employment), we shall expect to find, and have found, a divergence between the rules for '$\supset$' and the rules for 'if' (in its standard employment). Because 'if p, then q' *does* entail '$p \supset q$,' we shall also expect to find some degree of parallelism between the rules; for whatever is entailed by '$p \supset q$' will be entailed by 'if p, then q,' though not everything which entails '$p \supset q$' will entail 'if p, then q.' Indeed, we find further parallels than those which follow simply from the facts that 'if p, then q' entails '$p \supset q$' and that entailment is transitive. To laws (19)–(23) inclusive we find no parallels for 'if.' But for

(15) $(p \supset q) \cdot p \supset q$

(16) $(p \supset q) \cdot \sim q \supset \sim p$

(17) $p \supset q \equiv \sim q \supset \sim p$

(18) $(p \supset q) \cdot (q \supset r) \supset (p \supset r)$

we find that, with certain reservations,[3] the following parallel laws hold good:

(i)   (if p, then q; and p) $\supset q$

(ii)   (if p, then q; and not-q) $\supset$ not-p

(iii)   (if p, then q) $\supset$ (if not-q, then not-p)

(iv)   (if p, then q; and if q, then r) $\supset$ (if p, then r)

(One must remember that calling the formulae (i)–(iv) *laws* is the same as saying that, e.g., in the case of (iii), 'if p, then q' entails 'if not-q, then not-p.') And similarly we find that, for some steps which would be *invalid* for 'if,' there are corresponding steps that would be *invalid* for '$\supset$.' For example:

$$(p \supset q)\cdot q \therefore p$$
$$(p \supset q)\cdot \sim p \therefore \sim q$$

are invalid inference-patterns, and so are

if p, then q; and $q \therefore p$

if p, then q; and not-$p \therefore$ not-q.

[3] The reservations are important. For example, it is often impossible to apply entailment-rule (iii) directly without obtaining incorrect or absurd results. Some modification of the structure of the clauses of the hypothetical is commonly necessary. But formal logic gives us no guide as to which modifications are required. If we apply rule (iii) to our specimen hypothetical sentences, without modifying at all the tenses or moods of the individual clauses, we obtain expr   which are scarcely English. If we preserve as nearly as possible the ten   *structure*, in the simplest way consistent with grammatical requirements   the sentences:

> If the Germans had not won the war, they wo   invaded England in 1940.
> If half the staff had not been dismissed, Jor   not be in charge.
> If the match is not cancelled, it will not ra

But these sentences, so far from being logically   alent to the originals, have in each case a quite different sense. It is possible, at least in some such cases, to frame sentences of more or less the appropriate pattern for which one can imagine a use and which do stand in the required logical relationship to the original sentences (e.g., 'If it is *not* the case that half the staff *has* been dismissed, then Jones *can't be* in charge'; or 'If the Germans *did not win* the war, *it's only because they did not invade* England in 1940'; or even [should historical evidence become improbably scanty] 'If the Germans did not win the war, it can't be true that they invaded England in 1940'). These changes reflect differences in the circumstances in which one might use these, as opposed to the original, sentences. Thus the sentence beginning 'If Jones were in charge . . .' would normally (though not necessarily) be used by a man who antecedently knows that Jones is not in charge: the sentence beginning 'If it's not the case that half the staff has been dismissed . . .' by a man who is working towards the conclusion that Jones is not in charge. To say that the sentences are nevertheless logically equivalent is to point to the fact that the grounds for accepting either, would, in different circumstances, have been grounds for accepting the soundness of the move from 'Jones is in charge' to 'Half the staff has been dismissed.'

The formal analogy here may be described by saying that neither '$p \supset q$' nor 'if p, then q' is a simply convertible formula.

We have found many laws (e.g., (19)–(23)) which hold for '$\supset$' and not for 'if.' As an example of a law which holds for 'if,' but not for '$\supset$,' we may give the analytic formula '$\sim[(\text{if } p, \text{ then } q)\cdot(\text{if } p, \text{ then } \text{not-}q)]$.' The corresponding formula '$\sim[(p \supset q)\cdot(p \supset \sim q)]$' is not analytic, but (cf. (23)) is equivalent to the contingent formula '$\sim\sim p$.'

The rules to the effect that formulae such as (19)–(23) are analytic are sometimes referred to as 'paradoxes of implication.' This is a misnomer. If '$\supset$' is taken as identical either with 'entails' or, more widely, with 'if . . . then . . .' in its standard use, the rules are not paradoxical, but simply incorrect. If '$\supset$' is given the meaning it has in the system of truth-functions, the rules are not paradoxical, but simple and platitudinous consequences of the meaning given to the symbol.

Throughout this section, I have spoken of a 'primary or standard' use of 'if . . . then . . .,' or 'if,' of which the main characteristics were: that for each hypothetical statement made by this use of 'if,' there could be made just *one* statement which would be the antecedent of the hypothetical and just *one* statement which would be its consequent; that the hypothetical statement is acceptable (true, reasonable) if the antecedent statement, if made or accepted, would, in the circumstances, be a good gr____ or reason for accepting the consequent statement; and that the ____ of the hypothetical statement carries the implication either of u____ about, or of disbelief in, the fulfilment of both antecedent and co____ [4] Not all uses of 'if,' however, exhibit all these characteristics. ____icular, there is a use which has an equal claim to rank as standa____ which is closely connected with the use described, but which does not exhibit the first characteristic and for which the description of the remainder must consequently be modified. I have in mind what are sometimes called 'variable' or 'general' hypotheticals: e.g., 'If ice is left in the sun, it melts'; 'If the side of a triangle is produced, the exterior angle is equal to the sum of the two interior and opposite angles'; 'If a child is very strictly disciplined in the nursery, it will develop aggressive tendencies in adult life'; and so on. To a statement made by the use of a sentence such as these there corre-

---

[4] There is much more than this to be said about this way of using 'if'; in particular, about the meaning of the question 'whether the antecedent would be a good ground or reason for accepting the consequent' and about the exact way in which this question is related to the question of whether the hypothetical is true (acceptable, reasonable) or not.

sponds no single pair of statements which are, respectively, its antecedent and consequent. On the other hand, for every such statement there is an indefinite number of non-general hypothetical statements which might be called exemplifications, applications, of the variable hypothetical; e.g., a statement made by the use of the sentence 'If this piece of ice is left in the sun, it will melt.' To the subject of variable hypotheticals I shall return later.

Two relatively uncommon uses of 'if' may be illustrated respectively by the sentences 'If he felt embarrassed, he showed no signs of it' and 'If he has passed his exam, I'm a Dutchman (I'll eat my hat, etc.).' The sufficient and necessary condition of the truth of a statement made by the first is that the man referred to showed no sign of embarrassment. Consequently, such a statement cannot be treated either as a standard hypothetical or as a material implication. Examples of the second kind are sometimes erroneously treated as evidence that 'if' does, after all, behave somewhat as '⊃' behaves. The evidence for this is, presumably, the facts (i) that there is no connexion between antecedent and consequent; (ii) that the consequent is obviously not (or not to be) fulfilled; (iii) that the intention of the speaker is plainly to give emphatic expression to the conviction that the antecedent is not fulfilled either; and (iv) the fact that '$(p \supset q) \cdot \sim q$' entails '$\sim p$.' But this is a strange piece of logic. For, on any possible interpretation, 'if p, then q' has, in respect of (iv), the same logical powers as '$p \supset q$'; and it is just these logical powers that we are jokingly (or fantastically) exploiting. It is the absence of connexion referred to in (i) that makes it a quirk, a verbal flourish, an odd use of 'if.' If hypothetical statements were material implications, the statements would be not a quirkish oddity, but a linguistic sobriety and a simple truth.

Finally, we may note that 'if' can be employed not simply in making statements, but in, e.g., making provisional announcements of intention (e.g., 'If it rains, I shall stay at home') which, like unconditional announcements of intention, we do not call true or false but describe in some other way. If the man who utters the quoted sentence leaves home in spite of the rain, we do not say that what he said was false, though we *might* say that he lied (never really intended to stay in); or that he changed his mind. There are further uses of 'if' which I shall not discuss.

The safest way to *read* the material implication sign is, perhaps, 'not both . . . and not . . . .'

$$- (p \ \& \ -q)$$

17   J. A. Faris: INTERDERIVABILITY OF '⊃' AND 'IF' (1962)

Relation between if *and* ⊃ : *preliminary discussion.* Many people regard *if* as being essentially non-truth-functional in its use and are bewildered by the suggestion that it can be defined by the truth-table for ⊃ or that an *if-then* statement is true always and only when the corresponding ⊃ statement is true. The same sort of puzzlement does not arise in connexion, for example, with *or* and ∨ or with *and* and · . Although there may be doubt about the interderivability in general of *or* and ∨ the point of assigning to *or* the truth-table for ∨ is easily understood; for it is recognized that *or*, even if it may not always be used truth-functionally, is at least sometimes used truth-functionally in the way suggested. But with *if*, on the other hand, the position is quite different. An *if-then* statement is regarded as essentially asserting a connexion of some kind between antecedent and consequent; as we shall see later this appears incompatible with truth-functionality; consequently *if* unlike *or* and *and* is thought not to have a truth-functional use at all. Now whatever the truth may be about the relation between *if* and ⊃ I think that at least this extreme view that there can be no natural truth-functional use of *if* is very hard to defend although one can quite see how people come to adopt it. I shall begin by giving an example of a situation in which it seems quite natural to interpret *if* truth-functionally in accordance with the truth-table for ⊃.

Our example relating to a truth-functional use of *if* will be preceded for the sake of comparison by an analogous one concerned with *and*. Let us suppose that it is a condition for appointment to a certain post that the candidate should be over twenty-one and a graduate. If a certain candidate Robinson is to be regarded as satisfying this condition it must be the case that:

(i) Robinson is over twenty-one and Robinson is a graduate. It will be convenient to use abbreviations; we shall put *T* for *Robinson is over twenty-one* and *G* for *Robinson is a graduate*. (i) thus becomes:

(i)   *T* and *G*.

We shall call (i), in the present context, the qualification statement. Now there are four possibilities about truth-values for the propositions *T*

Reprinted by permission of the publishers from J. A. Faris, *Truth-functional Logic* (London, Routledge & Kegan Paul Ltd.; New York, Dover Publications, Inc.)

and G. In one of the possible cases, namely T and G both true, Robinson satisfies the condition; in the other three cases he fails to satisfy it. But also in the first case, T and G both true, the qualification statement (i) is true and in the other three cases the qualification statement is false. Thus the qualification statement is true if and only if Robinson satisfies the condition. We may set all this out in a table:

T	G	Condition satisfied	Truth-value of qualification statement (i)
1	1	Yes	1
1	0	No	0
0	1	No	0
0	0	No	0

On the other hand there might be a different condition of appointment namely that if the candidate is over twenty-one he should be a graduate. If Robinson is to be regarded as satisfying this condition it must be the case that

(ii) If T then G.

(ii) is in this case the qualification statement. Again there are four possibilities about truth-values for T and G. In the first case where T and G are both true clearly Robinson satisfies the condition; in the second case, where T is true but G is false, he fails to satisfy the condition; in the third and fourth cases, in both of which T is false, he satisfies the condition simply by not being over twenty-one; for clearly he either satisfies or fails to satisfy it and he cannot fail to satisfy it unless he is over twenty-one. Thus Robinson fails to satisfy the condition in the second case, where T is true and G is false, but satisfies it in all the other possible cases. Now what about the truth-value of the qualification statement? Surely, just as in the previous example, we must say that this statement is true if Robinson satisfies the condition and false if he fails to satisfy it. But, if so, the use of *if* in (ii) is truth-functional. For all we need to know about T and G in order to know whether the condition is satisfied or not are their truth-values. Further, the truth-table for *if* in this case will be exactly the same as the truth-table for $\supset$. Again a table brings these points out clearly:

T	G	Condition satisfied	Truth-value of qualification statement (ii)
1	1	Yes	1
1	0	No	0
0	1	Yes	1
0	0	Yes	1

Argument against the interderivability of if *and* $\supset$. *The paradoxes*. The example we have just been using does, I think, show that there are some occasions at least on which it would be natural and not just perverse to use *if* in a purely truth-functional sense. However, it by no means follows from this that in general *if* is used in a way in which *if* and $\supset$ are interderivable, and in fact very plausible arguments can be adduced in support of the contrary view that, at least as a general rule, *if* and $\supset$ are not interderivable. These arguments have their focus in what have been called the paradoxes of implication or of material implication and these we will now explain.

It can be seen from the truth-table for $\supset$ that the proposition $p \supset q$, (which is said to assert the material implication by p of q,) is false when p is true and q is false but true for all other possible values of p and q. Another way of saying exactly the same thing is to say that $p \supset q$ is true if p is false or q is true but otherwise it is false. In other words if a certain proposition p is false then whatever proposition q may be the proposition $p \supset q$ is true; and again if q is a true proposition then whatever proposition p may be $p \supset q$ is true. Now if we replace $\supset$ by *if-then* the sentence we have just written will read '. . . if a certain proposition p is false then whatever proposition q may be the proposition *if p then q* is true; and again if q is a true proposition then whatever proposition p may be the proposition *if p then q* is true.' This sentence now expresses the so-called *paradoxes of material implication*. They may also be put in rather different language: if $p \supset q$ is taken to assert that p implies q the paradoxes are that a false proposition implies any proposition and a true proposition is implied by any proposition. One or two examples will make it clear why these assertions are described as paradoxical. The proposition *Daniel Defoe lived in the fifteenth century* is false; hence according to those assertions if we take any other proposition whatever, say for example, *Men will land on the moon before 1970* the compound proposition:

(iii) If Daniel Defoe lived in the fifteenth century then men will land on the moon before 1970

is true. Again the proposition *Daniel Defoe lived in the fifteenth century* is said to imply the proposition *Men will land on the moon before 1970*. These statements are paradoxical because as many people understand the word *if* the proposition (iii) cannot be true unless there is some connexion between the proposition *Daniel Defoe lived in the fifteenth century* and the proposition about men landing on the moon; there is obviously, it seems, no connexion and yet if the interderivability of *if* and $\supset$ is allowed the proposition (iii) is true.

To take another example, relevant this time to the second paradoxical assertion, the proposition *2 + 2 = 4* is true. It follows, according to the second assertion, that the proposition:

(iv) If Cicero was a poet 2 + 2 = 4

is true. But again there seems to be no connexion between the proposition that Cicero was a poet and the proposition that 2 + 2 = 4; for this reason it seems very queer to call (iv) a true proposition.

These paradoxes are the basis of the main argument against the interderivability of *if* and $\supset$. They are also the basis of the main argument against the <u>synonymity</u> of *if* and $\supset$. This distinction must be explained before we go further. Propositions X and Y, as we have seen, are interderivable if and only if each of them can be inferred from the other alone. On the other hand X and Y are synonymous propositions if and only if they have the same meaning — or perhaps strictly we should say, if every sentence which expresses the proposition X has the same meaning as every sentence which expresses the proposition Y.

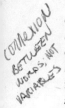

Now let us formulate briefly the arguments, based on the paradoxes, against interderivability and synonymity respectively. *Argument against interderivability.* There is some kind of connexion the existence of which between *p* and *q* is a necessary condition of the truth of *if p then q* but is not a necessary condition of the truth of $p \supset q$. Therefore it is possible for $p \supset q$ to be true when *if p then q* is false; and so *if* and $\supset$ are not interderivable. *Argument against synonymity.* There is some kind of connexion which is part of the meaning of *if p then q* but is not part of the meaning of $p \supset q$. Therefore *if* and $\supset$ are not synonymous.

In the next section we put forward an argument in support of interderivability. Part of our contention will be that the only kind of connexion which can plausibly be held to be a necessary condition of the truth of *if p then q* is also a necessary condition of the truth of *p ⊃ q*. If this is correct, the argument stated above against interderivability is destroyed; for its premise, despite the paradoxes, must be false. However, in case there should be misunderstanding it should be said that our argument for interderivability will not, by itself at least, destroy the argument against synonymity. Interderivability is not in general incompatible with non-synonymity. Consider the following propositions:

(A) The winner was the tallest and James was the winner.

(B) The winner was the tallest and James was the tallest.

These two propositions are interderivable but they are not synonymous.

Before we leave the subject of the paradoxes it ought I think to be pointed out that they are rather misleadingly described as paradoxes of *material implication*. To describe them thus is to suggest that the paradoxes concern the functor ⊃ in itself, and that paradox is involved, not merely in calling (iii) and (iv) true propositions, but even in calling the following proposition (v) and (vi) true:

(v) Daniel Defoe lived in the fifteenth century ⊃ Men will land on the moon before 1970.

(vi) Cicero was a poet ⊃ 2 + 2 = 4.

This would be a mistake. The functor ⊃ has no meaning except what is defined by the relevant truth-table. From the truth-table for ⊃ together with the falsity of the antecedent of (v) and the truth of the consequent of (vi) the truth of (v) and (vi) necessarily follows and there is no paradox whatsoever. What paradox there is arises only from taking ⊃ and *if-then* to be interderivable or synonymous.

Argument for interderivability. To show that *if* and ⊃ are interderivable we have to establish both the derivability of ⊃ from *if* and the derivability of *if* from ⊃; i.e. we have to establish both that (i) *p ⊃ q* is derivable from *if p and q* and that (ii) *if p then q* is derivable from *p ⊃ q*. The derivability of ⊃ from *if* hardly needs any proof; for everyone would agree that when *if p then q* is true it cannot be the case that *p* is true and *q* is false. But if it is not the case that *p* is true and *q* is false we know from the truth-table for ⊃ that *p ⊃ q* is true. But that *if p then q* is derivable for *p ⊃ q* certainly does require to be argued and to this we now proceed.

We said in section 8 that the existence of a certain connexion between p and q is commonly believed to be a necessary condition of the truth of *if p then q*. We have been regrettably vague about this connexion and we must now inquire what its character is. At first thought we might perhaps be inclined to say that the connexion is simply that q is derivable from p. This works all right for some cases; for example if p is *No Frenchmen were saved* and q is *No one who was saved was a Frenchman* then in the *if-then* proposition:

(i) If no Frenchmen were saved no one who was saved was a Frenchman,

q is certainly derivable from p. However, the suggestion in its present form does not always work. For if p is for example *Smith is taller than Jones* and q is *Smith is taller than Robinson* then in the *if-then* proposition:

(ii) If Smith is taller than Jones Smith is taller than Robinson,

q certainly cannot be derived from p (i.e. inferred from p alone). Yet (ii) is a very everyday sort of *if-then* proposition which may well be true and which any theory must be able to account for. Let us for the moment confine our attention to (ii), referring to the antecedent as p and to the consequent as q. Although q cannot be inferred from p alone it can be inferred from p together with the proposition,

(iii) Jones is at least as tall as Robinson.

Now it might perhaps be thought that (ii) can be true if and only if (iii) is true and that the connexion which is a condition of the truth of (ii) is simply the relationship asserted in (iii) or at least is based on this relationship. However, this cannot be right. Certainly (ii) will be true if (iii) is true but not *only* if (iii) is true. It is not difficult to think of an example to demonstrate that (ii) can be true even if (iii) is false. For example, if the following three propositions were true:

(iv) Every member taller than Jones is red-haired;
(v) Every red-haired member is taller than Robinson;
(vi) Smith is a member;

the proposition

(ii) If Smith is taller than Jones Smith is taller than Robinson

would also be true. But (iv), (v) and (vi) could quite well all be true even though (iii) were false; for example if Smith and Jones are the only members, Smith is red-haired and Jones not, and Smith, Robinson and Jones are respectively 6 ft., 5 ft. and 4 ft. tall then (iv), (v) and (vi) are true but (iii) is false. Hence in this case (ii) is true though (iii) is false. In other words the truth of (iii) though a sufficient is not a necessary condition of the truth of (ii). But the connexion about which we are inquiring has to be a necessary condition of the truth of *if p then q*.

From this suggestion we may pass on to one that is more promising. Perhaps the condition for the truth of *if p then q* is not that there should be a specified true proposition (as e.g. (iii) in our last example) from which together with p q is inferrible but simply that there should be *some* true proposition or propositions from which together with p q is inferrible. We may formulate this condition as follows:

(Condition E.) There is a set S of true propositions such that q is inferrible from p together with S.

The effect of this condition may be illustrated by reference to our previous example. If (iii) is a true proposition then there is a set S of true propositions, namely the set consisting of (iii) itself, such that q is inferrible from p together with S. Thus condition E is satisfied. On the other hand if (iii) is not true the condition may still be satisfied; for example if propositions (iv), (v) and (vi) are true there is a set S of true propositions, namely the set consisting of these three propositions, such that q is inferrible from p together with S. Thus condition E is again satisfied. We can imagine of course many different ways besides these two that we have mentioned in which condition E might be satisfied for this particular example.

It seems to me that, whatever propositions p and q may be, condition E is a sufficient and necessary condition of the truth of *if p then q*. I think it is sufficient because I think that in any case in which we believed that a set S existed as specified we should be prepared to assert *if p then q* and I think it is necessary because I think that in any case in which we believed that no such set existed we should be prepared to deny *if p then q*. It is to be understood of course that in a case in which q is inferrible from p alone the condition E is satisfied in that S may then be taken to be any set of true propositions whatever. If we may refer to an earlier example in which p was the proposition, *No Frenchmen were saved* and q was the proposition, *No one who was saved was a Frenchman* we see that in the case of the proposition

(i) If no Frenchmen were saved then no one who was saved was a Frenchman, the condition E is satisfied because since q is inferrible from p alone it is inferrible from any set S of true propositions together with p.

We take it then that condition E is a sufficient and necessary condition of the truth of *if p then q*; and we now return to the question of the relationship between *if p then q* and $p \supset q$. Now q can certainly be inferred from p and $p \supset q$. Accordingly if $p \supset q$ is true there is a set S of true propositions, namely the set consisting solely of the proposition $p \supset q$, such that q is inferrible from p together with S. It follows that if $p \supset q$ is true condition E is satisfied. But if condition E is satisfied *if p then q* is true. Consequently, if we are able to know that the proposition $p \supset q$ is true we are able to know that the proposition *if p then q* is true also whatever other truths or falsehoods there may be. That is to say *if p then q* is derivable from $p \supset q$. But we have already seen that $p \supset q$ is derivable from *if p then q*. It follows that the propositions *if p then q* and $p \supset q$ are interderivable.

The Logic of
Categorical Propositions

18 Franz Brentano: CRITICISMS OF
TRADITIONAL LOGIC (1874)

The fact that not every judgment refers to a conjunction of presented attributes and that the predication of one attribute of another
does not unavoidably characterize judgment is a truth which commonly
has gone unrecognized, but this is not so without exception. In his
criticism of the ontological proof of God, Kant made the pertinent
remark that in an existential proposition, i.e., in a proposition of the
form, "*A exists*," existence is "not a real predicate; that is, it is not a
concept of something capable of being added to the concept of a thing."
"It is," he said, "merely the positing of a thing, or of certain determi-
nations, as existing in themselves." But now instead of saying that the
existential proposition is not a categorical proposition at all, neither an
analytic one in the Kantian sense, i.e., one in which the predicate is included in the subject, nor a synthetic, in which the subject does not
contain the predicate, Kant let himself be misled into including the
proposition among synthetic propositions. For he said that just as the
"is" of the copula ordinarily places two concepts in a relationship to
each other, the "is" of the existential proposition "places the object in
relationship to my concept." "The object," he says, "is added on
synthetically to my concept." This was but a partial remedy, unclear

Reprinted with the kind permission of the trustees of the Brentano Foundation
and of the translator, Professor D. B. Terrell, from Brentano's *Psychologie vom
empirischen Standpunkt*, Vol. 2, Ch. 7, §7 and §15.

and full of contradictions. Herbart made an end of it when he clearly distinguished existential propositions from categorical as a special type. Other philosophers have sided with him on this point and not just his numerous followers but also, to a certain degree, those like Trendelenburg who usually polemicized against the Herbartian school.

But there is still more. Even if all thinkers do not already recognize the interpretation of the existential proposition we have advanced to be correct, nevertheless at present they all grant, without exception, another truth from which it can be inferred with the utmost stringency. Even those who misconstrue the nature of the "is" and "is not" in the existential proposition nevertheless have a completely correct judgment of the "is" and "is not" which is added on to a subject and a predicate as copula. If they believe that the "is" and "is not" in the existential proposition signify something in and of themselves, that the former brings the presentation of the predicate, "existence," to the presentation of the subject in order to combine them; on the other hand, as far as the copula is concerned they recognize that, being without any meaning when taken all by itself, it only supplements the expression of presentations so as to make them expressions of affirmative and negative judgments. Let us hear, for example, from John Stuart Mill, who is our opponent in the interpretation of the existential proposition: "A predicate and a subject," he says, "are all that is necessarily required to make up a proposition: but as we cannot conclude from merely seeing two names put together, that they are a predicate and a subject, that is, that one of them is intended to be affirmed or denied of the other, it is necessary that there should be some mode or form of indicating that such is the intention; some sign to distinguish a predication from any other kind of discourse . . . this function is more commonly fulfilled by the word *is*, when an affirmation is intended, *is not*, when a negation; or by some other form of the verb *to be*. The word which thus serves the purpose of a sign of predication is called the copula." He then expressly distinguishes this "is" or "is not" of the copula from that which includes the concept of existence within its meaning. That is not only Mill's theory, but it may be said of all who do not agree with us in the interpretation of the existential proposition. We find it to be advanced by grammarians and lexicographers as well as logicians. And when John Stuart Mill credits James Mill with first having clearly developed this interpretation he is very much mistaken. He might have been able, for example, to find it in entirely the same way in the Port Royal Logic.

Well then — it requires no more than this admission, which our opponents universally make with respect to the copula, in order to deduce from it that no other function can be ascribed to the "is" and "is not" of the existential proposition either. For it can be shown most clearly that every categorical proposition can be translated into an existential one without any change in meaning and that in that event the "is" and "is not" of the existential proposition takes the place of the copula.

I will prove this with some examples.

The categorical proposition, "Some man is sick," has the same meaning as the existential proposition, "A sick man exists," or "There is a sick man."

The categorical proposition, "No stone is living," has the same meaning as the existential proposition, "A living stone does not exist," or "There is no living stone."

The categorical proposition, "All men are mortal" has the same meaning as the existential proposition, "An immortal man does not exist," or "There is no immortal man."[1]

The categorical proposition, "Some man is not learned," has the same meaning as the existential proposition, "A non-learned man exists," or "There is a non-learned man."

Since all of the four classes of categorical judgments which logicians are accustomed to distinguish are represented in the four examples I chose,[2] the possibility of the linguistic transformation of categorical propositions into existential is generally proved; and it is clear that the "is" and the "is not" of the existential proposition are nothing but equivalents of the copula, and so they are not predicates and are entirely meaningless taken all by themselves.

Yet is the reduction we have given of the four categorical propositions to existential ones really correct? It might be challenged by Herbart himself, whom we previously called upon as a witness. For his interpretation of the categorical propositions was completely different from our own. He believed that every categorical proposition expresses

[1] Ordinary logic says that the judgments, "All men are mortal," and "No men are not mortal," are equipollent. The truth is that they are identical.

[2] The particular affirmative, the universal negative, and the so-called (mistakenly) universal affirmative and particular negative. The truth, as the above reduction to the existential formula reveals clearly, is that no affirmative judgment is universal (in general it must then be called a judgment with individual content (*Materie*)) and no negative judgment is particular.

a hypothetical judgment, that the predicate is ascribed to or denied of the subject only on a certain presupposition, namely the presupposition of the existence of the subject. It was on precisely this point that he based his attempt to prove that the existential proposition could not be interpreted as a categorical one. In our opinion, on the contrary, a categorical proposition corresponds to a judgment which can just as well be expressed in the existential form and the truly affirmative categorical propositions include within themselves the affirmation of the subject.[3] But, as much as we approve of Herbart's view as to the "being" of the existential proposition, we cannot say that we agree with his derivation of it. To us this seems to be an example which provides excellent confirmation of Aristotle's remark to the effect that mistaken premises can lead to a correct conclusion. It is too much, even impossible to expect us to believe that the proposition, "Some man is walking," or the one introduced above, "Some man is sick," includes the tacit presupposition, "If indeed there is a man." And likewise it is not only incorrect, but without the least semblance to favor it, to say that the proposition, "Some man is not learned," makes this presupposition. In the proposition, "No stone is living," I wouldn't know at all what the limitation, "If indeed there is a stone," is supposed to mean. If there were no stones, then it would certainly be just as true that there are no living stones as it is now, when stones do exist. Only in the example, "All men are mortal" (one of the so-called universal affirmative propositions) does there appear to be a limiting condition included. It seems to assert the conjunction of "man" and "mortal." This conjunction of man and mortal obviously does not exist if no man exists. And yet the existence of a man cannot be inferred from the proposition, "All men are mortal." Consequently it seems to assert the conjunction of man and mortal only under the presupposition of the existence of a man. Nevertheless a glance at the existential proposition equivalent to this categorical proposition resolves the whole difficulty. It reveals that the proposition is not truly an affirmation but a denial, and therefore something like what we just said about the proposition, "No stone is living," holds true of it.

[3] Those which are truly affirmative are, according to what has been mentioned in a preceding note, the so-called particular affirmative and negative propositions. Those propositions which are truly negative (to which the universal affirmative propositions belong) in the very nature of the case do not include the affirmation of the subject, since generally they do not affirm anything, but deny something. An earlier comment shows why they do not also include the denial of the subject.

Moreover, if here I attacked Herbart's doctrine that all categorical propositions are hypothetical propositions, I did so only in order to justify in detail my translations into existential propositions given above, not because in case Herbart were correct such a reduction would be impossible. On the contrary, what I said of the categorical propositions holds true of hypothetical propositions; they too can all be clothed in the existential form and it comes out that they are purely negative assertions. An example will suffice to show how the same judgment, without the slightest change, can be expressed just as well in the form of a hypothetical as in that of a categorical and an existential proposition. The proposition, "If a man behaves badly, he injures himself," is a hypothetical proposition. As far as its meaning is concerned, however, it is the same as the categorical proposition, "All men who behave badly injure themselves." And this again has no other meaning than the existential proposition, "A man who behaves badly and does not injure himself does not exist," or "There is no man who behaves badly and does not injure himself." The clumsy form taken by the expression of the judgment in the existential form makes it very understandable why language has found other syntactical clothing for it as well, but there is nothing in the differences among the three propositions except differences of linguistic expression, even though the famed philosopher of Königsberg let himself be misled by such differences into assuming fundamental differences of judgment and basing special a priori categories on these "relations of judgments."

The reducibility of categorical, indeed the reducibility of all propositions which express a judgment to existential propositions is consequently certain. And this serves in two ways to confute the mistaken opinion which would find that what distinguishes judgment from presentation is the fact that it has a conjunction of attributes as its content. In the first place, in the reduction of the categorical to the existential proposition, the "being" of the existential proposition replaces the copula and so lets it be known that it no more involves a predicate term than the latter does. Further, it is seen quite plainly how the compounding of several elements which was believed to be so essential for the general and the specific nature of judgments, the combination of subject and predicate is in fact nothing but a matter of linguistic expression. . . .

In logic, too, the failure to understand the essence of judgment necessarily created further errors. I have thought through the idea's consequences in this direction and discovered that it leads to nothing less than a complete overthrow, but also a reconstruction of elementary logic. Everything then becomes simpler, clearer and more exact. I will only point out the contrast between the rules of this reformed logic and the traditional logic in some examples, since to carry it out and justify it completely would naturally delay us too long and lead us too far away from our theme.

The following three main rules, which can be directly applied to each figure and are perfectly sufficient by themselves for the testing of every syllogism, take the place of the earlier rules of categorical arguments:

1. Every [valid] categorical syllogism includes four terms, of which two are complementary to each other and the other two occur twice.

2. If the conclusion is negative, then each of the premises has in common with it its quality and one of its terms.

3. If the conclusion is affirmative, then the one premise has the same quality and an identical term, the other has the opposite quality and a complementary term.

These are rules which a logician of the old school will not hear without immediate horror. Every syllogism is supposed to have four terms: and he has always damned the *Quaternio terminorum* as a fallacy. Negative conclusions are supposed to have purely negative premises; and he has always taught that nothing can be inferred from two negative premises. There is also supposed to be a negative judgment among the premises of the affirmative conclusion; and he would have sworn that it unavoidably required two affirmative premises. Indeed, there is no room left at all for a categorical inference from affirmative premises; and he had taught that affirmative premises are best, since, when a negative is adjoined to them, he called it the "Pejor pars." Finally, nothing at all is heard about "universal" and "particular" in the new rules; and he had had these expressions in his mouth all the time, as it were. And have his old rules not shown themselves to be so well-adapted for the testing of syllogisms that conversely the thousand inferences measured by their criterion are themselves now proof and confirmation for them? Are we supposed to acknowledge that the celebrated inference: "All men are mortal, Caius is a man, therefore Caius is mortal," and all of its companions are no longer valid? — That seems an impossible demand.

But the situation is not as bad as all that. The mistakes from which the earlier rules of the syllogism arose consisted in the misunderstanding of the nature of judgments as concerns their form and content. Consequently, when the rules were consistently adhered to in their application, the disadvantageous effects of the errors for the most part cancelled each other out.[4] Of all the inferences which were said to be valid according to the rules which prevailed until now, only those in four forms were invalid, whereas on the other hand, to be sure, a not unimportant number of correct forms were overlooked.[5]

The consequences for the theory of so-called immediate inference were more damaging. Not only is the correct rule of conversion, for example, that every categorical proposition is simply convertible (one must only be clear about the true subject and predicate), but according to the old rules many conversions were regarded as valid which in fact are invalid, and vice versa. There is the same result with the so-called inferences by subalternation and opposition.[6]

Also, it proves to be the case, strangely enough, that when the old rules are critically compared with each other, they at times contradict each other, so that what is to be designated as valid according to the one is to be designated as invalid according to the other.

19 P. F. Strawson: ORTHODOX CRITICISMS OF THE SYSTEM (1952)

The most interesting questions which have arisen about the traditional logic are questions concerning the interpretation of the system. One might be inclined to think that there could scarcely be a problem here; that, with certain reservations regarding the word 'some,'

[4] For example, if, owing to the misunderstanding of the propositions, it was said that there are three terms in a valid categorical inference, the same misunderstanding caused three terms to be seen in particular arguments when in fact there were four.

[5] The latter fact was also recognized by the English logicians mentioned before [Boole and Bain]. The four invalid forms of which I am speaking are Barapti and Felapton (AAI and EAO) in the third figure and Bamalip and Fesapo (AAI and EAO) in the fourth.

[6] The conversion of a so-called universal affirmative proposition into a particular affirmative is not permissible; the usual inferences by subalternation are all invalid, and of those by opposition, the inferences to the falsity of the so-called contraries as well as to the truth of the so-called subcontraries.

Reprinted by permission of the publisher from *Introduction to Logical Theory* by P. F. Strawson. Methuen & Co. Ltd. (London, 1952.)

the rules listed give a perfectly acceptable account of the logical powers of the words which figure as the constants of the system, as these words are most commonly used in ordinary speech; and that hence the solution of the interpretation-problem is simply to equate the constants of the system with those words in their standard or typical employment. I shall try to show in the end that, with a few reservations, this naïve view is also the correct one. It has been so frequently disputed, however, that it has become orthodoxy to deny it; and, indeed, to go further and maintain that the constants of the system cannot be given any interpretation such that (a) they have roughly the same meaning as in ordinary speech and (b) all the rules of the system hold good together for that interpretation. It is, in other words, maintained that no consistent interpretation can be found for the system as a whole which approximates to the naïve interpretation. I want to show that this thesis is false; and false in an important way. For in seeing just how it is false, we come to notice an important general feature of the ordinary use of language which is systematically neglected in modern formal logic. For the proper purposes of that logic, this neglect is unimportant; it becomes important only when it impairs our understanding of ordinary speech.

Criticisms of the traditional system have centered round the question of whether or not, in using a sentence of one of the four forms, we are to be regarded as committing ourselves to the existence of anything answering to the description given by the first term of the sentence. It is felt that this question cannot be left unanswered; for the answer to it makes a difference to the validity of the laws. It is argued that the usage of the ordinary words (e.g., 'all') corresponding to some of the constants of the system varies in this respect. Everyone agrees that it would be absurd to claim that the man who says 'All the books in his room are by English authors' has made a true statement, if the room referred to has no books in it at all. Here is a case where the use of 'all' carries the existential commitment. On the other hand, it is said, we sometimes use 'all' without this commitment. To take a classic example: the statement made by 'All moving bodies not acted upon by external forces continue in a state of uniform motion in a straight line' may well be true even if there never have been or will be any moving bodies not acted upon by external forces. The consistency-problem for the traditional system is then posed as follows. We must decide, with regard to each of the four forms, whether it carries the existential commitment or whether it does not. But, for any plausible decision, i.e., any decision which keeps the constants of the system reasonably close in sense to their use as words of ordinary speech, we find that some of the laws of the traditional system become invalid. It has generally been assumed that, in the case of the particular forms, i.e., I and O, only one decision was reasonable, viz., that they did carry the existential commitment; and that whichever decision was made for one of the universal forms, the same decision should be made for the other. So the problem reduced itself to a dilemma. Either the A and E forms have existential import or they do not. If they do, one set of laws has to be sacrificed as invalid; if they do not, another set has to go. Therefore no consistent interpretation of the system as a whole, within the prescribed limits, is possible. . . .

[Interpreting each of the traditional forms in terms of the predicative calculus and not giving existential import to the A and E forms gives the following translations: *

Table 1

$$A \quad \sim (\exists x)(fx . \sim gx) \text{ or } (x)(fx \supset gx)$$
$$E \quad \sim (\exists x)(fx . gx) \quad \text{ or } (x)(fx \supset \sim gx)$$
$$I \quad (\exists x)(fx . gx) \quad \text{ or } \sim (x)(fx \supset \sim gx)$$
$$O \quad (\exists x)(fx . \sim gx) \quad \text{ or } \sim (x)(fx \supset gx)$$

Of the traditionally sanctioned inferences, those which fail to hold on this interpretation are: conversion *per accidens* of the A and E, 'weakened' contraposition of the E, all the laws of the Square of Opposition except those involving contradictories, and nine of the twenty-four valid syllogisms (those involving inferences from two universal premises to a particular conclusion, e.g., AAI in the first figure.)

Interpreting each of the traditional forms in terms of the predicative calculus and giving existential import to the A and E forms gives the following translations:

Table 2

$$A \quad \sim (\exists x)(fx . \sim gx) . (\exists x)(fx)$$
$$E \quad \sim (\exists x)(fx . gx) . (\exists x)((fx)$$
$$I \quad (\exists x)(fx . gx)$$
$$O \quad (\exists x)(fx . \sim gx)$$

*I have summarized here the details of the dilemma. Ed.

This interpretation renders invalid the conversion *per accidens* of the E, the simple conversion of the E and several forms of the syllogism which depend upon it, the subcontrariety of I and O, and the contradictory relations between A and O and between E and I.]

The dilemma, then, is a clear one. It rests upon the assumption that the only two unambiguous interpretations of the system for which its constants approximate in sense to their ordinary use are the two just considered. Unless this assumption can be shown to be mistaken, the conclusion must be accepted that there is no consistent and acceptable interpretation of the system as a whole.

This conclusion, and the assumption upon which it rests, are in fact mistaken. It is perfectly possible to find interpretations for the A, E, I, and O forms for which all the laws of the traditional system hold good together. There are at least two distinct, though related, methods by which this can be done. One has only a limited and formalistic interest; the other illuminates some general features of our ordinary speech. But though they are very different in certain respects, the ways in which they operate to save the consistency of the system are closely related. I give the formalistic solution first, partly for the sake of completeness and partly for the light it casts on the second, or realistic, solution.

The first method consists simply in a further elaboration of the kind of interpretation in class or quantificational terms which we have been considering. It is a kind of *ad hoc* patching up of the old system in order to represent it, in its entirety, as a fragment of the new. The method is to encounter every breakdown in a traditional law by amending the class or predicative interpretation suggested in such a way as to secure its validity. . . .* So we have, as our final interpretation:

Table 3

A $\sim (\exists x)(fx . \sim gx) . (\exists x)(fx) . (\exists x)(\sim gx)$
E $\sim (\exists x)(fx . gx) . (\exists x)(fx) . (\exists x)(gx)$
I $(\exists x)(fx . gx) \lor \sim (\exists x)(fx) \lor \sim (\exists x)(gx)$
O $(\exists x)(fx . \sim gx) \lor \sim (\exists x)(fx) \lor \sim (\exists x)(\sim gx) .$

For this interpretation, all the laws of the traditional logic hold good together; and they hold good within the logic of classes or quantified formulae; as a part of that logic.

* The detailed working-out of this method has here been omitted. Ed.

So the consistency of the system can be secured in this way. But the price paid for consistency will seem a high one, if we are at all anxious that the constants 'all,' 'some,' and 'no' of the system should faithfully reflect the typical logical behaviour of these words in ordinary speech. It is quite unplausible to suggest that if someone says 'Some students of English will get Firsts this year,' it is a sufficient condition of his having made a true statement, that no one at all should get a First. But this would be a consequence of accepting the above interpretation for I. Note that the dropping of the implication of plurality in 'some' makes only a minor contribution to the unplausibility of the translation. We should think the above suggestion no more convincing in the case of someone who said 'At least one student of English will get a First this year.' The third table of translations, then, does, if anything, less than the other two to remove our sense of separation from the mother tongue.

So let us start again, taking the latter as our guide. And let us not be bound by the assumption from which all these difficulties have arisen; namely, that whatever interpretation we give to the four forms, it must be an interpretation in explicitly existential terms; that all statements of the four forms must be positively or negatively existential, or both. Suppose someone says 'All John's children are asleep.' Obviously he will not normally, or properly, say this, unless he believes that John has children (who are asleep). But suppose he is mistaken. Suppose John has no children. Then is it true or false that all John's children are asleep? Either answer would seem to be misleading. But we are not compelled to give either answer. We can, and normally should, say that, since John has no children, the question does not arise. But if the form of the statement were

$$\sim(\exists x)(fx \cdot \sim gx) \qquad \text{[Table 1]}$$

the correct answer to the question, whether it is true, would be 'Yes'; for '$\sim(\exists x)(fx)$' is a sufficient condition of the truth of '$\sim(\exists x)(fx \cdot \sim gx)$.' And if the form of the statement were either

$$\sim(\exists x)(fx \cdot \sim gx) \cdot (\exists x)(fx) \qquad \text{[Table 2]}$$
$$\text{or} \qquad \sim(\exists x)(fx \cdot \sim gx) \cdot (\exists x)(fx) \cdot (\exists x)(\sim gx) \qquad \text{[Table 3]}$$

the correct answer to the question would be that the statement was false; for '$\sim(\exists x)(fx)$' is inconsistent with both these formulae. But one does not happily give either answer simply on the ground that the subject-class is empty. One says rather that the question of the truth or falsity of the statement simply does not arise; that one of the conditions for answering the question one way or the other is not fulfilled.

The adoption of any of the explicitly existential analyses, whether it be a negatively existential one (Table 1) or a conjunction of negatively and positively existential components (Tables 2 and 3), forces us to conclude that the *non-existence* of any children of John's is sufficient to determine the truth or falsity of the general statement; makes it true for the first analysis, false for the other two. The more realistic view seems to be that the existence of children of John's is a necessary pre-condition not merely of the truth of what is said, but of its being *either* true *or* false. And this suggests the possibility of interpreting all the four Aristotelian forms on these lines: that is, as forms such that the question of whether statements exemplifying them are true or false is one that does not arise unless the subject-class has members.

It is important to understand why people have hesitated to adopt such a view of at least some general statements. It is probably the opera-tion of the trichotomy 'either true or false or meaningless,' as applied to statements, which is to blame. For this trichotomy contains a confusion: the confusion between sentence and statement. Of course, the sentence 'All John's children are asleep' is not meaningless. It is perfectly signifi-cant. But it is senseless to ask, of the *sentence*, whether it is true or false. One must distinguish between what can be said about the sentence, and what can be said about the statements made, on different occasions, by the use of the sentence. It is about statements only that the question of truth or falsity can arise; and about these it can sometimes fail to arise. But to say that the man who uses the sentence in our imagined case fails to say anything either true or false, is not to say that the sentence he pronounces is meaningless. Nor is it to deny that he makes a mistake. Of course, it is incorrect (or deceitful) for him to use this sentence unless (*a*) he thinks he is referring to some children whom he thinks to be asleep; (*b*) he thinks that John has children; (*c*) he thinks that the children he is referring to are John's. We might say that in using the sentence he *commits himself* to the existence of children of John's. It would prima facie be a kind of logical absurdity to say 'All John's children are asleep; but John has no children.' And we may be tempted to think of this kind of logical absurdity as a straightforward self-contradiction; and hence be led once more towards an analysis like that of Table 2; and hence to the conclusion that the man who says

'All John's children are asleep,' when John has no children, makes a false statement. But there is no need to be led, by noticing this kind of logical absurdity, towards this conclusion. For if a statement S presupposes a statement S' in the sense that the truth of S' is a precondition of the truth-or-falsity of S, then of course there will be a kind of logical absurdity in conjoining S with the denial of S'. This is precisely the relation, in our imagined case, between the statement that all John's children are asleep (S) and the statement that John has children, that there exist children of John's (S'). But we must distinguish this kind of logical absurdity from straightforward self-contradiction. It is self-contradictory to conjoin S with the denial of S' if S' is a necessary condition of the truth, simply, of S. It is a different kind of logical absurdity to conjoin S with the denial of S' if S' is a necessary condition of the *truth or falsity* of S. The relation between S and S' in the first case is that S entails S'. We need a different name for the relation between S and S' in the second case; let us say, as above, that S *presupposes* S'.

Underlying the failure to distinguish sentence and statement, and the bogus trichotomy 'true, false, or meaningless,' we may detect a further logical prejudice which helps to blind us to the facts of language. We may describe this as the belief or, perhaps better, as the wish, that if the uttering of a sentence by one person, at one time, at one place, results in a true statement, then the uttering of that sentence by any other person, at any other time, at any other place, results in a true statement. It is, of course, incredible that any formal logician should soberly believe this. It is, however, very natural that they should wish it were so; and hence talk as if it were so. And to those tempted to talk as if it were so, the distinction I have insisted upon between sentence and statement will not occur or will seem unimportant. Why this wish-belief should be natural to formal logicians, and what further effects it has, I shall discuss later.

What I am proposing, then, is this. There are many ordinary sentences beginning with such phrases as 'All . . .,' 'All the . . .,' 'No . . .,' 'None of the . . .,' 'Some . . .,' 'Some of the . . .,' 'At least one . . .,' 'At least one of the . . .' which exhibit, in their standard employment, parallel characteristics to those I have just described in the case of a representative 'All . . .' sentence. That is to say, the existence of members of the subject-class is to be regarded as presupposed (in the special sense described) by statements made by the use of these sentences; to be regarded as a necessary condition, not of the truth

simply, but of the truth or falsity, of such statements. I am proposing that the four Aristotelian forms should be interpreted as forms of statement of this kind. Will the adoption of this proposal protect the system from the charge of being inconsistent when interpreted? Obviously it will. For every case of invalidity, of breakdown in the laws, arose from the non-existence of members of some subject-class being compatible with the truth, or with the falsity, of some statement of one of the four forms. So our proposal, which makes the non-existence of members of the subject-class incompatible with either the truth or the falsity of any statement of these forms, will cure all these troubles at one stroke. We are to imagine that every logical rule of the system, when expressed in terms of truth and falsity, is preceded by the phrase 'Assuming that the statements concerned are either true or false, then . . .' Thus the rule that A is the contradictory of O states that, *if corresponding statements of the A and O forms both have truth-values*, then they must have opposite truth-values; the rule that A entails I states that, *if corresponding statements of these forms have truth-values*, then if the statement of the A form is true, the statement of the I form must be true; and so on. The suggestion that entailment-rules should be understood in this way is not peculiar to the present case. What is peculiar to the present case is the requirement that, in order for any statement of one of the four forms to have a truth-value, to be true or false, it is necessary that the subject-class should have members.

That the adoption of this suggestion will save the rules of the traditional system from breakdown is obvious enough for all the rules except, perhaps, those permitting, or involving the validity of, the simple conversion of E and of I. That the subject-class referred to in a statement of either of these forms must be non-empty in order for the statement to be true or false does not guarantee, in the case of the truth of an E statement or the falsity of an I statement, the non-emptiness of the predicate-class. This was the reason why the final interpretations of Table 3 required three components for each form instead of two. But, whilst this is true, it does not constitute an objection, nor lead to the breakdown of the rules as we are now to understand them. Thus perhaps a statement of the form '*x*E*y*' might be true while the corresponding statement of the form '*y*E*x*' was neither true nor false. But all that we require is that so long as corresponding statements of the forms '*x*E*y*' and '*y*E*x*' are both either true or false, they must either be both true or both false. This is secured to us by interpreting '*x*E*y*' as the form

of hosts of ordinary statements, beginning with 'No . . .' or 'None of the
. . .,' of the kind described in this section.

Similar considerations hold for I; though mention of I reminds us
of one not unimportant reservation we must make, before simply
concluding that the constants 'all,' 'some,' 'no' of the traditional system
can be understood, without danger to any of the rules, as having just
the sense which these words have in the hosts of ordinary statements of
the kind we are discussing. And this is a point already made: viz., that
'some,' in its most common employment as a separate word, carries an
implication of plurality which is inconsistent with the requirement that
O should be the strict contradictory of A, and I of E. So 'some,' occurring as a constant of the system, is to be interpreted as 'At least one . . .'
or 'At least one of the . . .,' while 'all' and 'no,' so occurring, can be
read as themselves.

The interpretation which I propose for the traditional forms has,
then, the following merits: (*a*) it enables the whole body of the laws of
the system to be accepted without inconsistency; (*b*) with the reservation
noted above, it gives the constants of the system just the sense which
they have in a vast group of statements of ordinary speech; (*c*) it empha-
sizes an important general feature of statements of that group, viz.,
that while the existence of members of their subject-classes is not a part
of what is asserted in such statements, it is, in the sense we have examined, presupposed by them. It is this last feature which makes it unplausible to regard assertions of existence as either the whole, or conjunctive or disjunctive parts, of the sense of such ordinary statements as
'All the men at work on the scaffolding have gone home' or 'Some of the
men are still at work.' This was the reason why we were unhappy about
regarding such expressions as '$(x)(fx \supset gx)$,' as giving the form of these
sentences; and why our uneasiness was not to be removed by the simple
addition of positively or negatively existential formulae. Even the
resemblance between 'There is not a single book in his room which is
not by an English author' and the negatively existential form '$\sim(\exists x)$
$(fx \cdot \sim gx)$' was deceptive. The former, as normally used, carries the presupposition 'books-in-his-room' and is far from being entailed by 'not-a-
book-in-his-room'; whereas the latter is entailed by '$\sim(\exists x)(fx)$.' So
it is that if someone, with a solemn face, says 'There is not a single
foreign book in his room' and then later reveals that there are no books
in the room at all, we have the sense, not of having been lied to, but of
having been made the victim of a sort of linguistic outrage. Of course

he did not *say* there *were* any books in the room, so he has not said anything false. Yet what he said gave us the right to assume that there were, so he has misled us. For what he said to be true (or false) it is necessary (though not sufficient) that there should be books in the room. Of this subtle sort is the relation between 'There is not a book in his room which is not by an English author' and 'There are books in his room.'[1] What weakens our resistance to the negatively existential analysis in this case more than in the case of the corresponding 'All'-sentence is the powerful attraction of the negative opening phrase 'There is not. . . .'

To avoid misunderstanding I must add one point about this proposed interpretation of the forms of the traditional system. I do not claim that it faithfully represents the intentions of its principal exponents. They were, perhaps, more interested in formulating rules governing the logical relations of more imposing general statements than the everyday ones I have mostly considered; were interested, for example, in the logical powers of scientific generalizations, or of other sentences which approximate more closely to the desired conditions that if their utterance by anyone, at any time, at any place, results in a true statement, then so does their utterance by anyone else, at any other time, at any other place. We have yet to consider how far the account here given of certain general sentences of common speech is adequate for all generalizations.

---

[1] Some will say these points are irrelevant to logic (are 'merely pragmatic'). If to call them 'irrelevant to logic' is to say that they are not considered in formal systems, then this is a point I should wish not to dispute, but to emphasize. But to logic as concerned with the relations between general classes of statements occurring in ordinary use, with the general conditions under which such statements are correctly called 'true' or 'false,' these points are not irrelevant. Certainly a 'pragmatic' consideration, a general rule of linguistic conduct, may perhaps be seen to underlie these points: the rule, namely, that one does not make the (logically) lesser, when one could truthfully (and with equal or greater linguistic economy) make the greater, claim. Assume for a moment that the form 'There is not a single . . . which is not . . .' were *introduced* into ordinary speech with the same sense as '$\sim(\exists x)(fx \cdot \sim gx)$.' Then the operation of this general rule would inhibit the use of this form where one could truly say simply 'There is not a single . . .' (or '$\sim(\exists x)(fx)$'). And the operation of this inhibition would tend to confer on the introduced form just those logical presuppositions which I have described; the form would tend, if it did not remain otiose, to develop just those differences I have emphasized from the logic of the symbolic form it was introduced to represent. The operation of this 'pragmatic rule' was first pointed out to me, in a different connexion, by Mr. H. P. Grice.

Regimentation

20 P. F. Strawson: TWO KINDS OF LOGIC

I. FORMAL LOGIC: APPLICATIONS AND LIMITATIONS

Language is used for a variety of purposes. The normal use of some sentences is to give orders; of others, to ask questions; of yet others, to take oaths, to convey greetings, to make apologies, or to give thanks. When sentences are used in any of these ways it makes no sense to inquire whether what is said is true or false. But the normal use of an indefinitely large number of sentences is to say things to which this inquiry is appropriate. Such sentences as these I have called, by an easily understood brachylogy, 'statement-making sentences.' To know the meaning of a sentence of this kind is to know under what conditions someone who used it would be making a true statement; to *explain* the meaning is to *say* what these conditions are. One way of giving a partial account of these conditions is to say what some of the entailments of the sentence are. For to say that one sentence entails another is to say that a statement made by the use of the first is true only if the corresponding statement made by the use of the second is true; and to say that one sentence entails and is entailed by another is to say that a statement made by the use of the first is true if, and only if, the corresponding statement made by the use of the second is true. This might make us think that to give the two-way entailments (the logical equivalents) of a statement-making sentence is all that can be done, in the way of *saying*,

Reprinted by permission of the publisher from *Introduction to Logical Theory* by P. F. Strawson. Methuen & Co. Ltd. (London, 1952.)

to give its meaning. And since the meaning of sentences can sometimes be explained simply by talking, we may think that, in such cases, this is all that ever *need* be done; that where talking can explain, this is the only kind of talking we can do and the only kind we need do.

To think this is to make a mistake, though a common one. Let us return to the point that to explain the meaning of a statement-making sentence is to say under what conditions someone who used it would be making a true statement: and let us call this 'giving the rules of use' of the sentence. We have just noticed the temptation to think that the only kind of rules involved are entailment-rules. I want to show, first, that this view is false, and, second, that the fact of its falsity imposes an unavoidable limitation on the scope and application of formal logic. The limitation in question is not one to be deplored or to be welcomed. It is one to be noticed; for the failure to notice it leads to logical mythology.

It is a fact I have remarked upon before, that the questions, whom a sentence is uttered by, and where and when it is uttered, may be relevant to the question of whether a true statement is made by its utterance. The same sentence in different mouths may be used to make one true, and one false, statement ('My cat is dead'); the same sentence in the same mouth at different times may be used to make one true, and one false, statement ('My cat is dead'); and so on. (Not only is this true of the majority of the statement-making sentences we use in ordinary speech. It is also an unavoidable feature of any language we might construct to serve the same general purposes. But I shall not try to prove this; for it is with ordinary discourse that I am concerned.) Since this is so, the assertion that a sentence S entails a sentence S′ cannot be generally taken to mean that if any statement made by the use of the first is true, then any statement made by the use of the second would be true. It must rather be taken to mean the following: If, at some time, at some place, in the mouth of some speaker, the utterance of S results or would result in a true statement, then the utterance of S′ at that time, at that place, in the mouth of that speaker, would result in a true statement. So the entailments of S may tell us to what *kind* of situation S may be correctly applied; they do not give general instructions enabling us to determine whether, in the mouth of a certain speaker, at a certain time, at a certain place, S is being applied to a situation of that kind. Such general instructions can be given; but not by entailment-rules. Entailment-rules, as the above schematic formulation shows, abstract from the time and place of the utterance and the identity of the utterer: so they cannot tell the whole story about the conditions under which a sentence is used to make a true statement, unless the sentence is one of which it is true that, if its utterance by any-one, at any time, at any place results in a true statement, then its utter-ance by anyone else, at any other time, at any other place, results in a true statement.

Entailment-rules, then, must be supplemented by rules of another kind. We may call these 'referring rules.' Referring rules take account of what entailment-rules abstract from, viz., the time and place of the utterance and the identity of the utterer. Examples of referring rules are: the word 'I' is correctly used by a speaker to refer to himself; the word 'you' is correctly used to refer to the person or persons whom the speaker is addressing; one of the correct uses of the present tense is for the description of states of affairs contemporaneous with the describing of them; the past tense is correctly used to indicate that the situation or event reported is temporally prior to the report. Elucidation of some or all of the uses of such words as 'the,' 'a,' 'over there,' 'he,' 'they,' 'now,' 'here,' 'this,' 'those' are elucidations of referring rules; so are some discussions of the uses of the many tenses of verbs. Consideration of these and other examples shows that the description I gave of the factors taken account of by referring rules (viz., time and place of utter-ance, and identity of the speaker) must be generously interpreted. These factors embrace many distinguishable features of what, in a wide sense of the word, might be called the *context* of an utterance. A refer-ring rule lays down a *contextual requirement* for the correct employment of an expression. But the fact that the contextual requirement is satis-fied is not a part of what is *asserted* by the use of a sentence containing an expression governed (in this use) by a referring rule: it is, rather, pre-supposed by the use of the expression, in the sense of 'presupposed' which I introduced in Chapter 6.* Thus, if someone says, 'He will die in the course of the next two months,' it is linguistically outrageous to reply, 'No, he won't' *and then give as one's reason* 'He's dead already.' If the event has already taken place, the question whether it will take place within the next two months or not is a question which does not arise. 'He's dead already' disputes the presupposition that his death lies in the future, that he is not dead already. But it does not *contradict* the original statement, since to do this would be to admit its presupposi-

* See above, p. 223. Ed.

tions; and hence does not contradict anything entailed by the original statement. The fact that the fulfilment of the contextual requirement is not part of what is asserted by the use of a sentence containing an expression governed by a referring rule thus involves and is involved by the distinction between referring rules and entailment-rules.

Formal logic is concerned with the meanings of sentences only in so far as these can be given by entailment-rules. Indeed, its concern is far more limited than this suggests, for only a relatively small subclass of highly general entailment-rules are of interest to the logician. Hence formal logic systematically ignores the referring element in ordinary speech. This fact helps to explain the preoccupation of formal logic with certain types of sentence; and helps to explain also the popularity among logicians of certain collateral doctrines such as I discussed in Chapter 6. From the logician's point of view, the ideal type of sentence is one of which the meaning is entirely given by entailment-rules; that is, it is one from which the referring element is absent altogether; that is, roughly, it is one of which it is true that if its utterance at any time, at any place, by any speaker, results in a true statement, then its utterance at any other time, at any other place, by any other speaker, results in a true statement. Almost the only types of contingent sentence (i.e., sentence the utterance of which would result in a contingent statement) which seem able fully to realize this ideal are positively and negatively existential sentences, of which some forms are studied by the predicative calculus, or sentences compounded of these. That sentences of this sort may realize the ideal is easily seen. For the main, though not the only, referring elements, of sentences which contain such elements, are of two types: (1) the time-indications, relative to the moment of utterance of the sentence, which are given by the tenses of verbs; (2) the logical subjects, i.e., the separate words or phrases used to pick out the object or objects, person or persons, etc., which are being referred to. Neither of these elements need be present in a sentence exemplifying one of the positively or negatively existential forms studied in the calculus. For (1), as we have already seen, '$(\exists x)$' must be interpreted as, if not temporally ambiguous, either timeless or omnitemporal; and (2) since such a sentence is existential, it need contain no expression which functions as a logical subject. Of course, in so far as we attempt to cast ordinary empirical statements into one of these forms, we may find one or both of these types of referring element in the subordinate clauses of the resulting existential sentence. But the logician is concerned with the form; and here he seems to have found a form which *can* be exemplified by sentences entirely free from referring elements.

A qualification must be added here. It is not quite true that the only contingent sentences which answer to this ideal of independence of context of utterance are those sentences which are entirely free from referring elements. For law-sentences in general answer to this ideal; and therefore subject-predicate law-sentences answer to it; for although they contain a referring element of the second type, the reference is to an open class, and is therefore independent of contextual conditions.

All necessary statements may be said to answer, though in a different way, to the ideal of independence of context. For sentences embodying necessary statements are merely the analogues of higher-order sentences stating entailments, or else other logical relations which can be re-expressed as entailments. Their use is not to describe or report or forecast. They embody entailment-rules, and, like them, abstract from contextual conditions. So one does not in making them refer to any part of the world, or to any stretch or moment of the world's history; and the present tense, in which they are generally, though not necessarily, framed, is, not the omnitemporal, but the timeless present. We have already seen that, with certain safeguards, the symbolism of modern logic may be used in writing some of them.

I shall return later to the consideration of the sentences which do answer to the logician's ideal. But first I want once more to stress the obvious fact that the vast majority of the statement-making sentences we ever have, or might have, occasion to use in ordinary speech do not answer to it. For in this contrast between the logically ideal type of sentence and the types we mostly employ is the final explanation of many facts which I have mentioned in earlier chapters; particularly in the last three. For example, it explains how it is that many features of the use of ordinary speech which are sufficiently general to deserve consideration under such a title as 'The Logic of Language' are necessarily omitted from consideration under the narrower title 'Formal Logic.' Here I may instance such features as the uses of 'a' and 'the'; the presupposition-relation between certain subject–predicate statements and certain existence-statements; the functions of the various grammatical tenses. Second, it explains the *acharnement* with which differing types of subject-predicate statements are assimilated to negatively and/or positively existential forms, with the result that both their general character and the differences between them are obscured. This is a natural consequence; for the formal logician is reluctant to admit, or even envisage the possibility, that his analytical equipment is inadequate for the dissection of most ordinary types of empirical statement. Third, it explains the myth of the logically proper name and reveals the full importance of the myth. The logically proper name is envisaged as a type of referring expression which shall be free from the unideal characteristics which all referring expressions possess. If there did exist a class of expressions the meaning of each of which was identical with a single object, then of course the use of any expression of that class to refer to the appropriate object would be independent of contextual conditions. A contingent sentence of the form 'fx,' where the predicate replacing 'f' was omnitemporal and the individual expression replacing 'x' was an expression of this class, would have the ideal characteristic that, if its utterance at any time, at any place, in the mouth of any speaker, resulted in a true statement, then its utterance at any other time, at any other place, in the mouth of any other speaker, would result in a true statement. Now the whole structure of quantificational logic, with its apparatus of individual variables, seems, or has seemed to most of its exponents, to require, for its application to ordinary empirical speech to be possible, that there should exist individual referring expressions which could appear as values of the individual variables. That is to say, the whole structure has seemed to presuppose the existence of simple predicative sentences of the form 'fx.' The belief in logically proper names made it possible to assume both that there were such sentences and that they were of the logically ideal type; and thus helped to preserve the illusion that formal logic was an adequate instrument for the dissection of ordinary speech. In fact, there *are* such sentences, but they are *not* of the logically ideal type. Finally, the preoccupation with the ideal type of sentence explains the persistent neglect of the distinction between sentence and statement. For, in the case of sentences of the ideal type, the distinction really *is* unimportant. Such a sentence whenever it is used, is used to make one and the same statement; the contextual conditions of its use are irrelevant to the truth or falsity of that statement. To this type of sentence the otherwise bogus trichotomy 'true, false, or meaningless' may be harmlessly applied. . . .

II. TYPE-DIFFERENCES AND FORMATION-RULES

We have seen that at an early stage in the development of any logical system rules should be laid down prescribing what combinations of the symbols of the system are permissible. These are the formation-rules of the system. Expressions framed in accordance with them are called well-formed; and combinations of symbols which violate them are said to be ill-formed. Ill-formed expressions are without meaning: the deductive or testing technique of the system cannot be applied to them; and, when the system is interpreted, no sense is given to such expressions. The framing of formation-rules obviously presupposes the classification of the constants and variables of the system into different types. For to give formation-rules is to say what classes of symbols of the system can significantly figure in combinations of certain kinds with other types of symbols of the system. When the system is given a linguistic interpretation, this classification of expressions into types is obviously carried over into the domain of words and phrases: it applies to the verbal expressions which can figure as values of the variables of the system, and to the verbal expressions used to interpret its constants. So we may expect to find some restrictions on the significant combinations of the expressions of ordinary language, which are analogous to the formation-rules of a linguistically interpretable system. And, so long as we do not insist overmuch on their strictness, we do find such analogies. We find them, we may say, in the rules (some of the rules) of grammar. Grammarians, like logicians, classify expressions into types. Given that a sentence is to contain an expression of one grammatical type, then the rules of grammar will often lay down requirements concerning other types of expression it must contain and, sometimes, the method of their arrangement. If these requirements are not satisfied, then no sentence, or an ungrammatical sentence, is obtained. 'Ungrammatical' is, roughly speaking, the linguistic analogue of 'ill-formed.' To take some examples. (1) The formation-rules of the propositional calculus require that '·' or '$\lor$' should be flanked at least by two statement-variables in a well-formed expression. Grammar describes the role of conjunctions like 'or' and 'and' as that of joining two like clauses or phrases. (2) In a formal system which made a notational distinction between one-place and two-place predicates, there would be a formation-rule to the effect that a two-place predicate required at least two individual variables or expressions to figure in a well-formed expression. Compare this with the grammatical requirement that a transitive verb should have both a subject and an object. (3) Logic does not allow 'xyz' as a well-formed expression. Grammar does not allow 'Tom, Dick, Harry' as a sentence.

It is clear that the parallels could be multiplied. It is also clear that they cannot be pressed at all closely. Grammatical classifications are of many different kinds, are difficult to formulate clearly, and not always easy to apply. This is natural; for they deal with living or once-living languages and not with invented symbolisms. Formal classifications are precisely stated, and can be made as easy to apply as he who chooses the symbolism desires. No sense is given to expressions which violate the formation-rules of a system. But many ungrammatical sentences make sense, and so do many expressions which are not sentences at all, but which, if written, would be written between full stops; and context may confer upon a single word the force of a sentence. Even where the detailed analogies seem at their closest, they may break down: 'Either there will be war or not' is a perfectly good sentence; but '$p \vee \sim$' is an ill-formed expression.

Although the analogies cannot be pressed too closely, it is evident that, where they exist, they have a common root. Earlier we saw how the *formal* distinction between individual and predicative variables reflects the *functional* distinction between referring to something and describing it; and how this is correspondingly reflected by the *grammatical* distinction between subject and predicate. The formation-rule that an individual variable must be escorted by a predicative variable, the grammatical rule that a sentence must have a predicate as well as a subject, have their root in the necessary fact that no statement is made by referring alone. Similarly, the grammatical need which conjunctions have for two clauses, the formal need which statement connectives have for two statement-variables, alike reflect a cluster of tautologies: as that, for example, one cannot say that one thing is conditional upon another without indicating *both* what is conditional *and* upon what it is conditional. It might be asked why distinguish the root tautology from the formal or grammatical requirement? The answer is that the linguistic devices by which statements of different kinds are made might conceivably have been quite different from those we are familiar with. Both the grammatical rules and the formation-rules reflect, not only the root tautology, but the kind of linguistic devices we actually employ.

So the formation-rules of a system, which rigidly proscribe certain combinations of expressions as nonsense, have genuine connexions with those grammatical rules which yield no more than a presumption against certain kinds of combinations of words making sense. They both reflect very general necessities of language. The formation-rules of a system are related to their grammatical analogues somewhat as the entailment-rules of a system are related to their analogues in ordinary speech: the former are rigid and systematic, the latter flexible and unsystematic.

Now we saw that entailments of sufficient generality to interest the formal logician were not the only entailments to be found in ordinary speech. Similarly, we find that the grammatical requirements which are analogous to formation-rules are not the only requirements a sentence must satisfy if it is to make sense. No grammatical rule is infringed by saying that the cube root of ten is three miles away or that there is a loud smell in the drawing-room. But to say either of these things would be, if not to talk nonsense, at least to say something which had no literal or straightforward sense. The sentences 'He knows French well' and 'He knows French slowly' have the same grammatical structure; but whereas the first makes sense as it stands, the second can be given a sense only by taking it as bad English for, e.g., 'He is slowly getting to know French' or 'He can read French slowly' or 'He can understand French when it is spoken slowly.' Similarly, 'The average tax-payer is dissatisfied with the Budget' makes straightforward sense, whereas 'The average tax-payer died yesterday' would be a joke, an epigram, or a piece of nonsense.

It seems, then, that there are additional restrictions, besides those laxly imposed by grammar, on the ways in which words may be combined to make literal sense. We may refer to these as type-restrictions or type-rules; for they rule out combinations of expressions of certain types. Some have been tempted to assimilate violation of type-restrictions to self-contradictions. But this seems a mistake. The reason why 'loud smell' makes no sense is not that smells, like murmurs, are necessarily soft. Referring to something as a smell proscribes as senseless the question whether it is loud or not loud: it does not commit the speaker to one of two incompatible answers to the question. Instead of assimilating non-grammatical type-restrictions to non-formal entailments, we had better recognize a parallel relationship: between grammatical type-restrictions and non-grammatical type-restrictions on the one hand; and between formal entailments (i.e., entailments of the generality which interests the logician) and non-formal (lexicographers') entailments on the other. No one, after all, would want to assimilate grammatical rules to highly general entailments.

There is a certain metaphysical view, opposed to the conclusions of the last section, to which a preoccupation with formal logic may incline us. It may be summarily expressed as the view that the only irreducible type-differences are those which formal logic recognizes; that all other type-differences between expressions are ultimately explicable as differences between the logical forms of the sentences which contain them. This requires explanation. Formal logic commits us to a distinction in type between singular referring expressions (values of individual variables) and predicative expressions (values of predicative variables). But obviously the considerations of the last section require us to make further type-distinctions within each of these types. For example, the names of human qualities and the names of individual human beings may alike figure as singular referring expressions. But not everything that can, with literal significance, be said of individual human beings can, with literal significance, be said of individual human qualities; and conversely. To put it very roughly: the ranges of expressions with which the names of men and the names of men's qualities can be significantly combined are different. It can sometimes be plausibly maintained, however, that a singular statement about a human quality is logically equivalent to a general statement about human beings. In such a case we may be encouraged to say that the difference in type between expressions playing formally similar roles in formally similar sentences has been reduced to a difference in form between sentences about things of the same type (viz., human beings). Sometimes it is said that the translation of the singular into the general statement discloses the 'real' logical form of the former.

This manoeuvre has several interesting features. If we commit ourselves to the last of the steps mentioned, then we are giving to the expression 'logical form' a quite different *sense* from any in which we have used it hitherto. For why, of the two equivalent sentences, should we choose to say that the general sentence reveals the 'real' form of the singular sentence rather than the reverse? Why should we think of the reduction, of the elimination of a certain type of expression, as going in that direction rather than the other? The only answer can be that we think of expressions referring to individual human beings as more 'fundamental' or 'basic' in type than expressions referring to human qualities. For suppose our general sentence is written in the form '$(x)(fx \supset gx)$,' with the appropriate values for 'f' and 'g.' Then the corresponding formula of the form 'fx' will take, as values of the individual variable, expressions referring to individual human beings. The original singular sentence, equivalent to the general sentence, itself exemplified the formula 'fx,' but had, as the value of 'x,' the name of a quality. So one says that '$(x)(fx \supset gx)$' was the real form of the original sentence rather than 'fx,' only if one thinks of individual variables as somehow basically designed to indicate gaps to be filled by designations of individual people rather than designations of qualities. One can speak, *in this way*, of the real logical form of a sentence or statement only if one has already selected a certain type of expression as the basic type in terms of which 'real logical form' is to be defined. Thus the real logical form of a sentence S will be given by the formula exemplified by a sentence S' which is (1) equivalent to the sentence S and (2) contains no expressions of non-basic types and no subsidiary formulae such that a variable, free in that formula, would take an expression of a non-basic type as a value. This is a far cry from the sense in which we have used 'logical form' up to now.

Even if we forswear this last step, and hence refrain from introducing new elements into the notion of logical form, it remains true that the general programme of explaining type-differences, other than formal-grammatical ones, along these lines, presupposes the selection of one type of expression as the type par excellence of individual expression. This selection will in its turn dictate the selection of one type of predicative expression as the type par excellence. This selection of basic types will yield a range of sentences of the form 'fx' such that any individual expression occurring in any of them can be significantly combined with any predicative expression occurring in any of them. As far as these sentences are concerned, the formal difference in type between individual and predicative expressions will *coincide* with the difference between the two basic types of expression selected. From sentences of this range we can construct (by truth-functional composition, quantification, or any other means recognized in our formal logic) more complex sentences, which will not, however, contain any expression of any further types except those officially recognized in our logic (or our grammar). Now the general programme of explanation of type-differences can theoretically be carried out if, and only if, for every sentence containing expressions of non-basic types there is a logically equivalent sentence in which these expressions are eliminated in favour of expressions of the basic types, together with whatever devices for constructing complex sentences are recognized in our formal logic (or our grammar). If we could show a reasonable presumption that this programme of translations could be carried out, we might reasonably claim to have explained all type-differences in terms of those recognized by formal logic (or grammar), together with the entailment-rules sanctioning the translations.

Much metaphysics consists in the attempt to show that this programme (or a part of it) could theoretically be carried out. Sense-impressions have been among the candidates for the designata of the basic individual expressions; so have material objects. There is, however, no reason for supposing that the programme can be carried out; and there are many good reasons for supposing that it cannot.

When the reductionist programme is combined with belief that the truth-functional and quantificational systems give an adequate analysis of the means of framing complex statements, then the metaphysical pull of formal logic is at its most powerful. For then we have the belief that modern symbolic systems, together with ordinary entailment-rules, give a completely adequate map of the logic of language in its statement-making aspect. In this section I have indicated yet another field — that of distinctions of type — in which this claim is unfounded.

III. THE LOGIC OF LANGUAGE

In discussing the logic of ordinary language I have frequently used the word 'rule.' I have spoken of entailment rules, referring rules, type-rules. The word is not inappropriate: for to speak of these and other 'rules' is to speak of ways in which language may be *correctly* or *incorrectly* used. But though not inappropriate, the word may be misleading. We do not judge our linguistic practice in the light of antecedently studied rules. We frame rules in the light of our study of our practice. Moreover, our practice is a very fluid affair. If we are to speak of rules at all, we ought to think of them as rules which everyone has a licence to violate if he can show a point in doing so. In the effort to describe our experience we are continually putting words to new uses, connected with, but not identical with, their familiar uses; applying them to states of affairs which are both like and unlike those to which the words are most familiarly applied. Hence we may give a meaning to sentences which, at first sight, seem self-contradictory. And hence, though some have incautiously spoken of the violation of type-rules as resulting in sentences which, though neither ungrammatical nor self-contradictory, are nonsense, it is in fact hard to frame a grammatical sentence to which it is impossible to imagine some sense being given; and given, not by arbitrary *fiat*, but by an intelligible, though probably figurative, extension of the familiar senses of the words and phrases concerned.

In speaking of entailment-rules we make use of the distinction between analytic and synthetic (or contingent) statements. In speaking of type-rules we make use of the distinction between the literal and the figurative use of language. But we must not imagine these distinctions to be very sharp ones, any more than we must imagine our linguistic rules to be very rigid. Very often we may hesitate between saying, of two uses of a word, that one is literal and the other figurative, and saying that they are just two different, though equally literal, senses of the word. Sometimes we shall be uncertain whether to say that a word is being used in the same sense, or different senses. And these notions — of figurative and literal senses, of different senses and the same sense — are, with all their imprecision, indispensable to explaining what we mean by type-distinctions and type-rules. Similarly, we may very often hesitate to say whether a given sentence is analytic or synthetic; and the imprecision of this distinction, as applied to ordinary speech, reflects an imprecision in the application of the notion of entailment to ordinary speech.

This fluidity in our rules, and this imprecision in the distinctions they involve, are things we must be aware of if we aim at a realistic study of the logic of ordinary speech. But though they make such a study more complicated and less tidy than the study of formal systems, they do not make it impossible. In a way, the awareness of them makes it easier; for if we realize that we are at best describing only the standard and typical uses of certain kinds of expression, we shall be less disconcerted by untypical cases.

Side by side with the study of formal logic, and overlapping it, we have another study: the study of the logical features of ordinary speech. The second study can illuminate the first, and can by it be illuminated or obscured. Much of this book is concerned with the interrelations between the two. I have given, in outline, some examples of the kinds of distinction we can draw, and the kinds of generalization we can make, in pursuing this second study. The most important general lesson to be learnt from them is that simple deductive relationships are not the only kind we have to consider if we wish to understand the logical workings of language. We have to think in many more dimensions than that of entailment and contradiction, and use many tools of analysis besides those which belong to formal logic. The scope of the second study is further greatly extended if, instead of restricting our attention to the statement-making use of language, we consider also some of the many other uses it may have. Nor, in this study, are we confined to linguistic minutiae; although the detailed examination of small linguistic differences may be absorbing enough. For in trying to discover the answers to questions of such forms as 'What are the conditions under which we use such-and-such an expression or class of expressions?' or 'Why do we say such-and-such a thing and not such-and-such another?,' we may find ourselves able to frame classifications or disclose differences broad and deep enough to satisfy the strongest appetite for generality. What we shall not find in our results is that character of elegance and system which belongs to the constructions of formal logic. It is none the less true that the logic of ordinary speech provides a field of intellectual study unsurpassed in richness, complexity, and the power to absorb.

21 Willard Van Orman Quine: AIMS AND CLAIMS OF REGIMENTATION (1960)

Opportunistic departure from ordinary language in a narrow sense is part of ordinary linguistic behavior. Some departures, if the need that prompts them persists, may be adhered to, thus becoming ordinary language in the narrow sense; and herein lies one factor in the evolution of language. Others are reserved for use as needed.

In relation to the concerns of this book, those departures have interested us less as general aids to communication than as present aids to understanding the referential work of language and clarifying our conceptual scheme. Now certain such departures have yet a further purpose that is decidedly worth noting: simplification of theory. A striking case is the use of parentheses. To say of parentheses that they resolve ambiguities of grouping gives little notion of their far-reaching importance. They enable us to iterate a few selfsame constructions as much as we please instead of having continually to vary our idioms in order to keep the grouping straight. They enable us thus to minimize our stock of basic functions, or constructions, and the techniques needed in handling them. They enable us to subject long expressions and short ones to a uniform algorithm, and to argue by substitutions of long expressions for short ones, and vice versa, without readjustments of context. But for parentheses or some alternative convention[1] yielding the foregoing benefits, mathematics would not have come far.

Simplification of theory is a central motive likewise of the sweeping artificialities of notation in modern logic. Clearly it would be folly to burden a logical theory with quirks of usage that we can straighten. It is the part of strategy to keep theory simple where we can, and then, when we want to apply the theory to particular sentences of ordinary language, to transform those sentences into a "canonical form" adapted to the theory. If we were to devise a logic of ordinary language for direct use on sentences as they come, we would have to complicate our rules of inference in sundry unilluminating ways. For example, we would have to make express provision for the contrasting scope connotations of 'any' and 'every.' Again we would have to incorporate rules on agreement of tense, so as to disallow inference e.g. of 'George married a widow' from 'George married Mary and Mary is a widow.' By developing our logical theory strictly for sentences in a convenient canonical form we achieve the best division of labor: on the one hand there is theoretical deduction and on the other hand there is the work of paraphrasing ordinary language into the theory. The latter job is the less tidy of the two, but still it will usually present little difficulty to one familiar with the canonical notation. For normally he himself is the one who has uttered, as part of some present job, the sentence of ordinary language concerned; and he can then judge outright whether his ends are served by the paraphrase.

The artificial notation of logic is itself explained, of course, in ordinary language. The explanations amount to the implicit specification of simple mechanical operations whereby any sentence in logical nota-

[1]Łukasiewicz has pointed out that the benefits of parentheses can be gained without their aid by adopting a prepositive symbol for each basic construction (in the sense of §11) and fixing, for each such construction, the number of terms or sentences that it is to admit as immediate components. See Tarski, *Logic, Semantics, and Metamathematics* (Oxford, 1956), p. 39.

tion can be directly expanded, if not into quite ordinary language, at least into semi-ordinary language. Parentheses and variables may survive such expansion, for they do not always go over into ordinary language by easy routine. Commonly also the result of such mechanical expansion will display an extraordinary cumbersomeness of phrasing and an extraordinary monotony of reiterated elements; but all the vocabulary and constituent grammatical constructions will be ordinary. Hence to paraphrase a sentence of ordinary language into logical symbols is virtually to paraphrase it into a special part still of ordinary or semi-ordinary language; for the shapes of the individual characters are unimportant. So we see that paraphrasing into logical symbols is after all not unlike what we all do every day in paraphrasing sentences to avoid ambiguity. The main difference apart from quantity of change is that the motive in the one case is communication while in the other it is application of logical theory.

In neither case is synonymy to be claimed for the paraphrase. Synonymy, for sentences generally, is not a notion that we can readily make adequate sense of; and even if it were, it would be out of place in these cases. If we paraphrase a sentence to resolve ambiguity, what we seek is not a synonymous sentence, but one that is more informative by dint of resisting some alternative interpretations. Typically, indeed, the paraphrasing of a sentence S of ordinary language into logical symbols will issue in substantial divergences. Often the result S′ will be less ambiguous than S, often it will have truth values under circumstances under which S has none, and often it will even provide explicit references where S uses indicator words. S′ might indeed naturally enough be spoken of as synonymous with the sentence S″ of semi-ordinary language into which S′ mechanically expands according to the general explanations of logical symbols; but there is no call to think of S′ as synonymous with S. Its relation to S is just that the particular business that the speaker was on that occasion trying to get on with, with help of S among other things, can be managed well enough to suit him by using S′ instead of S. We can even let him modify his purposes under the shift, if he pleases.

Hence the importance of taking as the paradigmatic situation that in which the original speaker does his own paraphrasing, as laymen do in their routine dodging of ambiguities. The speaker can be advised in his paraphrasing, and on occasion he can even be enjoined to accept a proposed paraphrase or substitute another or hold his peace;

but his choice is the only one that binds him. A foggy appreciation of this point is expressed in saying that there is no dictating another's meaning; but the notion of there being a fixed, explicable, and as yet unexplained meaning in the speaker's mind is gratuitous. The real point is simply that the speaker is the one to judge whether the substitution of S' for S in the present context will forward his present or evolving program of activity to his satisfaction.

On the whole the canonical systems of logical notation are best seen not as complete notations for discourse on special subjects, but as partial notations for discourse on all subjects. There are regimented notations for constructions and for certain of the component terms, but no inventory of allowable terms, nor even a distinction between terms to regard as simple and terms whose structure is to be exhibited in canonical constructions. Embedded in canonical notation in the role of logically simple components there may be terms of ordinary language without limit of verbal complexity. A *maxim of shallow analysis* prevails: *expose no more logical structure than seems useful* for the deduction or other inquiry at hand. In the immortal words of Adolf Meier, where it doesn't itch don't scratch.

On occasion the useful degree of analysis may, conversely, be such as to cut into a simple word of ordinary language, requiring its paraphrase into a composite term in which other terms are compounded with the help of canonical notation. When this happens, the line of analysis adopted will itself commonly depend on what is sought in the inquiry at hand; again there need be no question of the uniquely right analysis, nor of synonymy.

Among the useful steps of paraphrase there are some, of course, that prove pretty regularly to work out all right, whatever plausible purposes the inquiry at hand may have. In them, one may in a non-technical spirit speak fairly enough of synonymy, if the claim is recognized as a vague one and a matter of degree. But in the pattest of paraphrasing one courts confusion and obscurity by imaging some absolute synonymy as goal.

To implement an efficient algorithm of deduction is no more our concern, in these pages, than was the implementation of communication. But the simplification and clarification of logical theory to which a canonical logical notation contributes is not only algorithmic; it is also conceptual. Each reduction that we make in the variety of constituent constructions needed in building the sentences of science is a simplification in the structure of the inclusive conceptual scheme of science. Each elimination of obscure constructions or notions that we manage to achieve, by paraphrase into more lucid elements, is a clarification of the conceptual scheme of science. The same motives that impel scientists to seek ever simpler and clearer theories adequate to the subject matter of their special sciences are motives for simplification and clarification of the broader framework shared by all the sciences. Here the objective is called philosophical, because of the breadth of the framework concerned; but the motivation is the same. The quest of a simplest, clearest overall pattern of canonical notation is not to be distinguished from a quest of ultimate categories, a limning of the most general traits of reality. Nor let it be retorted that such constructions are conventional affairs not dictated by reality; for may not the same be said of a physical theory? True, such is the nature of reality that one physical theory will get us around better than another; but similarly for canonical notations.

SUGGESTIONS FOR FURTHER READING

GENERAL

Most elementary logic textbooks are of relatively little interest philosophically. Among exceptions are W. V. Quine's *Methods of Logic* (New York, Holt, Rinehart and Winston, 1950, 1959), especially Part IV, which, for the beginner in logic, provides an introduction to the views of one of the most distinguished contemporary philosopher-logicians. P. F. Strawson's *Introduction to Logical Theory* (New York, John Wiley & Sons, Inc., 1952) is an introductory textbook by one of the most distinguished of those who might be called contemporary anti-logicians. David Mitchell's *An Introduction to Logic* (London, Hutchinson University Library, 1962) takes Strawson's book "as a model and as a challenge." Gary Iseminger's *An Introduction to Deductive Logic* (New York, Appleton-Century-Crofts, 1968) attempts to raise philosophical issues in approximately the order in which the selections in this anthology are arranged.

Two books may be mentioned in the history of logic. I. M. Bochenski's *A History of Formal Logic* (Notre Dame, Ind., University of Notre Dame Press, 1961) is mainly a selection of original texts. W. C. and M. H. Kneale's *The Development of Logic* (Oxford, Oxford University Press, 1962) is a monumental survey of the history of logic.

Among books which deal in more advanced ways with a variety of problems in the philosophy of logic, the following may be mentioned: G. H. von Wright's *Logical Studies* (London, Routledge & Kegan Paul, 1957); Gustav Bergmann's *Logic and Reality* (Madison, University of Wisconsin Press, 1964) and *Meaning and Existence* (Madison, University of Wisconsin Press, 1960); and W. V. Quine's *From a Logical Point of View* (Cambridge, Mass., Harvard University Press, 1953, 1961) and *The Ways of Paradox* (New York, Random House, 1966).

Some books which deal with the philosophy of logic in its relation to other areas, such as the philosophy of language, are Morton White's *Toward Reunion in Philosophy* (Cambridge, Mass., Harvard University Press, 1956), L. J. Cohen's *The Diversity of Meaning* (New York, Herder and Herder, 1963), and W. V. Quine's *Word and Object* (Cambridge, Mass., The M.I.T. Press, 1960).

Finally, other anthologies in logical theory and related areas should be mentioned, including Paul Benacerraf and Hilary Putnam's *Philosophy of Mathematics: Selected Readings* (Englewood Cliffs, N. J., Prentice-Hall, Inc., 1964), Irving M. Copi and James A Gould's *Contemporary Readings in Logical*

Theory (New York, Macmillan, 1967), and P. F. Strawson's *Philosophical Logic* (Oxford, Oxford University Press, 1967).

PROPOSITIONS

Arguments somewhat like Frege's for the existence of propositions appear in G. E. Moore's *Some Main Problems of Philosophy* (New York, Macmillan, 1953), Chapter III. Criticisms of the notion can be found in P. Marhenke, "Propositions and Sentences," in *Meaning and Interpretation* (University of California Publications in Philosophy, Vol. 25), pp. 273-298, and in R. Cartwright, "Propositions," in *Analytical Philosophy*, R. J. Butler, ed. (Oxford, Basil Blackwell & Mott, Ltd., 1962). In Strawson's *Introduction to Logical Theory*, pp. 3-4, 9-12, the notion of "statement" is introduced. Mitchell, in *An Introduction to Logic*, pp. 105-109, gives reasons for preferring "proposition" to "statement."

LOGICAL TRUTH

Quine, in *From a Logical Point of View*, Chapter II, appears to question the very existence of the distinction between logical and factual truth. Among many responses to Quine's argument, the following may be mentioned: B. Mates, "Analytic Sentences," *Philosophical Review*, Vol. 60 (1951), P. F. Strawson and H. P. Grice, "In Defense of a Dogma," in R. Ammerman's *Classics of Analytic Philosophy* (New York, McGraw-Hill, 1965), and H. Putnam, "The Analytic and Synthetic" in *Scientific Explanation, Space, and Time* (Minnesota Studies in the Philosophy of Science, Vol. III), pp. 358-397.

J. S. Mill also appears to have denied the existence of the distinction by insisting that laws of logic are only empirical generalizations. See *A System of Logic* (New York, Harper & Bros., 1874), pp. 204ff, reprinted in Copi and Gould's *Readings in Logic* (New York, Macmillan, 1964), pp. 163-165. E. Nagel's "Logic Without Ontology," in H. Feigl and W. Sellars, *Readings in Philosophical Analysis* (New York, Appleton-Century-Crofts, 1949), criticizes Mill's view and gives a survey of some other attempts to deal with the notion of logical truth, as well as offering suggestions of its own.

ENTAILMENT

The modal notions involved in the systems of Lewis and of Anderson and Belnap have given rise to various difficulties which Quine, most notably, has repeatedly insisted on. See, for example, his "The Problem of Interpreting Modal Logic," *Journal of Symbolic Logic*, Vol. 12 (1947), pp. 42-48, and the exchange between R. B. Marcus and Quine in *Synthese*, Vol. 27 (1962), pp. 303-330.

For other general discussions of the notion of entailment, see J. F. Bennett, "Meaning and Implication," *Mind*, N. S. Vol. 63 (1954), pp. 451-463, and T. J. Smiley, "Entailment and Deducibility," *Proceedings of the Aristotelian Society*, Vol. 59 (1959), pp. 233-254.

EXISTENCE AND BEING

A classical statement of the philosophically-inclined logician's attitude towards the notion of existence, together with some of the consequences of this attitude for such philosophically controversial matters as proofs of the existence of God and assertions of the existence of universals, may be found in W. Kneale's "Is Existence a Predicate?" in Feigl and Sellars' *Readings in Philosophical Analysis*. G. E. Moore's discussion of Kneale's paper can be found under the same title, in A. G. N. Flew's *Logic and Language* (*Second Series*) (Oxford, Basil Blackwell, 1955). The "multi-vocalism" of Ryle, mentioned by White, may be seen in *The Concept of Mind* (London, Hutchinson's University Library, 1949), p. 23.

ONTOLOGICAL COMMITMENT

Discussions of issues surrounding the notion of ontological commitment may be found in W. Sellars, *Science, Perception and Reality* (London, Routledge & Kegan Paul, 1963), Chapter 8, and in A. Donagan, "Universals and Metaphysical Realism," *The Monist*, Vol. 47 (1963), pp. 211-246. The particular ontological issue which Donagan explicitly discusses, the question of the "ontological status" of universals, is dealt with in D. Pears, "Universals," in Flew's *Logic and Language* (*Second Series*). Donagan talks about this article as well as Selections 4 and 12 of this anthology. See also N. Goodman's "A World of Individuals," from J. M. Bochenski, A. Church, and N. Goodman, *The Problem of Universals* (Notre Dame, Ind., University of Notre Dame Press, 1956).

QUANTIFICATION AND EXISTENCE

For a controversy rather like the one in the selections see the articles, one by C. H. Langford and one by J. A. Chadwick, each under the title "On Propositions Belonging to Logic," *Mind*, N. S., Vol. 36 (1927), pp. 342-346, and pp. 347-353. For Quine's views, mentioned by Cohen in Selection 15, see *From a Logical Point of View*, Chapter IX.

TRUTH—FUNCTIONS AND ORDINARY LANGUAGE

It is interesting to read almost any logic textbook which introduces the standard propositional calculus to see what tack the author takes with respect to apparent disparities between the notions defined in the system, such as "material implication," and the concepts they are supposed to help us understand, such as "if . . . then." A particularly full discussion appears in R. Neidorf, *Deductive Forms* (New York, Harper & Row, 1967).

THE LOGIC OF CATEGORICAL PROPOSITIONS

The interpretation of categorical propositions which Brentano advances is also advanced by Boole. See Kneale and Kneale, *The Development of Logic*, pp. 404ff. For the presentation of this view in the form of a dilemma for the traditional account, see A. Ambrose and M. Lazerowitz, *Logic: The Theory of Formal Inference* (New York, Holt, Rinehart and Winston, 1961), pp. 34ff. For a discussion of the difference between Strawson's attitude towards modern logic and his attitude towards traditional logic, see P. Geach, "Mr. Strawson on Symbolic and Traditional Logic," *Mind*, N. S., Vol. 72 (1963), pp. 125-128.

The notion of "presupposing" to which Strawson appeals in Selection 19 originally appeared in his "On Referring," reprinted in R. Ammerman, *Classics of Analytic Philosophy*. This article was a discussion of Russell's "Theory of Descriptions," itself a classic example of the application of logical techniques to philosophical problems, in this case problems such as those which led Meinong to distinguish a kind of being which belongs to things like Pegasus, which are apparently referred to by propositions such as "Pegasus does not exist." Quine gives a brief account of Russell's theory in Selection 12. One of Russell's own presentations of the theory and his reply to Strawson's criticisms also appear in Ammerman, *Classics of Analytic Philosophy*.

REGIMENTATION

Strawson has written further on these issues in "Carnap's Views on Constructed Systems Versus Natural Languages in Analytic Philosophy," in *The Philosophy of Rudolf Carnap*, P. A. Schilpp (ed.) (LaSalle, Illinois, Open Court, 1963), pp. 503-518. Gilbert Ryle, a leading "informal" logician, has expressed similar views in "Formal and Informal Logic," in his *Dilemmas* (Cambridge, Cambridge University Press, 1954).

One of the most interesting ways to pursue these issues is to read Quine's and Strawson's discussions of one another's views. Quine's review of Strawson's *Introduction to Logical Theory* appears in *The Ways of Paradox*, pp. 135-155. Strawson's review of Quine's *From a Logical Point of View* appears under the title "A Logician's Landscape," in *Philosophy*, Vol. XXX (1955), pp. 229-237, and his review of *The Ways of Paradox* appears under the title "Paradoxes, Posits and Propositions," in *The Philosophical Review*, Vol. LXXVI (1967), pp. 214-219. Strawson, in "Singular Terms, Ontology, and Identity," *Mind*, N. S., Vol. 65 (1956), pp. 433-454, discusses Quine's view, adumbrated in Selection 12 above and discussed in more detail in *Word and Object*, pp. 181-186, that "singular terms" are "eliminable."